THE HISTORY OF THE SOCIAL SCIENCES SINCE 1945

This compact volume covers the main developments in the social sciences since the Second World War. Chapters on economics, human geography, political science, psychology, social anthropology, and sociology will interest anyone wanting short, accessible histories of those disciplines, all written by experts in the relevant field; they will also make it easy for readers to make comparisons between disciplines. The final chapter proposes a blueprint for a history of the social sciences as a whole. Whereas most of the existing literature considers each of the social sciences separately from one another, this volume shows that they have much in common; for example, they have responded to common problems using overlapping methods, and cross-disciplinary activities have been widespread. The focus throughout the book is on societal pressures on knowledge production rather than just theoretical lineages.

This book is noteworthy because it

- is the first book that puts together histories of the main social sciences since the Second World War, each of which is written by a discipline specialist,
- enables readers to realise that what they see as specific to their own discipline is, in fact, common to several,
- contains a chapter that proposes a blueprint for a history of the social sciences as a whole.

Roger E. Backhouse was a lecturer at the University College London and at the University of Keele, before moving to the University of Birmingham in 1980, where he has been Professor of the History and Philosophy of Economics since 1996. In 2009, he took a part-time position at Erasmus University, Rotterdam. After writing two textbooks on macroeconomics, he moved into the history of economics and methodology, on which he has published many articles in leading journals, including *History of Political Economy, Journal of the History of Economic Thought,* and *European Journal of the History of Economic Thought.* His books include *History of Modern Economic Analysis* (1985), *Economists and the Economy* (1994), *Truth and Progress in Economic Knowledge* (1997), and *The Penguin History of Economics* (2002) [published in North America as *The Ordinary Business of Life* (2002)]. Books he has edited include *The Cambridge Companion to Keynes* (with Bradley W. Bateman). He has been review editor of the *Economic Journal,* editor of the *Journal of Economic Methodology,* and associate editor of the *Journal of the History of Economic Thought.*

Philippe Fontaine is Professor of Economics in the Department of Economics at the École normale supérieure de Cachan and a Senior Fellow of the Institut universitaire de France. In 2003–2004, he was Ludwig Lachmann Research Fellow at the Department of Philosophy of the London School of Economics and Political Science. Professor Fontaine is the co-editor (with Roger E. Backhouse) of *The Unsocial Social Science? Economics and Neighboring Disciplines since 1945* (forthcoming). He has written for a number of journals, including *Economics and Philosophy, History of Political Economy, Isis, Science in Context,* and the *British Journal of Sociology.* He is associate editor of the *Revue de philosophie économique.* In 2005, Professor Fontaine received the Best Article Award of the Forum for the History of Human Science. In 2008, he was the recipient of the prix d'excellence en sciences sociales (Foundation Mattei Dogan/CNRS).

The History of the Social Sciences since 1945

Edited by

ROGER E. BACKHOUSE

and

PHILIPPE FONTAINE

CAMBRIDGE
UNIVERSITY PRESS

CAMBRIDGE UNIVERSITY PRESS
Cambridge, New York, Melbourne, Madrid, Cape Town, Singapore,
São Paulo, Delhi, Dubai, Tokyo, Mexico City

Cambridge University Press
32 Avenue of the Americas, New York, NY 10013-2473, USA

www.cambridge.org
Information on this title: www.cambridge.org/9780521717762

First published 2010

Printed in the United States of America

A catalog record for this publication is available from the British Library.

Library of Congress Cataloging in Publication data
Backhouse, Roger, 1951–
The history of the social sciences since 1945 / Roger E. Backhouse, Philippe Fontaine.
    p.   cm.
Includes bibliographical references and index.
ISBN 978-0-521-88906-3 (hardback)
1. Social sciences – History – 20th century.   I. Fontaine, Philippe, 1960–   II. Title.
H51.B243 2010
    300.9–dc22   2010007253

ISBN 978-0-521-88906-3 Hardback
ISBN 978-0-521-71776-2 Paperback

Contents

Notes on Contributors

Robert Adcock is Assistant Professor of Political Science at George Washington University. His research focuses on nineteenth- and twentieth-century Anglo-American thought, specifically the history, philosophy, and methods of the social sciences, and their relationship to the evolution of liberalism. He is the co-editor of *Modern Political Science: Anglo-American Exchanges since 1880* (2007).

Mitchell G. Ash is Professor of Modern History, head of the Working Group in History of Science, and Speaker of the Ph.D. program "The Sciences in Historical Context" at the University of Vienna. He is author or editor of eleven books and numerous articles and chapters in the following research fields: the relations of science, politics, society, and culture in German-speaking Europe since 1850; forced migration and scientific change during and after the Nazi era; and the history of modern psychology and psychoanalysis. Publications in the latter field include *Gestalt Psychology in German Culture 1890–1967: Holism and the Quest for Objectivity* (1995) and *Psychology's Territories: Historical and Contemporary Perspectives from Different Disciplines* (first editor, with Thomas Sturm, 2007).

Roger E. Backhouse is Professor of the History and Philosophy of Economics at the University of Birmingham and Erasmus University Rotterdam. His books include *The Ordinary Business of Life / The Penguin History of Economics* (2002) and *The Cambridge Companion to Keynes* (co-edited with Bradley W. Bateman, 2006).

Mark Bevir is a Professor in the Department of Political Science, University of California, Berkeley. He is the author of *The Logic of the History of Ideas* (1999), *New Labor: A Critique* (2005), *Key Concepts of Governance* (2009), and *Democratic Governance* (2010) and co-author with R. A. W. Rhodes of

Interpreting British Governance (2003), *Governance Stories* (2006), and *The State as Cultural Practice* (2010).

Philippe Fontaine is Professor of Economics in the Department of Economics at the École normale supérieure de Cachan and a Senior Fellow of the Institut Universitaire de France. With Roger E. Backhouse, he is the co-editor of *The Unsocial Social Science? Economics and Neighboring Disciplines Since 1945* (forthcoming).

Ron Johnston is Professor in the School of Geographical Sciences at the University of Bristol. His publications on geography and its history include *Geography and Geographers: Anglo-American Human Geography since 1945* (6th ed., with James Sidaway, 2004) and the co-edited *Dictionary of Human Geography* (5th ed., 2009).

Adam Kuper is the author of a number of studies in the history of anthropology, including *Anthropologists and Anthropology: The Modern British School* (3rd ed., 1996), *The Chosen Primate* (1996), and *Culture: The Anthropologists' Account* (1999). His most recent book is *Incest and Influence: The Private Life of Bourgeois England* (2009). He is a Fellow of the British Academy.

Jennifer Platt is Emeritus Professor of Sociology at the University of Sussex. Her most recent book is *The British Sociological Association: A Sociological History* (2003), and she edited *Introductions to Sociology: History, National Traditions, Paedagogies*, a monograph on national textbook traditions, for *Current Sociology* (2008, vol. 36, no. 2). Her current work is on the social structure of international Anglophone sociology.

Preface

In January 2006, we initiated a seminar series, held at the Centre for Philosophy of Natural and Social Science (CPNSS), at the London School of Economics and Political Science, on the history of postwar social science. This was an experiment to create an audience for reflection on the history of the social sciences in general. To start the series, we decided to have papers on the six core social sciences, providing general perspectives against which further work could be placed. In subsequent years, after obtaining the support of the Leverhulme Trust, we explored interdisciplinary figures in social science and a series of social problems.

These papers made us realize the importance of this interdisciplinary approach to the history of the social sciences. There is already work on this, but only as part of histories that have a much longer time frame: historical research on the postwar social sciences remains overwhelmingly discipline based. So we approached Cambridge University Press with a proposal for a short volume based on chapters by four of the participants in the seminar and outsiders. This book is the result.

We do not claim to offer a comprehensive or unified history of the social sciences since the Second World War. Contributors were provided with a common list of themes and were asked to address the ones they considered relevant to the discipline they were discussing, but no attempt has been made to homogenise the chapters, which reflect the different disciplinary backgrounds and concerns of their authors, as well as the peculiarities of the social sciences under consideration. Although the chapters on the six disciplines do discuss relations with other social sciences, albeit to a limited extent, they remain histories of individual disciplines. In the concluding chapter we seek to build on these discussions by sketching an account of how one might move towards a history of the social sciences as a whole. Though it is arguing for a more integrated history of the social sciences, it does little more than provide the evidence that, we believe, is needed to make the case that such a history is needed. Though it suggests taking the subject in a new direction, we could not have written it without having read the preceding chapters alongside one another. We therefore suggest that, despite its limitations, the book represents a significant step toward the more comprehensive history that we believe needs to be written.

We wish to thank the Leverhulme Trust, the CNRS Projet international de coopération scientifique (PICS #3758), and the CPNSS for their support. We are also indebted to Robert Adcock, Mitchell G. Ash, David Engerman, Daniel Geary, Craufurd Goodwin, Ron J. Johnston, Jennifer Platt, and Donald Winch for their comments on drafts of the chapters we have written together. We also wish to thank our editor at Cambridge University Press, Scott Parris, for his encouragement and feedback on what we have done and an anonymous reader for invaluable comments on the volume as a whole. It goes without saying that we, not they, are responsible for any errors that remain.

R. E. B.

P. F.

THE HISTORY OF THE SOCIAL SCIENCES SINCE 1945

Introduction

Roger E. Backhouse and Philippe Fontaine

The Social Sciences and Their Histories

In the past decade or so, there have been a number of retrospective surveys of the histories of the social sciences. For instance, to mark the centenary of the American Political Science Association, the *American Political Science Review*, widely viewed as the premier scholarly research journal in that field, published a centennial issue of some twenty-five articles on the "evolution of political science" with special emphasis on the period since the Second World War. Likewise, to celebrate its hundredth anniversary, the American Sociological Association sponsored *Sociology in America* (Calhoun 2007), a 900-page volume that, as one reviewer (Geary 2008) put it, placed more emphasis on the history of the discipline than on its current state. These volumes attest to the depth of research being undertaken on the history of these disciplines; however, interest in the histories of other disciplines may be less. For example, the American Economic Association did not choose to mark its centenary two decades ago in a similar way, and it seems unlikely that its leading journal, the *American Economic Review*, will devote an issue to historical reflection on its first hundred years. Nonetheless, there is a significant amount of work being undertaken on the recent history of the discipline.[1]

Historical work on what Ross (1993, p. 99) has called the "core social sciences in the U.S." has been undertaken, despite the fact that history has increasingly been seen as irrelevant to the shaping of theory.[2] However,

---

[1]   The main concentration of such work is probably in the annual supplements to the journal *History of Political Economy*.

[2]   Here we are concerned not so much with the uses of history across the social sciences (see Monkkonen 1994) as with the significance of their disciplinary histories. It should be noted that there is also increasing interest in the history of the social sciences from intellectual historians who have no institutional connections with the social sciences.

virtually all of this work either focuses on one social science in isolation or considers the social sciences in the context of specific historical problems. There are hardly any attempts to write their history as a whole. An exception to this generalization is Daniel Bell's *The Social Sciences Since the Second World War* (1982). As befits a work included in *The Great Ideas Today*, Bell's book identifies key innovative ideas and even makes some effort to contextualize them. Conscious that Auguste Comte's hope "to present a unified view of man's knowledge through the unity of science" had not been realized, Bell noted that "there is a sense today that we are probably farther from that ambition than at most times in our intellectual history" (p. 10). This, together with his sociological outlook, may explain why he does not offer much in the way of historicizing the developments of the social sciences as a whole. Another exception is the special issue of *Dædalus* on the transformation of academic culture in America after the Second World War. The essays on economics and political science contain material that is of great value to a historian of modern social science, but it is the three essays on cross-disciplinary comparisons (Hollinger 1997, Katznelson 1997, Schorske 1997) that represent the most valuable efforts to build upon the disciplinary histories of several social sciences.[3]

Much more momentous than either of these is the collection of essays edited by Theodore Porter and Dorothy Ross (2003), *The Modern Social Sciences*, published as volume VII of *The Cambridge History of Science*. This offers a systematic coverage without suffering from the historiographic limitations of Bell's book. The history it offers is of the social sciences since the late eighteenth century. If one is trying to understand the deeper roots of the modern social sciences, this approach is especially helpful – the late eighteenth century is a key period without which the nineteenth-century origins of much social science cannot be understood. However, if one is trying to understand the social sciences since the Second World War, it suffers from a number of disadvantages if only because there is simply not enough space to explore recent events in sufficient detail. Furthermore, possibly because of the different focus that results from adopting a long time frame, the volume's coverage of interrelations among the social sciences in this period does not go as far as one might hope. Disciplinary histories are integrated in a chapter

---

[3]   Collini distinguished between "discipline history," which "offers an account of the alleged historical development of an enterprise the identity of which is defined by the concerns of the current practitioners of a particular scientific field" (1988, p. 388) and a broader "intellectual history," which cannot be reduced to "an assemblage of 'discipline-histories' " (p. 390). On the definition of intellectual history, see Collini (1985).

by Ross and in eight chapters dealing with the "internationalization of the social sciences," as well as in fourteen chapters on "social science as discourse in public and private life."[4] Given the objectives of the volume as a whole, this structure has much to commend it; however, it means that, although there are accounts of the social sciences in Latin America, Africa, and major Asian countries, there are no essays on the social sciences as a whole in North America or Europe, the main centers of academic social science in this period.[5]

When Porter and Ross (2003, pp. 1–10) introduced their volume, they had to be attentive to changes in terminology – what are now known as the social sciences had been called, in different contexts, moral and human sciences. These changes were associated with different perceptions of what this group of disciplines covered: was psychology, for example, a social science or a natural science, closer to biology? Such disagreements over the use of the word "social" were accompanied by disputes over whether, or in what sense, they were "sciences," the difference between French and English usages of the word being a factor. Here, dealing with a narrower period that did not see the same changes in the institutional setting of the social sciences, we do not need to pay such attention to these shifts in terminology, although the scientific status of the social sciences was repeatedly questioned, particularly by outsiders, and the boundaries between the social and the human sciences varied from one country to another. Though these questions have not disappeared – in particular, the claim of the social sciences to the title "science" is disputed as hotly as ever, especially when some failure in the public arena can be blamed on their inadequacies – the institutionalization of the social sciences in academia makes them less of an issue.

More directly relevant is the question of which disciplines are to be covered. Clearly economics, political science, sociology, and social anthropology must be included: on this, there is no disagreement. Though there may be reasonable doubts whether it is a social science at all (Calhoun 1992, p. 170), we also include psychology because it was central to many cross-disciplinary research ventures in the social sciences after the Second

---

[4]   These are the headings to Parts III and IV of the volume.

[5]   Heilbron, Guilhot, and JeanPierre (2008) explore the possibility of a transnational history of the social sciences. Regarding the lack of histories of the social sciences as whole, two other exceptions can be mentioned: Scott Gordon's (1991) *The History and Philosophy of Social Science* and the *Fontana History of the Human Sciences* by Roger Smith (1997). Yet, in these two volumes, little attention is paid to the postwar era.

World War. The final inclusion is human geography, a discipline that came to be seen as a social science after the Second World War.[6]

While these six disciplines span the modern social sciences, they are not the only choices that could legitimately have been made. Even in a period when their institutionalization within academia has imparted rigidity, the boundaries of the social sciences and their relationships have remained fluid. There were many cross-disciplinary ventures, some of which challenged conventional disciplinary boundaries and some of which accepted them. They might be based, as was Parsons's reconceptualization of sociology "as the unifying center of an interdisciplinary nexus" (Nichols 1998, p. 83), on an overarching theoretical framework.[7] Alternatively, they might be based on no more than a pragmatic, commonsense view that social scientists tackling common problems ought to work together, exemplified by area studies, a self-consciously cross-disciplinary network of academic departments and research centers set up in the 1950s and 1960s to tackle problems relating to the Soviet Union, Africa, Latin America, and parts of Asia (see pp. 193–4). In other cases, such as management science (or its various branches from marketing to accountancy), there emerged what effectively have become independent disciplines but, because of their practical, applied orientation, they never became core social science disciplines. There were also disciplines that were partly within social science yet retained strong identifications outside of it. Social history drew on sociology and might be considered the counterpart of human geography, concerned with time rather than space. However, though it was subject to many of the same intellectual fashions as the social sciences, it retained a separate disciplinary identity linked to history and the humanities (see Sewell 2005). Linguistics can also be seen as a social science but, like social history, it extends outside

---

[6]   Though he was more concerned with the definition of the "behavioral sciences," Berelson (1963, p. 1), who served as director of the Behavioral Sciences Program of the Ford Foundation from 1951 to 1957, listed anthropology, economics, history (not geography), political science, psychology, and sociology under the term social sciences. He regarded the American versions of anthropology, psychology, and sociology as the core disciplines of the behavioral sciences and included as well parts of political science, law, psychiatry, geography, biology, economics, and business and history (p. 2). Kenneth Prewitt (2005, p. 222) notes that "the social sciences formed themselves in the now familiar five core disciplines: anthropology, economics, political science, psychology, and sociology." Joel Isaac (2007) provides an informative survey of the history of Cold War studies since 1990. He notes "a burgeoning research front: the history of the American human sciences during the Cold War" (p. 727). Interestingly, by the term "human sciences," he means: philosophy, psychology, economics, sociology, and anthropology.

[7]   On the place of *The Structure of Social Action* of 1937 in Parsons's effort, see Camic (1989).

the social sciences as usually understood. Law offers another example of a discipline outside of what is traditionally considered social science yet draws heavily on its frameworks, whether via criminology or via the various approaches of bringing together law and economics. There have also been attempts (such as communication studies) to spin new disciplines from established ones. The lesson to be drawn is that, using Calhoun's (1992) apt phrase, the social sciences are part of a complex "project of a general understanding of social life," reinforcing the argument that the histories of the different social sciences need to be considered together.

While the ideal is, without doubt, a comprehensive history of the social sciences as a whole that explores both developments within each discipline and the networks of interdisciplinary engagements that helped frame disciplinary identities, such a history is some way off. Although much useful work has been undertaken on the history of the social sciences since the Second World War, there remain significant gaps in our knowledge so that the task of synthesis is only at a preliminary stage. The type of synoptic work, achieved by *The Cambridge History* in relation to the post-Enlightenment creation of the social sciences, is not yet possible. Yet much can be learned simply from placing the histories of the different social sciences alongside each other, as is done here, in Chapters 2 to 7. Doing so enables us to answer a number of questions that are central to any understanding of the social sciences as a whole, and that pave the way toward an integrated history (see Chapter 8).

Recognizing that the histories of our six social sciences share common features but also exhibit significant differences, we asked contributors to prepare their chapters in a way that fitted the discipline about which they were writing. We suggested a number of questions that contributors might consider, although emphasizing that they were only illustrative of potentially significant themes.

1. Was the Second World War a significant dividing line in the orientation and development of social scientific knowledge for all disciplines?
2. Has the development of social science disciplines been teaching or research driven, and what have been the effects of this?
3. How important was the influence from the United States and, more broadly, how important were national traditions within the social sciences?
4. What were the relationships among the various social sciences?
5. What were the relationships with the natural sciences?
6. Was the size of the various communities significant in any respects?

7. What was the role of professional societies in the development of social science disciplines?
8. What was the role of the Cold War and politics, including the radical movements of the 1960s and the rise of neoliberalism?
9. How was dissent handled?

Though the contributors could not be expected to respond to all of these questions – most were phrased in a way that was not especially conducive to a treatment centered on disciplinary history – their accounts provide a basis on which an intellectual history of the various social sciences could be contemplated.

Professionalism, Methods, and Disciplinary Identity

The six chapters that follow reveal much about the perceived identities of the different disciplines as they evolved in response to the challenges facing social scientists during this period. Mitchell G. Ash starts Chapter 2 by pointing to the peculiar place of psychology, "suspended between methodological orientations derived from the physical and biological sciences, and a subject matter extending into the social and human sciences" (p. 16). This location helps to explain the variety found within psychology and also the tensions and dynamics within a discipline that is in some ways closer to being an assemblage of different fields than a single discipline. After the Second World War, a growing number of psychologists endorsed a "sociotropic" orientation and accordingly emphasized the social scientific dimension of the discipline (see Capshew 1999, pp. 155–158). Interestingly, at the very same time, "biotropic" psychology experienced a relative retreat, economists embraced the model of the natural sciences with much enthusiasm. In Chapter 3, Roger E. Backhouse argues that the Second World War brought economists together with mathematicians, statisticians, engineers, and, more generally, natural scientists in a way that had profound consequences for how the discipline was conceived. Whereas in psychology, the rapprochement with the social sciences reinforced the discipline's protean identity, the increasingly scientistic ambitions of economists served to consolidate a strong disciplinary identity based on their image "as the practitioners of a rigorous, dispassionate, and apolitical discipline" (Bernstein 2001, p. 152).

Chapter 4 on political science, by Robert Adcock and Mark Bevir, focuses instead on the narrative of Americanization. Although all the chapters tackle this issue, Americanization was particularly prominent in political science because American scholars were at the forefront of the so-called behavioral revolution of the 1950s and 1960s. This involved a shift away from normative problems (increasingly placed in courses in political philosophy) towards the study of how political processes worked in modern societies. The comparatively late establishment of political science in academia and the transatlantic differences within the field also contributed to the question of Americanization being more central to discussions of disciplinary identity in a field characterized by multiple approaches and several subfields.[8] Jennifer Platt, in Chapter 5 on sociology, a discipline that entertained a complex and changing relationship with political science after the Second World War, shows that, even though the fragmentation of the discipline may be less than that in political science, one can hardly escape questioning "the extent to which there has been one sociology with a shared history" (p. 102). Rather than attempt a conventional history, which would, perhaps almost inevitably, give the subject more unity than she believes it has, she confines herself to outlining some of the key features of world sociology. She provides not a single history but a series of histories, ranging from the discipline's demography to its research methods.

The remaining chapters structure their histories around peculiar features of their disciplines. In Chapter 6, Adam Kuper seeks to locate social anthropology firmly in its colonial setting, which made it originally a specifically European enterprise. It was a discipline pursued in elite academic institutions within what were then the world's leading colonial powers. During and after the Second World War, when the United States displaced Britain as the dominant world power and the effects of decolonization began to shake the British Empire, the anthropological landscape changed in many ways. Where the First World War had played no minor role in accelerating the emancipation of anthropology from sociology, making the differences between traditional and modern societies much more meaningful than the simple question of backwardness, the Second World War strengthened the orientation toward the study of different cultures and, in the process, reinforced the vision of the relativism of Western cultural principles even among highly industrialized countries. Building on the legacy of Franz Boas, American anthropologists acquired greater visibility on the

---

[8] Michael Kenny (2004) shows that the fate of British political studies in the 1950s and 1960s can hardly be understood as a mere conversion to American models, which is not to say that the American version of political science did not weigh on British debates. Robert Adcock and Mark Bevir (2005) point to the historiographic significance of the opposition between the British study of politics, with its emphasis on historical and cultural particulars, and the more ideologically scientist American science of politics.

international academic scene. Though the ongoing international influence of British social anthropology makes it inappropriate to characterize the developments of anthropology in the Western world after the Second World War as a simple story of Americanization, the relative institutional slowing down of social anthropology and concomitant recognition of sociology in Britain from the mid-1960s facilitated the development of cultural anthropology in the United States.

In contrast with social anthropology, the dynamics of human geography, as Ron Johnston points out in Chapter 7, are explained by its absence from the elite academic institutions. Geography was represented only by the *National Geographic* and school geography teaching. Learning about maps and exotic places might be an important part of the curriculum, and responsibility for training geography teachers might fall upon universities, but for many years human geography lacked the research base that would justify it as an academic discipline.

In all these accounts, with the possible exception of social anthropology for which the interwar period was at least as important, the Second World War was much more than a symbolic dividing line, for it generally strengthened the social sciences, laying the foundations for their postwar expansion: psychologists were needed to conduct personnel assessment and allocation, to treat and reduce psychological casualties of war, and to understand how best to undermine enemy morale; sociologists, political scientists, and social anthropologists were needed to understand the societies within which and against which the Allied powers were fighting; geographers were needed for cartography and for their knowledge of remote parts of the world; and economists were needed to plan the war effort, helping to allocate resources efficiently, and as generalized, technical problem solvers.

The nature of the war's impact, however, varied considerably across disciplines. Psychology experienced enormous growth on the clinical side, with massive numbers of women entering the profession, especially in the "softer" subfields such as developmental and educational psychology. In contrast, sociology managed to keep itself apart from social work, the closest equivalent to clinical psychology. However, despite these differences, all disciplines encountered new tools with strong methodological implications, from the quantitative techniques that posed challenges to much prewar economics to the sample survey, a major tool for postwar sociology and political science.

The most obvious feature of all the social sciences after 1945 was their rapid growth. In psychology, this was associated with specialization, illustrated by the rapid emergence of a clear divisional structure within the American Psychological Association. By the 1970s, the differences were sufficiently great that complaints were raised that there was no unity to the subject. The discipline held itself together by enforcing methodological conventions, laying out how research was to be conducted and evaluated. Economics did not have the same problem. There was specialization and discussion of method (in the early postwar years, concerning the role of mathematics), but by the 1960s, economics had become more unified. Postwar expansion played an important role here, for the influx of economists from wartime service caused an unusually rapid generational shift, favoring the spread of mathematical and statistical methods, although this happened much more slowly than has often been suggested.

The history of sociology fits neither of these models. Before the Second World War, many sociologists had entertained hopes that sociology might be the master discipline among the social sciences, performing a "grand synthetic function." After 1945, other, perhaps less grandiose, aims appeared, especially in the United States, with a growing number of sociologists making a profession of linking theory to data collection. There was also a contrast with economics in that, far from providing opportunities for economists with experience to practice their subject outside academia, rapid expansion resulted in new staff often having qualifications outside sociology, making for diversity within the discipline. Human geographers, too, came from a range of academic backgrounds (see Robic 2003, p. 384), though, for them, the problem was the lack of a substantial research base to a discipline that was dominated by the need to teach undergraduates and to train school teachers. For very different reasons, in neither human geography nor social anthropology was there postwar expansion to rival that seen by other social sciences.

Another interesting feature of social science disciplines after 1945 was their endorsement of theory. It is unclear whether this turn should be located precisely after the Second World War, as some of its origins can be found in prewar developments, but it is fair to say that by the late 1940s an increasing number of social scientists recognized the necessity for a more theoretical outlook. As shown in several of the contributions to this book, that development may well have been obscured by historians' obsession with the use of new techniques and tools after the Second World War. Economists, political scientists, human geographers, and social anthropologists, as well as sociologists inspired by Parsons, began to develop identities in which theory was more central than had been the case before the war. This is not to say that social scientists had previously neglected theory but rather that they became more self-conscious of the need for a theoretical basis for the facts they were studying. In part this was because scientific theory helped differentiate lay and expert knowledge.

When we talk of the social science disciplines after the Second World War, there is a tendency to treat them as single entities, as if continuing national traditions were of minor importance to their development. Stories of international homogenization often present the intellectual and institutional changes that characterized the social sciences after 1945 as the outcome of a process of Americanization. Most contributors acknowledge that the significance of the American social sciences after the Second World War can be seen as the effect of their sheer size, combined of course with American wealth and cultural power. Though size may be a necessary condition for dominance or influence, it is hardly sufficient in itself. Thus, American influences seem to have played a significant role in economics where a strong disciplinary identity reinforced the effects of size, but they were less of a factor in psychology where these were offset by the fragmentation of the field and the difficulty any approach faced in claiming hegemony over the psychological discourse in the public sphere. In these cases as in many others, when taken too literally, narratives of Americanization can be misleading.

As many scholars such as Bell (1982) have noted, the 1960s and 1970s were a highly significant period for the social sciences. Hunter Crowther-Heyck (2006) has argued that a new patronage regime began to take shape in the late 1950s and early 1960s, which became dominant by 1970 at a time when a number of social scientists began to show concern about the fragmentation of their fields. The move from the first system, characterized by the prominence of several private foundations, the Social Science Research Council, and a variety of military research agencies, to the second system, which centered on the National Science Foundation and the National Health Institutes, was especially significant because it marked a shift from the cross-disciplinary research ventures following the Second World War to the more specialized orientations that characterized the social science disciplines from the early 1970s. One interesting, and subtle, argument advanced by Crowther-Heyck is that "the program officers of the second system tended to see applied social science as the application or dissemination of existing social scientific knowledge, whereas the behavioralists had seen new, fundamental research as an essential part of solving practical problems" (p. 434). By 1970, it would seem that the "policy orientation … that cuts across the existing specializations" and that Harold Lasswell (1951, p. 3) endorsed in the programmatic *Policy Sciences* had retreated.

The changes affecting the funding structure of the social sciences occurred at a time when various social movements were placing increasing pressure on policy makers to change society. These were often mediated by governmental agencies, though in the case of student agitation some social scientists experienced social discontent first-hand. As is well known, the degree of permeability to social change is highly variable across the social sciences, from the rather impenetrable economics to the more open sociology, but none of them could ignore the social movements of the 1960s altogether. As Backhouse explains, in economics there was concern that the discipline was ignoring issues such as poverty, inequality, and discrimination, and, despite a number of initiatives aimed at broadening the scope of the discipline, these topics remained confined to its periphery. The image of academic neutrality that economists were able to construct for themselves was preserved. In political science, as Adcock and Bevir point out, the story is not very different, though the political debates of the 1960s played a significant role in transforming political theory, which was once the common core in the American discipline, into a locus of hostility to the discipline's mainstream.[9] Insofar as the permeability to external forces is connected with a discipline's sense of identity, one will not be surprised that sociology, which, according to Platt, "did not always have a clear identity distinct from that of other social sciences" (p. 102), proved especially receptive to the movements of the 1960s. For instance, Platt notes the influence of the women's movement in "redefining issues and topics of research and theorising" (p. 107). That the greater openness of sociology to social change may have encouraged the disappearance of core areas in the field (as noted by Crane and Small 1992, p. 230) is an open question, but given the identity crisis of the field that emerged in the 1970s, it deserves to be asked. Johnston, in his chapter, notes geography's growing pluralism after 1970 without, however, suggesting an identity crisis. Here again, one of the main criticisms leveled at the discipline was its irrelevance to many of the hot questions of

---

[9] James Farr notes that "[r]iots in America's cities, assaults against the Cold War policies, and protests in the United States and Europe over the Vietnam war exacerbated debates within the discipline" and that a "left-leaning Caucus for a New Political Science was formed in 1967, critical of the APSA for having 'failed to study, in a radically critical spirit, either the great crises of the day or the inherent weakness of the American political system' " (2003, p. 325). Rogers Smith offers a similar account but notes that "after the debunking phase of the late 1960s and early 1970," "[t]here was still no alternative approach to studying politics that was genuinely more rigorous and produced more scientific knowledge than the prevailing versions of behavioralism" (1997, p. 262). Ira Katznelson (1997) provides a very useful account of the way the effects (or lack thereof) of the convulsions of the 1960s on various scholarly disciplines have been approached.

the day including poverty, inequality, and civil rights. And the alternative, as emphasized by Johnston, was Marxism, with British geographer David Harvey as one of its main proponents. Yet, the radicals' arrival was soon eclipsed by the "cultural turn" from the late 1980s.

All in all, it seems that the effects of the events of the 1960s, though certainly far from negligible, were considerably mitigated by the increasing professionalization of the social science disciplines after the Second World War. Their political participation in the various social movements notwithstanding, when it came to analyzing human behavior and society, social scientists continued to have more in common with each other than with political activists wishing to change society.

Toward a History of the Social Sciences as a Whole

As we have shown in the previous discussion, much can be learned from placing histories of the different social sciences alongside each other. Such an approach, however, inevitably has limitations. The most obvious reason is that it minimizes the role played by cross-disciplinary research ventures.[10] From the histories of individual social sciences, one would never guess that the period was one in which cross-disciplinary ventures proliferated, driven by both demand from sponsors and intellectual forces. Governments and funding bodies, such as Ford, Rockefeller, and Carnegie, all highly influential in creating social science disciplines in the twentieth century, put resources into trying to solve societal problems, many of which were perceived to require a multidisciplinary approach combining a variety of perspectives.[11] Other ventures went even further toward integrating the social sciences in that they were interdisciplinary, seeking to achieve greater cross-fertilization among the disciplines themselves. There were also researchers, including Kenneth Boulding, Talcott Parsons, Anatol Rapoport, and Herbert Simon, who saw themselves as general social scientists trying to combine the tools and theories of various social sciences into a coherent whole.

The concluding chapter explores ways in which we can move beyond the histories of individual disciplines toward seeing the social sciences as a

---

[10] Following Cohen-Cole (2007), we find it useful to distinguish between "interdisciplinary" situations, involving the exchange of intellectual tools, and "multidisciplinary" situations, implying researchers working in parallel. The term "cross-disciplinary" is used to refer to either situation whenever a greater degree of precision is dispensable.

[11] Steuer (2003) offers a snapshot of the ways in which different social sciences tackle the same problems.

whole, but without imposing a false unity on what was a diverse, albeit closely connected, collection of disciplines. It includes substantial discussions of the cross-disciplinary activities neglected in disciplinary histories and on which there has been too little systematic research. It also constructs a number of different contexts against which the social sciences developed, thus sketching a broader picture within which the narrower pictures offered by the disciplinary histories are located.

The last chapter argues that there are limitations to the type of disciplinary history that is offered in the preceding six chapters, including the chapter written by one of the editors. We would stress, however, that it arose directly from reflecting upon those chapters, identifying common themes and areas where the disciplinary histories needed to be augmented. The book as a whole, therefore, represents not a unified history of the social sciences since 1945, but a first step toward the construction of such a history. More significantly, it reflects the complexity of even the modern social sciences and hence the need to approach it from a variety of perspectives. In that respect, the social sciences are like the societies that form their subject matter: just as different social sciences view the same problems from contrasting perspectives, perhaps historians of the social sciences should be seen less as writing the histories of clearly identifiable social science disciplines and more as looking at different dimensions of a broader, albeit far from unified, social science.

REFERENCES

Adcock, Robert and Mark Bevir. 2005. The History of Political Science. *Political Studies Review* 3.1:1–16.

Bell, Daniel. 1982. *The Social Sciences since the Second World War*. New Brunswick, NJ: Transaction Press.

Berelson, Bernard. 1963. Introduction to the Behavioral Sciences. In B. Berelson, ed., *The Behavioral Sciences Today*. New York and London: Basic Books.

Bernstein, Michael A. 2001. *A Perilous Progress: Economists and Public Purpose in Twentieth-Century America*. Princeton, NJ and Oxford: Princeton University Press.

Calhoun, Craig. 1992. Sociology, Other Disciplines, and the Project of a General Understanding of Social Life. In Terence C. Halliday and Morris Janowitz, eds., *Sociology and Its Publics: The Forms and Fates of Disciplinary Organization*. Chicago, IL and London: University of Chicago Press.

   ed. 2007. *Sociology in America: A History*. Chicago, IL and London: University of Chicago Press.

Camic, Charles. 1989. Structure after 50 years: The Anatomy of a Charter. *American Journal of Sociology* 95.1:38–107.

Capshew, James H. 1999. *Psychologists on the March: Science, Practice, and Professional Identity in America, 1929–1969*. Cambridge: Cambridge University Press.

Cohen-Cole, Jamie. 2007. Instituting the Science of Mind: Intellectual Economies and Disciplinary Exchange at Harvard's Center for Cognitive Studies. *British Journal for the History of Science* 40.4:567–97.

Collini, S. 1985. What is Intellectual History? *History Today* 35.10:46–8.

1988. "Discipline History" and "Intellectual History": Reflections on the Historiography of the Social Sciences in Britain and France. *Revue de synthèse* 3.4:388–99.

Crane, Diana and Henry Small. 1992. American Sociology since the Seventies: The Emerging Identity Crisis in the Discipline. In Terence C. Halliday and Morris Janowitz, eds., *Sociology and Its Publics: The Forms and Fates of Disciplinary Organization.* Chicago, IL and London: University of Chicago Press.

Crowther-Heyck, Hunter. 2006. Patrons of the Revolution. Ideals and Institutions in the Postwar Behavioral Science. *Isis* 97.3:420–46.

Farr, James. 2003. Political Science. In T. M. Porter and D. Ross, eds., *The Cambridge History of Science, vol. 7 (The Modern Social Sciences).* Cambridge: Cambridge University Press.

Geary, Daniel. 2008. Every Social Scientist Her Own Historian. *Modern Intellectual History* 5.2:399–410.

Gordon, Scott. 1991. *The History and Philosophy of Social Science.* London and New York: Routledge.

Heilbron, Johan, Nicolas Guilhot and Laurent Jeanpierre. 2008. Toward a Transnational History of the Social Sciences. *Journal of the History of the Behavioral Sciences* 44.2:146–60.

Hollinger, David A. 1997. The Disciplines and the Identity Debates, 1970–1995. *Dædalus* 126:333–51.

Isaac, Joel. 2007. The Human Sciences in Cold War America. *Historical Journal* 50.3:725–46.

Katznelson, Ira. 1997. From the Street to the Lecture Hall: The 1960s. *Dædalus* 126:311–32.

Kenny, Michael. 2004. The Case for Disciplinary History: Political Studies in the 1950s and 1960s. *British Journal of Politics and International Relations* 6.4:565–83.

Lasswell, Harold D. 1951. The Policy Orientation. In D. Lerner and H.D. Lasswell, eds., *The Policy Sciences: Recent Developments in Scope and Method.* Stanford, CA: Stanford University Press.

Monkkonen, Erich H., ed. 1994. *Engaging the Past: The Uses of History across the Social Sciences.* Durham, NC and London: Duke University Press.

Nichols, Lawrence T. 1998. Social Relations Undone: Disciplinary Divergence and Departmental Politics at Harvard, 1946–1970. *American Sociologist* 29.2:83–107.

Porter, Theodore M. and Dorothy Ross, eds. 2003. *The Cambridge History of Science, vol. 7 (The Modern Social Sciences).* Cambridge: Cambridge University Press.

Prewitt, Kenneth. 2005. The Two Projects of the American Social Sciences. *Social Research* 72.1:219–36.

Robic, Marie-Claire. 2003. Geography. In T.M Porter and D. Ross, eds., *The Cambridge History of Science, vol. 7 (The Modern Social Sciences).* Cambridge: Cambridge University Press.

Ross, Dorothy. 1993. An Historian's View of American Social Science. *Journal of the History of the Behavioral Sciences* 29.2:99–112.

Schorske, Carl E. 1997. The New Rigorism in the Human Sciences. *Dædalus* 126:289–309.

Sewell, William H. 2005. The Political Unconscious of Social and Cultural History, or, Confessions of a Former Quantitative Historian. In G. Steinmetz, ed., *The Politics of Method in the Human Sciences: Positivism and its Epistemological Others*. Durham, NC: Duke University Press.

Smith, Roger. 1997. *The Fontana History of the Human Sciences*. London: Fontana.

Smith, Rogers M. 1997. Still Blowing in the Wind: The American Quest for a Democratic, Scientific Political Science. *Dædalus*, 126:253–87.

Steuer, Max. 2003. *The Scientific Study of Society*. Boston, Dordrecht and London: Kluwer.

2

Psychology

Mitchell G. Ash

Introduction

Psychology occupies a peculiar place among the sciences, suspended between methodological orientations derived from the physical and biological sciences, and a subject matter extending into the social and human sciences. A field with such a vast domain might well be called protean, or at the least a transdiscipline. The struggle to create a science encompassing both subjectivity – conscious or unconscious mental processes and motives – as well as observable behavior, and the interrelated effort to develop professional practices utilizing that science's results, provide interesting examples for the extension and also the limits of such scientific ideals as objectivity, measurability, repeatability, and cumulative knowledge acquisition. In addition, psychologists' struggles to live by such methodological ideals while competing with others to fulfill multiple public demands for their services illuminates both the formative impact of science on modern life, and the effects of technocratic hopes on science.

There has been a broad shift in the historiography of psychology over the past twenty years from the achievements of important figures and the history of psychological systems and theories, to the social and cultural relationships of psychological thought and practice. [For comprehensive overviews, see Smith (1998) and Danziger (1990, 1997).] In the process, the interrelationships of psychological research and societal practices with one another, and with prevailing cultural values and institutions in different times and places, have become clearer. Elsewhere I have tried to bring out certain common threads in this varied narrative. (For example, Ash, 2001, 2003, 2007; I have drawn upon these articles and other previous publications in this chapter.) One of those common threads is that the history of psychology has been a continuous struggle by multiple participants to occupy and define a sharply contested, but never clearly bounded, discursive and practical field. The emergence and institutionalization of both the discipline and the profession called "psychology" are often portrayed as acts of liberation from philosophy or medicine, but these efforts to establish scientific or professional autonomy never completely succeeded. A second common thread is that the histories of psychology as a science, of the psychological profession, of reflexive psychological practices in general are inseparable, at least in the twentieth century.

In consideration of all this, it is clear that this chapter is not and cannot be about the philosophers' constructs called "psychology" or "philosophy of mind," for several reasons. The first reason is banal, but perhaps worthy of mention nonetheless: I am a historian of science, not a philosopher; my institutional socialization has given me knowledge interests and trained me to raise questions rather different from those of philosophers. The second reason follows from the first, but is perhaps less banal: as a historian, I believe that it is both methodologically inappropriate and empirically incorrect to speak as though there were such a thing as "psychological objects" or "mind," as such, without pausing to ask just how such concepts have been defined and used, and in this sense constructed, in different contexts over time.

A simple distinction between "scientific" and "folk" psychologies does not relieve us from the necessity of such considerations. So-called "scientific" psychology has been unable to agree on common definitions of its own terms, and has, since 1945, become hopelessly fragmented institutionally as well, as I will show in the discussion following. On the other side of the supposed divide, as Martin Kusch (1999) and others have suggested, "folk" (or, as I prefer to call it, everyday) psychology is also a social construction that is just as subject to change over time as are the concepts of scientific or professional psychology. As I will try to show here, more careful consideration of such contexts and historical changes over time indicates that various segments of psychological science have defined, used, or constructed aspects of the psychical in rather different ways during the postwar period, in part due to complex interactions with other disciplines and with particular segments of society.

Space is not available here to discuss all of these results (detailed studies of such interactions are presented in Ash and Sturm 2007). What I can present is a sketch, necessarily lacking in detail, of three subtopics within a vast domain. In the first part of the chapter, I will briefly survey institutional developments, focusing on two key trends: inner-disciplinary fragmentation, resulting in the emergence of subdisciplines with different semantic/conceptual and methodological resources; and internationalization as Americanization, with certain countervailing crosscurrents. In part two of the chapter, I will sample some results of this fragmentation, focusing on the subfields of cognitive science and social psychology. Finally, I will address the topic of reflexivity, as both a cognitive and social process that has become increasingly characteristic of psychology – and perhaps also of other human sciences – in the past few decades.

Institutional Fragmentation, "Americanization," and the Alternatives

In the United States, the postwar years saw explosive expansion and differentiation in both the scientific and professional realms of psychology. The establishment of a divisional structure within the American Psychological Association (APA) in 1947 – already negotiated during the war – reflected this process. Initially seven divisions were proposed: General, Clinical, Educational, Business and Industrial, Consulting, Psychometric Society, and the Society for the Psychological Study of Social Issues, which had been founded in 1936 (Capshew 1999, esp. pp. 67; Dewsbury 1997). Today there are fifty-four APA Divisions, including one (Division 26) for the Society for the History of Psychology with its own scholarly journal. (For a current list see http://www.apa.org/about/division/index.aspx, consulted on February 28, 2010.) Despite the optimism of the time, it proved difficult to subsume all aspects of psychology's protean identity within single university departments or graduate programs (Capshew 1999, esp. pp. 205 ff.). At present, it is often possible to obtain doctorates in General or Experimental, Developmental, Clinical, and Social Psychology from the same university. (For fascinating, but quite exceptional efforts to overcome such fragmentation at Harvard's Department of Social Relations or Yale's Institute of Human Relations, see Backhouse and Fontaine 2010.)

By the 1970s, both the sheer numbers of psychologists (over 70,000 then and roughly 150,000 today) and the international representation of psychology had reached levels that could not have been imagined fifty years earlier. The growth was worldwide, but more than two-thirds of the total number were and remain Americans. From the point of view of social history, the most important aspect of this growth is the openness of both the discipline and the profession to women. Already noticeable in the pre–World War II period, this openness continued – indeed increased – from the 1950s onward. According to a National Science Foundation survey for the years 1956–58, for example, 18.49 percent (2,047) of all American psychologists were women – the highest percentage for any single discipline. Today more than half the doctorates in the field issued in the United States go to women (Rossiter 1997: Tables 1 and 3, p. 170 and p. 175, respectively. Contemporary data appear on p. 172 f.). However, the gender concentration in particular specialties that began in the 1920s (Furumoto 1987) continued, with women being most numerous in developmental and educational psychology (i.e., the "softer" subfields) and men in experimental, industrial, and personnel psychology (the "harder" subfields).

Such numbers as those presented and the extent of the institutional anchorage of psychology in the United States were more than sufficient to ensure that the research and professional practices institutionalized there would spread throughout the world. "Americanization" understood in this sense was, however, by no means automatic. The reception of American-style psychology occurred at different rates in different countries. In Western Europe, outside of Germany and France, the predominance of American and British work in academic psychology was secure by 1970. For example, citation rates for English-language publications in the leading Dutch psychology journal rose from 20 percent in 1950 to over 70 percent in 1970; by then, the citation rate of American publications in social psychology dissertations was well over 90 percent (van Strien 1997; for a perspective emphasizing initiatives by local psychologists reaching out to selected American partners, see Thue 2006).

American predominance was contested during the Cold War era, not only in the Soviet Union (see Kozulin 1984; Jorawsky 1989, Part V; Janousek and Sirotkina 2003), but also, though with at best partial success, by dissident, local-language movements in the West, most notably in France and Germany. The most important exceptions to the overall trend in terms of scientific impact were the near-worship of Jean Piaget by developmental psychologists (Flavell 1963), and the positive reception of applications of factor analysis to personality testing and diagnostics by British psychologists Hans Eysenck (1953, 1994) and Raymond Cattell (1966; see also Cattell and Scheier 1961). In cognition research, too, British work such as that of Frederick C. Bartlett (1932, 1958) and Donald E. Broadbent (1958), as well as the work of Soviet theorists such as Alexander R. Luria (1966, 2005), were mobilized to lend respectability and theoretical sophistication to the resurgent field in the United States.

During this period, psychology in the two German states became itself a laboratory for Cold War science. In West Germany, a striking continuity from the Nazi period emerged during the late 1940s and early 1950s. Of the fifteen full professors of psychology at universities in the Federal Republic of Germany (FRG) in 1955, twelve had begun their careers under Nazism or in military psychology; many of those who had held professorships in 1943 also did so in 1953, though often not in the same institutions (Mattes 1985). Many of these chair-holders had been dismissed or prevented from acquiring positions in the Soviet zone or in the early GDR and had subsequently migrated to the FRG. After an intense controversy with both nationalistic and generational dimensions, this older generation was supplanted by younger advocates of American-style psychology, which meant data-driven research and statistical presentation and assessment of results, by the 1960s (Métraux 1985).

In East Germany, continuity with the past was most clearly evident in the appointment of Kurt Gottschaldt, a former student of the Gestalt psychologists who had carried out extensive twin studies at the Kaiser Wilhelm Institute for Anthropology in the Nazi era, to a full professorship at the Humboldt University in East Berlin (Ash 1995, chap. 22; Ash 1999). The context here was the decision by East German party and state officials to utilize "bourgeois" scientists for pragmatic reasons until a "new intelligentsia" could be trained. By the late 1950s, however, Gottschaldt came under pressure from proponents of a "Marxist-Leninist" psychology, some of whom were located, ironically, in Wilhelm Wundt's Leipzig (Busse 2004). He departed for the West in 1962, but his successor in Berlin, Friedhart Klix, skillfully presented his own mixture of Soviet-style cognition research and American information-processing approaches as being in tune with the cybernetics-led "scientific-technical revolution," which was then being propagated by the East German party leadership (Klix 1966; for the context, see Segal 2004).

A brief remark may be permitted here on psychology in the so-called "developing world." Small laboratories and departments for psychology had been established in Asian, African, and Latin-American countries long before 1945, and European and American investigators had begun studying the behavior and mental processes of "non-Western" people early in the twentieth century. The discipline expanded in these areas during the post-war period, though not nearly at the same speed as in the United States and Western Europe. Particularly interesting in this regard is the emergence of a specialty called "cross cultural" psychology, which, after modest beginnings, expanded rapidly during the 1960s and 1970s. In this subfield ambivalences of postcolonialism acquired visibility before the term itself became fashionable. Whereas the founders of the specialty initially thought it sufficient to "validate" existing (Western) research and diagnostic procedures in non-Western locales, critics of such approaches soon challenged the universalistic claims on which they were based as a species of cultural imperialism, advocated paying attention to the psychological aspects of non-Western cultural traditions, and supported "indigenization" movements. (For further discussion, see Blowers and Turtle 1987; Petzold 1987; Hartnack 2001.)

The professional history of psychology after 1945 also continued to be affected by contingent local circumstances. The rise of clinical psychology in the United States, for example, was originally driven by the need to deal with large numbers of mentally ill veterans after World War II. (For overviews, see Gilgen 1982, chap. 9; Routh 1994.) The initially established division of labor between test-based clinical diagnostics and psychiatric treatment soon became complicated, as clinicians engaged in a wide variety of psychotherapies, often though not always inspired by psychoanalysis. The new field ultimately brought forth its own basic research in both clinical and academic settings, which led to the emergence of scientific communities based on methodological norms quite different from those of experimental or developmental psychologists. This was the background of the controversy over "clinical versus statistical prediction" during the early 1950s (Meehl 1954). In addition, an eclectic, so-called "humanistic" psychology movement arose in opposition to both behaviorism and psychoanalysis, and became widely popular in psychotherapy, social work, and the emerging field of counseling psychology (DeCarvalho 1991).

In Germany, as in the rest of Europe, the rise of clinical psychology came approximately ten years later than in the United States. Here, however, in contrast to the United States, the supremacy of personality diagnostics and its quantitative tools had already been established in basic research before the professionalization of the clinical field. Another important difference indicative of a persistent European tradition was that clinical training in academic settings was based far more on cognitive and behavioral techniques than on psychoanalysis. Barriers to the academic institutionalization of psychoanalytic research and training in the universities proved surmountable only in exceptional cases, such as that of the Sigmund Freud Institute in Frankfurt am Main under Alexander Mitscherlich (Dehli 2007).

Scientific Impacts of Institutional Fragmentation

Given the spectacular growth in the sheer size of the discipline, specialization was inevitable. The process had already begun decades before 1945, and by the mid-1950s discerning observers had become aware that specialization and subspecialization were having an impact on the content and practices of the field. Put in social historical terms, subcommunities were creating their own terms of trade. Fragmentation was most obvious in the different research practices institutionalized in experimental, social, and personality psychology (discussed in the following), but complaints that the discipline had lost any semblance of intellectual unity had become endemic by the 1970s. At least two related issues characterized the discussion of that period: (1) an intellectually sterile, but historically revealing, debate on whether psychology was "preparadigmatic" as Thomas Kuhn appeared to claim in *The Structure of Scientific Revolutions;* and (2) a related discussion of the unity of psychology's subject matter, resolved by compromise in basic textbooks by adding the term "experience" to "behavior" without any actual agreement on the content of either term. (For extended discussions of the unity – or disunity – of psychology as a science, see Koch [1959–63], and the papers in Koch and Leary 1985, Part I.)

The second issue has had far greater long-term impact than the first on the development of the discipline. In the 1950s, whether psychology should even try to claim that its subject matter is the mental, that is, subjective, world (which is what most people have always thought it was), appeared to be in conflict with operationalistic conventions stating that "real" science only exists when some sort of measurement – that is, hard data about observables – is involved. That is the primary reason why psychology was defined in the 1950s mainly as a science of behavior. But by the 1960s, the utter absurdity of even calling the science "psychology" if its subject matter did not or could not include mental events and processes had finally dawned on most of those involved, and the so-called "cognitive revolution" had broken the behaviorists' predominance in any case (see the following). The discipline then redefined itself with a dual subject matter, but without really agreeing on what the two defining terms meant or how they related to one another.

Common across subfields were methodological conventions: an emphasis on standardizing experimentation by "operationalizing" variables, distinguishing "independent" from "dependent" variables, and using statistical significance testing to evaluate results. (On the postwar triumph of statistics, see Danziger 1990 and Capshew 1999, chap. 10.) An increasingly fragmented field held itself together, if it actually did so, by enforcing such methodological conventions on ever-widening groups of researchers by way of the increasingly extensive guidelines in the *Publication Manual* of the APA (Bazerman 1987). Among the results were a relative lack of interest in field research and phenomenological exploration, and, by implication, the prestructuring even of basic research to suit the needs of an expert society. (For the wider context see Porter 1995.)

Beneath this loosely woven net of methodological convention, substantive differences persisted. In educational psychology, for example, the preferred research tools were not "classical" experimentation but the correlational methods pioneered by Francis Galton. This contrasted markedly with the laboratory tools preferred by neobehaviorist learning theorists, who claimed at least implicitly to be providing the basic science that educators required. (On learning theory, see Hilgard 1987, esp. chap. 6; cf. Smith 1992.) In 1957, Lee Cronbach even spoke of the rival research communities of educational and experimental psychologists as "two disciplines" (Cronbach 1957). A comparable methodological split occurred in experimental social psychology and personality theory. In a broad survey of the field, Dorwin Cartwright (1959) spoke openly of "hard" and "soft" or "messy" methods to distinguish learning theory from social and personality psychology. Meanwhile, developmental psychology went its own way, taking the work of Jean Piaget as a touchstone for numerous studies closely related, as the earlier work of Arnold Gesell and others in the 1920s had been, to the practical needs of schools for age-related developmental norms.

The following case studies are presented here as necessarily incomplete indications of the issues at stake in a "hard" field, cognitive science – which later came to be called (by some) cognitive neuroscience – and a "soft" field, social psychology. In both subdisciplines, methodological conventions (e.g., regarding the proper way to design experiments), played roles that were as significant as substantive issues. In cognition research and neuroscience, however, the iconic roles of research tools – first the computer, then neuroimaging equipment – went beyond conformity to methodological convention, and achieved substantive impact. (For consideration of the roles of paper tools such as questionnaires in personality and social psychology, see Strack and Schwarz 2007.)

Case 1: Cognitive (Neuro)science

In experimental psychology, neobehaviorist-learning theory was challenged in the late 1940s and 1950s via a revival of cognition research by advocates of the so-called "new look" and information-processing approaches. Cognitive science was not limited to psychology, of course, but was a multidisciplinary project from the start (Gardner 1985/1996). Among its components were: (a) computer science, with its associated artificial intelligence (AI), and cybernetics groups (on the extension of metaphors from cybernetics to other disciplines, see, e.g., Heims 1993 and Edwards 1996); (b) philosophers of mind following Wittgenstein's remarks on psychology, among others; and (c) experimental psychologists trying to swim against the neobehaviorist tide and bring cognitive processes back into the mainstream of their discipline while retaining the semblance of natural scientific rigor. Each of these research communities remained largely self-contained at first, because each was affiliated institutionally with different disciplines; this resulted in considerable tensions at interdisciplinary gatherings. But the tensions were not only institutional in origin: the machine dreams of the early AI community were not easily married with the struggle to re-establish the autonomy of the psychological events and processes against the very different reductionism of behaviorist learning theory. I focus here briefly on two issues: the impact of machine metaphors since the 1950s, and the (only apparently) more recent challenge of brain research.

Very soon after the emergence of computer science and cybernetics during World War II and of information theory soon afterward, talk of "information processing" as a way of describing sensory, and subsequently lower-level cognitive, processes began to proliferate. By the late 1950s, it was common to speak of an information-processing model of sensory and cognitive processes, or even of mind per se; by the 1980s the model had become a "paradigm" (see, e.g., Mulder 1983). In hindsight, it appears obvious that the term was actually a metaphor, but it was nonetheless powerful. Metaphors have often served as a kind of glue, binding together different disciplines and also linking the sciences with the wider culture. (For examples from the nineteenth century, see Rabinbach 1990.) A certain conceptual imprecision generally accompanies such linkages; no one seems to mind, as long as it appears fruitful to continue using imported language. Whether synapses actually work the same way that vacuum tubes do, as cybernetics seemed to imply, whether Claude Shannon's information theory could ever have had much to do with entropy in physical systems, or whether talk of genetic "codes" transmitting information had much to do with Shannon's information theory, seemed not to matter, at least at first. The machines were there, they "processed" information, and their technical prowess was getting rapidly more impressive. One irony seems obvious in retrospect: just as cognitive scientists were beginning to succeed in their struggle against behaviorists for supremacy in experimental psychology, they seemed to become enthralled with cybernetics, a reductionist program in its own right.

As stated earlier, psychologists made strenuous efforts to maintain the unity of the discipline, despite obvious fragmentation, by enforcing methodological conventions on all participants. One of these was the use of statistical significance testing to establish reliability of research results. One of the problematic implications of this convention became clear in the 1980s and 1990s in the debate over computational models of mind. In this case, psychologists seeking instruments of control via standardized inference provided tools such as Baysian statistics, which then generated metaphors and concepts, the acceptance of which was easier because the tools were already in frequent use. The scientists then found the instruments informing their theorizing, or they found themselves claiming, quite implausibly, that "normal" subjects not socialized into the use of these techniques nonetheless solve problems the way they do, by applying "incomplete" or "naïve" versions of statistical inference (Gigerenzer 1992; Gigerenzer and Goldstein 1996; Gigerenzer and Sturm 2007).

The interaction of psychology and neuroscience in the postwar era is a superb example of the degree to which interest in psychological subject matter is influenced by the availability, constraints, and development of instrumentation. This is in part a question of theory-method alignments, but it is also a question of disciplinary power and preferences. Instrumentation from brain research, such as the electroencephalograph (EEG), has played a significant role in cognitive science for decades, in combination with other methods taken from experimental psychology (Rösler 2005). At the same time, brain researchers have long claimed to have privileged access to the psyche (Hagner 1996; Borck 2005a, 2005b). Current brain research, and particularly neuroimaging and other visualization techniques, are now having such a major impact on cognitive science that a leading segment of the field has been renamed cognitive neuroscience. Recent neuroscience maintains that all affective-emotional processes are coupled to neural processes in specific brain regions. Though they acknowledge that attempts to delineate the neurobiological foundations of affective-emotional states and of psychiatric disorders with the aid of structural and functional imaging methods are still very preliminary, they nonetheless maintain that states of the psyche can be visualized by modern neuroimaging methods (see, e.g., Roth et al. 2007). If there is anything to such controversial claims, they would have fundamental implications for any model of or metaphor for the mind.

In this case, one might well ask two questions: first, what in fact is being "imaged," psychical or neuronal processes? And, second, are the techniques in question only instrumental or also rhetorical? Are psychological processes now being made visible by neuroscientific apparatus, as some neuroscientists clearly want to argue, or are pieces of equipment and spectacular images being used as tools in a rhetorical strategy to make people *believe* that this has happened?

In a recent paper, Michael Hagner (2007) provocatively describes what he calls the "fictional" elements in current (over)confident proclamations by neuroscientists and their allies in the media. In Hagner's view, poetic

dreams about brain mirrors and mind reading dating from the nineteenth century or even earlier have been kept alive mainly by the sense of
uncanny possibility that they evoke. The simple fact that a category mistake
is involved – that the metabolic processes in the brain being recorded by
neuroimaging techniques obviously do not "think" in any coherent sense of
the word – suggests, in his view, that the current controversy may say more
about the need to make exaggerated claims in order to gain media attention, and thus to use cultural resources to attract research support, than
they do about the science involved.

Case 2: Social Psychology

In social psychology, the main trends in the early postwar years were
two: continuation of the effort to subject social behavior to experiment,
leading, as some have claimed, to the progressive removal of the "social" as
such from the field; and the continuation of efforts begun during the 1930s
to make social psychology more relevant to social and political problems.
Both of these trends were complicated by the impact of émigrés from Nazi
Germany.

Experimental studies of social influence on perception by Solomon Asch
and of prejudice by Gordon Allport and others captured the imagination
of many in the field in the 1950s (Asch 1952; Allport 1954). Common to
these studies was specific construction of the "social" as group impact on
individual behaviors or attitudes. This was partly due to the acceptance of
methodological conventions shared with learning theorists. Among these
were the injunctions to "operationalize" variables as well as results, and
to distinguish "dependent" and "independent" variables (Danziger 1992).
That this need not have happened the way it did is shown by the case of Kurt
Lewin (for the following, see esp. Ash 1992).

Lewin was a Berlin-based German Jewish psychologist who resigned his
position in 1933 before he could be dismissed by the Nazis, and accepted
a research stipend at Cornell supported by the Rockefeller Foundation.
After moving to the Child Welfare Research Station at the University of
Iowa in 1934, he carried out, with American collaborators, research on
"authoritarian," "democratic," and "laissez-faire" behavioral styles in children's play groups that made him famous (Lewin, Lippitt and White 1939). In
each group the role of the group leader, and thus a kind of individual-group
influence, was central; the notion that leadership and democracy were not
only not incompatible, but also that a particular kind of leadership (facilitating rather than dominating) was essential to democratic behavior, was

attractive as a contrast to continental Europe's authoritarian regimes. Most impressive to contemporaries, however, was the visual evidence provided by Lewin's films of his subjects and the fact that he had succeeded in studying the behavior of groups *as groups*, and not only the impact of groups on individuals or vice-versa.

This success encouraged Lewin to inaugurate a program he called "action research," the purpose of which was to collaborate with members of socially disadvantaged groups in order to study their behaviors, while at the same time giving them the means of changing that behavior (Lewin 1948). (On the origins of the term "action research," see Bargal 2006.) His open support for American democracy and his optimism about the potential of education to achieve social change impressed the progressive segment of his discipline sufficiently that he was elected president of the Society for the Psychological Study of Social Issues in 1939, only three years after he had helped to found it.

After his sudden death from a heart attack in 1947 at the age of fifty-seven, Lewin's prestige reached its high point. In the obituaries that followed, he was celebrated as the founder of experimental social psychology; Edward Tolman (1948) went so far as to call him the most important thinker in the history of psychology after Freud. Indeed, many of Lewin's terms, including "life space" and "marginal affiliation," entered the vocabulary of American psychology (Bierbrauer 1992, p. 329). Nonetheless, particularly in experimental social psychology, the field in which he made his greatest impact in America, his experiments with "authoritarian" and "democratic" groups, though greatly admired, were not accepted or imitated as exemplars for research design. Instead of the behavior of groups as groups, the preferred subject matter of social psychology remained the influence of groups on the behavior of individuals. Moreover, rather than establishing laboratory settings in which group behavior could be observed directly, social psychologists preferred to work as described previously, that is, according to standardized methodological rules that prescribed clear differentiation between "independent" and "dependent" variables. With that, the holistic presuppositions on which Lewin had based his approach ceased to apply (Danziger 1992, 2000). A number of Lewin's former collaborators tried to work in the style he had taught them, and some of them were among the founders of the approach called "ecological psychology" in the 1960s (Barker and Wright 1955; Barker 1968).

In the case of *The Authoritarian Personality* (Adorno et al. 1950), the picture is even more complex, but equally ironic. As I have shown elsewhere (Ash 2005), *The Authoritarian Personality* study, begun during the

Second World War and published in 1950, was by no means only the real-
ization of a research program conceived by the Frankfurt School, but the
result of a complex synthesis of three cultures of scientific practice, each of
which was itself a synthesis of multiple components: (a) the combination
of late Marxist "critical theory" and empirical social research practiced by
the Frankfurt School since the late 1920s; (b) the personality theory, based
on in-depth clinical interviews, practiced by Viennese psychologist Else
Frenkel-Brunswik; and (c) the statistical correlation methods practiced by
the Americans R. Nevitt Sanford and Daniel Levinson. When it appeared,
the study played to widespread worries among American liberals that fascist
and anti-Semitic attitudes were not limited to Nazi Germany. The popularity of such studies was symptomatic of a widespread tendency of the period
to psychologize, and thus individualize, social problems (Samelson 1986;
Herman 1996).

Many accepted the central claim of the study, that racist prejudices are
rooted deeply in psychology and are therefore not likely to be eliminated
completely, even in liberal democracies. Nonetheless, a certain ambivalence
expressed itself in the methodological criticisms that began to appear very
soon after the study was published – some of these criticisms came, interestingly enough, from other émigrés (Jahoda and Christie, 1954). Though
some criticisms, for example, the point that all of the test items were formulated as negatives, were justified, the emphasis on such problems to the
exclusion of content issues can surely be interpreted as resistance against
accepting the study's disquieting results. A sign of the McCarthy era was
the accusation that the study paid too little attention to authoritarian
tendencies among liberals and leftists. Nonetheless, the fundamental results
of the book have stood the test of time to a remarkable extent. In particular Frenkel-Brunswik's concept "intolerance of ambiguity" was shown in
the 1990s to be valuable in studies of xenophobia (Oesterreich 1993; Stone,
Lederer and Christie 1993).

Reflexivity

James Capshew (2007) has described an increasing emphasis on what
he calls "reflexivity" in psychology since World War II. By "reflexivity"
Capshew means, first of all, the awareness that psychologists are themselves part of the subject matter of their own discipline, and, second, that
working on people's selves, meaning their identities and personal problems,
has become an increasingly important purpose of psychological practice.
As Capshew, Morawski (1992, 2007), and others have shown, reflexivity

in the first sense – the awareness that psychologists are part of their own research – was initially suppressed during the formative period of academic psychology, but has become an increasingly acknowledged feature of methodological reflection and more general psychological thinking within the discipline since the 1940s.

One reason for the increase in such reflections is the increasing demand for reflexive knowledge and expertise to help clients work on themselves, meaning their identities and personal problems. Both are indicators of what Roger Smith has called "psychological society," meaning "a significant sense in which everyone in the twentieth century ... became her or his own psychologist, able and willing to describe life in psychological terms" (Smith 1998, p. 577). The irony that the demand for tools to achieve *individuality* could become such a widespread *social* phenomenon appears obvious in retrospect. Smith suggests that this phenomenon both draws upon and helps to sustain the authority of at least certain parts of psychology, just as psychologists respond in varied ways to the corresponding need for expert assistance in self-improvement, or for expert repair of damaged selves.

"Mind games" of various kinds have been around for a very long time. A random list of examples would include Zen practices, the spiritual exercises of St. Ignatius de Loyola, the agonized "soul-searching" of English and American Puritans, as well as the passionate introspections of Karl Philip Moritz and his colleagues in the German *Magazin für Erfahrungsseelenkunde* in the late eighteenth century (Moritz et al. 1783–1793). In the 1920s, approaches emerged that could be called reflexive or self-applications of psychology, which were offered to wider publics and not only to self-styled elites or the adepts of sects. One example is the autosuggestive relaxation technique developed by the German psychotherapist Johannes Heinrich Schultz (1991) in the 1930s, which he called "autogenic training"; the method is still in use.

From such modest beginnings, an entire field of reflexive practices has emerged, with particular intensity since the 1960s. In this field, mixtures of everyday and expert psychological knowledge have been given the appearance of technical tools and put on offer by a wide variety of practitioners to improve productivity through self-knowledge or group awareness in management training workshops, to raise the quality of child-rearing, or to increase individual well-being in numerous kinds of psychotherapy (Herman 1996, 2003; Moscowitz 2001; for historical background, see Shamdasani 2005). Nikolas Rose (1990, 1996) and others have suggested that these techniques, and the "work on one's self" they all claim to involve, have become a fundamental feature of late modern societies and cultures (see Conclusion).

Sabine Maasen (2007) has compared the self-help literature of the 1920s to that of today, focusing particularly on constructions of the concept of will in the two periods. As Maasen argues, in modern life, the government of others is closely linked with practices in which free individuals are enjoined to govern themselves as both free and responsible subjects. To this end, self-help manuals do not themselves prescribe any particular action or values, but offer to "train" us to decide for ourselves. This self-help literature often refers to psychological knowledge and the practices of counseling and psychotherapy, but it also draws from other sources, such as manuals designed to refine manners and educate virtues. While in the 1920s self-help manuals aimed to help male employees establish strong, fixed identities, today's self-help books and techniques advocate (male and female) "enterprising selves," capable of managing various tasks efficiently.

Conclusion

By the 1980s, if not earlier, psychology, which had been a multifaceted but predominantly European discursive and practical field at the turn of the century, had spread around the world; but at the same time it had become deeply dependent economically, institutionally, and culturally on American research styles and professional practices. When and to what extent the kinds of obsessions with psychological topics typical of American popular culture came to pervade European or even non-Western cultures cannot be considered in detail here. But it was clear even to casual visitors by the 1980s that psycho-babble and the associated group workshop culture had become as firmly anchored at least in Western European, especially German, middle- and upper middle-class culture, as in its American counterpart.

How much of this is caused by, and how much is an effect of developments in the discipline called psychology remains an open question. Kenneth Gergen (2007) argues that a cyclical interaction of everyday and academic psychology has worked particularly prominently in the case of so-called "mental deficits." As psychological concepts such as "depression" have been used more frequently in ordinary life, he claims, people come to be seen – and to see themselves – more often and more easily as mentally ill, or at least to conceptualize their difficulties in psychopathological terms. As they seek professional help more frequently, psychology reacts to this increasing demand, and the cycle continues. Gergen explains such cycles by arguing that psychological phenomena are socially constructed in any case, and that such constructions depend in turn on intellectual and financial interests. However, though he calls the process "colonization," he acknowledges that it need not result from deliberate strategies by psychologists in order to be effective.

Historians love ironies; one such irony is perhaps the most significant result of these complex developments. I refer to the contrast between American predominance in both academic and professional psychology worldwide, and the insecure standing of trained psychologists in America itself. Vagueness and confusion in the use of the term "psychologist" in public discussion have been remarkably consistent over time; the term itself lacks legal protection in any case. All this, not to mention the omnipresence of self-help books, which are often placed on the psychology shelves of many bookstores whether their authors are psychologists or not, indicates that even in the United States, where most of the world's psychologists live and work, trained academics and professionals can hardly claim hegemony over psychological discourse in the public sphere to the degree that physical scientists can in their fields.

Given this incomplete victory in the century-long struggle for scientific and professional autonomy and authority in psychology, it might well be asked why such a shakily legitimated field has acquired such an important role in twentieth-century culture and society. Roger Smith's notion of "psychological society," cited earlier, may be of some help here, but it cannot answer the causal question, except by suggesting that developments within psychology are responses to demand, which in turn shape subsequent demand by organizing supply, as Gergen (2007) suggests. Nikolas Rose (1990, 1996), in contrast, has argued that psychological practices make possible particular kinds of social authority, assembled at first *ad hoc*, then grafted onto all activities connected with the stewardship of human conduct in liberal-democratic polities, from law and penal administration to education and parenting. No single profession has monopolized the codification and certification of these activities, aimed at simplifying the administration of modern life by producing calculable individuals and manageable social relations. Precisely because it is so diffuse and widespread, on this view, psychological knowledge shapes the practices of welfare states and justifies them with a rationale, according to which individuals are required to be free and to feel obligated to correct or repair defects if they fail to cope on their own. Such an interpretation could explain why reflexive practices, nicely epitomized in the phrase "working on one's self" or "working on a relationship," have become the norm in late modern societies.

A further implication of such views is that psychology's alleged objects themselves – mind, behavior, and the self – are not simply invariant fixtures of the species, but may have cultural as well as natural histories. These histories also require study in order to understand the historical development of scientific discourse about them. Such questions have only recently received the attention they deserve, despite the long-standing focus on "mentalities" in cultural history. (For important first steps in this direction, see Staeuble 1991 and Porter 1997. For more recent studies, see Egighian 2004; Egighian, Killen and Leuenberger 2007, and the literature cited there.) Whether the "self" or "selves" now being evoked or constructed in recent cultural histories has anything to do with the "self" described in (social) psychological research (discussed, e.g., in Sturm 2007) is another matter entirely.

REFERENCES

Adorno, T. W., Frenkel-Brunswik, E., Levinson, D. & Sanford, N. (1950). *The Authoritarian Personality*. New York: Harper & Row.

Allport, G. (1954). *The Nature of Prejudice*. Reading, MA: Addison-Wesley.

Asch, S. E. (1952). *Social Psychology*. New York: Prentice-Hall.

Ash, M. G. (1992). Cultural Contexts and Scientific Change in Psychology: Kurt Lewin in Iowa. *American Psychologist*, 47, 198–207.

(1995). *Gestalt Psychology in German Culture 1890–1967: Holism and the Quest for Objectivity*. Cambridge & New York: Cambridge University Press.

(1999). Kurt Gottschaldt and Psychological Research in Nazi and Socialist Germany. In: K. Macrakis & D. Hoffmann (Eds.), *Science under Socialism: East Germany in Comparative Perspective*, pp. 286–301, 360–365. Cambridge, MA: Harvard University Press.

(2001). Psychology: Historical and Cultural Perspectives. In: Neil J. Smelser & Paul Baltes (Eds.), *International Encyclopedia of the Social and Behavioral Sciences*, pp. 12399–12405. Oxford: Pergamon.

(2003). Psychology. In: D. Ross & T. Porter (Eds.), *The Modern Social Sciences* (*The Cambridge History of Science*, Vol. 7), pp. 251–274. Cambridge & New York: Cambridge University Press.

(2005). Learning from Persecution: Émigré Jewish Social Scientists' Studies of Authoritarianism and Anti-Semitism after 1933. In: B. Meyer & M. Kaplan (Eds.), *Jüdische Welten. Juden in Deutschland vom 18. Jahrhundert bis in die Gegenwart* (*Festschrift für Monika Richarz*), pp. 271–294. Göttingen: Wallstein Verlag.

(2007). Psychological Thought and Practice – Historical and Interdisciplinary Perspectives. In: M. G. Ash & T. Sturm (Eds.), *Psychology's Territories: Historical and Contemporary Perspectives from different Disciplines*, pp. 1–27. Mahwah, NJ & London: Lawrence Erlbaum Associates.

Ash, M. G. & Sturm, T. (Eds.) (2007). *Psychology's Territories: Historical and Contemporary Perspectives from Different Disciplines*. Mahwah, NJ: Lawrence Erlbaum Associates.

Backhouse, R. E. & Fontaine, P. (2010). Towards a History of the Social Science. In: R. E. Backhouse & P. Fontaine (Eds.), *The History of the Social Sciences since 1945*, pp. 184–233. Cambridge: Cambridge University Press.

Bargal, D. (2006). Personal and Intellectual Influences Leading to Lewin's Paradigm of Action Research. *Action Research*, 4, 367–388.

Barker, R. (1968). *Ecological Psychology: Concepts and Methods for Studying the Environment of Human Behavior.* Stanford, CA: Stanford University Press.

Barker, R. & Wright, H. (1955). *Midwest and Its Children: The Psychological Ecology of an American Town.* Evanston, IL: Row, Peterson & Co.

Bartlett, F. C. (1932). *Remembering.* Cambridge: Cambridge University Press.

(1958). *Thinking.* New York: Basic Books.

Bazerman, C. (1987). Codifying the Social Scientific Style: The APA "Publication Manual" as a Behaviorist Rhetoric. In: J. S. Nelson, D. McCloskey & A. Megill (Eds.), *The Rhetoric of the Human Sciences: Language and Argument in Scholarship and Public Affairs*, pp. 125–143. Madison, WI: University of Wisconsin Press.

Bierbrauer, G. (1992). Ein Sozialpsychologe in der Emigration. Kurt Lewins Leben, Werk und Wirkungsgeschichte. In: E. Böhne & W. Motzkau-Valeton, *Die Künste und die Wissenschaften im Exil 1933–1945*, pp. 313–332. Heidelberg: Winter.

Blowers, G. H. & Turtle, A. M. (Eds.) (1987). *Psychology Moving East: The Status of Western Psychology in Asia and Oceania.* Boulder, CO/Sydney: Westview Press.

Borck, C. (2005a). *Hirnströme. Eine Kulturgeschichte der Elektroencephalographie.* Göttingen: Wallstein Verlag.

(2005b). Writing Brains: Tracing the Psyche with the Graphical Method. *History of Psychology*, 8, 79–94.

Broadbent, D. E. (1958). *Perception and Communication.* Oxford: Pergamon.

Busse, S. (2004). *Psychologie in der DDR. Die Verteidigung der Wissenschaft und die Formung der Subjekte.* Weinheim: Beltz Verlag.

Capshew, J. (1999). *Psychologists on the March: Science, Practice and Professional Identity in America, 1929–1969.* Cambridge and New York: Cambridge University Press.

(2007). Reflexivity Revisited: Changing Psychology's Frame of Reference. In: M. G. Ash & T. Sturm (Eds.), *Psychology's Territories: Historical and Contemporary Perspectives from Different Disciplines*, pp. 343–356. Mahwah, NJ: Lawrence Erlbaum.

Cartwright, D. (1959). Lewinian Theory as a Contemporary Systematic Framework. In: S. Koch (Ed.), *Psychology: A Study of a Science, Vol. 4. General Systematic Formulations*, pp. 7–91. New York: McGraw-Hill.

Cattell, R. B. (Ed.) (1966). *Handbook of Multivariate Experimental Psychology.* New York: Rand McNally.

Cattell, R. B. & Scheier, I. H.(1961). *The Meaning and Measurement of Neuroticism and Anxiety.* New York: The Ronald Press.

Cronbach, L. (1957). The Two Disciplines of Scientific Psychology. *American Psychologist*, 12, 671–684.

Danziger, K. (1990). *Constructing the Subject: Historical Origins of Psychological Research.* Cambridge and New York: Cambridge University Press.

(1992). The Project of an Experimental Social Psychology: Historical Perspectives. *Science in Context*, 5, 309–328.

(1997). *Naming the Mind: How Psychology Found its Language.* London: Sage Publications.

(2000). Making Social Psychology Experimental: A Conceptual History, 1920–1970. *Journal of the History of the Behavioral Sciences*, 36, 329–347.

DeCarvalho, R. J. (1991). *The Founders of Humanistic Psychology.* New York: Praeger.

Dehli, M. (2007). *Leben als Konflikt. Zur Biographie Alexander Mitscherlichs.* Göttingen: Wallstein Verlag.

Dewsbury, D. A. (Ed.) (1997). *Unification through Division: Histories of the Divisions of the American Psychological Association*, 2 vols. Washington, DC: American Psychological Association.

Edwards, P. N. (1996). *The Closed World: Computers and the Politics of Discourse in Cold War America*. Cambridge, MA: MIT Press.

Egighian, G. (2004). The Psychologization of the Socialist Self: East German Forensic Psychology and its Deviants, 1945–1975. *German History*, 22, 181–205.

Egighian, G., Killen, A. & Leuenberger, C. (Eds.) (2007). *The Self as Project: Politics and the Human Sciences, Osiris*, Vol. 22. Chicago, IL: University of Chicago Press.

Eysenck, H. J. (1953). *The Structure of Human Personality*. London: Methuen.

(1994). *Dimensions of Personality*. New York: Transaction.

Flavell, J. (1963). *The developmental psychology of Jean Piaget*. New York: Van Nostrand.

Furumoto, L. (1987). On the Margins: Women and the Professionalization of Psychology in the United States 1890–1940. In: M. G. Ash & W. R. Woodward (Eds.), *Psychology in Twentieth-Century Thought and Society*, pp. 93–114. New York/Cambridge: Cambridge University Press.

Gardner, H. (1985/1996). *The Mind's New Science*. New York: Basic Books. First published 1985.

Gergen, K. (2007). Colonizing the Self in Psychology and Society. In: M. G. Ash & T. Sturm (Eds.), *Psychology's Territories: Historical and Contemporary Perspectives from Different Disciplines*, pp. 149–168. Mahwah, NJ: Lawrence Erlbaum.

Gigerenzer, G. (1992). From Tools to Theories: Discovery in Cognitive Psychology. *Science in Context*, 5, 329–350.

Gigerenzer, G. & Goldstein, D. G. (1996). Mind as Computer: Birth of a Metaphor. *Creativity Research Journal*, 9, 131–144.

Gigerenzer, G. & Sturm, T. (2007). Tools=Theories=Data? On Some Circular Dynamics in Cognitive Science. In: M. G. Ash & T. Sturm (Eds.), *Psychology's Territories: Historical and Contemporary Perspectives from Different Disciplines*, pp. 305–342. Mahwah, NJ: Lawrence Erlbaum.

Gilgen, A. R. (1982). *American Psychology since World War II: A Profile of the Discipline*. Westport, CN: Greenwood Press.

Hagner, M. (1996). Der Geist bei der Arbeit: Überlegungen zur visuellen Repräsentation cerebraler Prozesse. In: C. Borck (Ed.), *Anatomien medizinischen Wissens*, pp. 259–286. Frankfurt am Main: Fischer Verlag.

(2007). Thought Reading, Brain Mirror, Neuroimaging: Insight into the Brain or the Mind? In: M. G. Ash & T. Sturm (Eds.), *Psychology's Territories: Historical and Contemporary Perspectives from Different Disciplines*, pp. 287–303. Mahwah, NJ: Lawrence Erlbaum.

Hartnack, C. (2001). *Psychoanalysis in Colonial India*. Delhi: Oxford University Press.

Heims, S. J. (1993). *Constructing a Social Science for Postwar America: The Cybernetics Group*. Cambridge, MA: MIT Press.

Herman, E. (1996). *The Romance of American Psychology*. Berkeley, CA: University of California Press.

(2003). Psychologism and the Child. In: T. M. Porter & D. Ross (Eds.), *The Modern Social Sciences (The Cambridge History of Science*, Vol. 7), pp. 649–662. Cambridge: Cambridge University Press.

Hilgard, E. R. (1987). *Psychology in America: A Historical Survey*. Orlando, FL: Harcourt, Brace Jovanovich.

Jahoda, M. & Christie, R. (Eds.) (1954). *Studies in the Scope and Method of "The Authoritarian Personality": Continuities in Social Research*. Glencoe, IL: The Free Press.

Janousek, J. & Sirotkina, I. (2003). Psychology in Russia and Central and Eastern Europe. In: T. M. Porter & D. Ross (Eds.), *The Modern Social Sciences (The Cambridge History of Science*, Vol. 7), pp. 431–445. Cambridge: Cambridge University Press.

Jorawsky, D. (1989). *Russian Psychology: A Critical History*. Oxford: Basil Blackwell.

Klix, F. (1966). *Information und Verhalten*. Berlin/GDR: Deutscher Verlag der Wissenschaften.

Koch, S. (Ed.) (1959–1963). *Psychology: A Study of a Science*, 6 vols. New York: McGraw-Hill.

Koch, S. & Leary, D. E. (Eds.) (1985). *A Century of Psychology as Science*. New York: McGraw-Hill.

Kozulin, A. (1984). *Psychology in Utopia. Toward a Social History of Soviet Psychology*. Cambridge, MA: MIT Press.

Kusch, M. (1999). *Psychological Knowledge: A Social History and Philosophy*. London: Routledge.

Lewin, K., Lippitt, R. & White, R. K. (1939). Patterns of Aggressive Behavior in Experimentally Created "Social Climates." *Journal of Social Psychology*, 10, 271–299.

Lewin, K. (1948). *Resolving Social Conflicts*. New York: Harper & Row.

Luria, A. R. (1966). *Human Brain and Psychological Processes*. New York: Harper & Row.

(2005). *Autobiography of Alexander Luria: A Dialogue with the Making of Mind*. Mahwah, NJ: Lawrence Erlbaum.

Maasen, S. (2007). Governing By Will – The Shaping of the Will in Self-Help Manuals. In: M. G. Ash & T. Sturm (Eds.), *Psychology's Territories: Historical and Contemporary Perspectives from Different Disciplines*, pp. 111–128. Mahwah, NJ & London: Lawrence Erlbaum Associates.

Mattes, P. (1985). Psychologie im westlichen Nachkriegsdeutschland – Fachliche Kontinuität und gesellschaftliche Restauration. In: M. G. Ash & U. Geuter (Eds.), *Geschichte der deutschen Psychologie im 20. Jahrhundert. Ein Überblick*, pp. 201–224. Opladen: Westdeutscher Verlag.

Meehl, P. E. (1954). *Clinical versus Statistical Prediction*. Minneapolis, MN: University of Minnesota Press.

Métraux, A. (1985). Der Methodenstreit und die "Amerikanisierung" der Psychologie in der Bundesrepublik 1950–1970. In: M. G. Ash & U. Geuter (Eds.), *Geschichte der deutschen Psychologie im 20. Jahrhundert. Ein Überblick*, pp. 225–251. Opladen: Westdeutscher Verlag.

Morawski, J. G. (1992). Self Regard and Other Regard: Reflexive Practices in American Psychology, 1890–1940. *Science in Context*, 5, 281–308.

(2007). Scientific Selves: Discerning Subjects and Experimenters in Experimental Psychology in the United States, 1900–1935. In: M. G. Ash & T. Sturm (Eds.), *Psychology's Territories: Historical and Contemporary Perspectives from Different Disciplines*, pp. 129–148. Mahwah, NJ: Lawrence Erlbaum.

Moritz, K. P., Maimon, S. , Pockels, C. F. et al. (Eds.) (1783–1793). *Gnothi Sauthon, oder: Magazin zur Erfahrungsseelenkunde*. Berlin: Mylius.

Moscowitz, E. (2001). *In Therapy We Trust: America's Obsession with Self-Fulfillment*. Baltimore, MD: Johns Hopkins University Press.

Mulder, G. (1983). The Information Processing Paradigm: Concepts, Methods and Limitations. *Journal of Child Psychology and Psychiatry*, 24, 19–35.

Oesterreich, D. (1993). *Autoritäre Persönlichkeit und Gesellschaftsordnung. Der Stellenwert psychologischer Faktoren für politische Einstellungen*. Weinheim: Beltz Verlag.

Petzold, M. (1987). The Social History of Chinese Psychology. In: M. G. Ash & W. R. Woodward (Eds.), *Psychology in Twentieth-Century Thought and Society*, pp. 213–232. New York/Cambridge: Cambridge University Press.

Porter, R. (Ed.) (1997). *Rewriting the Self: Histories from the Renaissance to the Present*. London: Routledge.

Porter, T. M. (1995). *Trust in Numbers: The Pursuit of Objectivity in Science and Public Life*. Princeton, NJ: Princeton University Press.

Rabinbach, A. (1990). *The Human Motor: Energy, Fatigue and the Origins of Modernity*. New York: Basic Books.

Rösler, F. (2005). From Single-Channel Recordings to Brain-Mapping Devices: The Impact of Electroencephelography on Experimental Psychology. *History of Psychology*, 8, 95–117.

Rose, N. (1990). *Governing the Soul*. London: Routledge.

(1996). *Inventing Our Selves: Psychology, Power and Personhood*. Cambridge & New York: Cambridge University Press.

Rossiter, M. (1997). Which Science? Which Women? In: S. G. Kohlstedt & H. E. Longino (Eds.), *Women, Gender and Science: New Directions (Osiris*, Vol. 12), pp. 169–185. Chicago, IL: University of Chicago Press.

Roth, G., Münte, T. F. & Heinze, H. J. (2007). Can Psychological Processes Be Made Visible by Current Brain Research? In: M. G. Ash & T. Sturm (Eds.), *Psychology's Territories: Historical and Contemporary Perspectives from Different Disciplines*, pp. 251–273. Mahwah, NJ: Lawrence Erlbaum.

Routh, D. K. (1994). *Clinical Psychology since 1917: Science, Practice, and Organization*. New York: Plenum Press.

Samelson, F. (1986). Authoritarianism from Berlin to Berkeley: On Social Psychology and History. *Journal of Social Issues*, 42, 191–208.

Schultz, J. H. (1991). *Das Autogene Training: Konzentrierte Selbstentspannung. Versuch einer klinisch-praktischen Darstellung*. Stuttgart: Thieme. First published 1932.

Segal, J. (2004). Kybernetik in der DDR: Dialektische Beziehungen. In: Claus Pias (Ed.), *Cybernetics/Kybernetik: The Macy-Conferences 1946–1953*, Vol. 2, pp. 227–251. Zürich/Berlin: Diaphanes.

Shamdasani, S. (2005). "Psychotherapy": The Invention of a Word. *History of the Human Sciences*, 18, 1–22.

Smith, L. D. (1992). On Prediction and Control: B. F. Skinner and the Technological Ideal of Science. *American Psychologist*, 47, 216–223.

Smith, R. (1998). *The Norton History of the Human Sciences*. New York: W. W. Norton.

Staeuble, I. (1991). "Psychological Man" and Human Subjectivity in Historical Perspective. *History of the Human Sciences*, 4, 417–432.

Stone, W. F., Lederer, G. & Christie, R. (Eds.) (1993). *Strength and Weakness: The Authoritarian Personality Today*. New York: Springer.

Strack, F. & Schwarz, N. (2007). Asking Questions: Measurement in the Social Sciences. In: M. G. Ash & T. Sturm (Eds.), *Psychology's Territories: Historical and Contemporary Perspectives from Different Disciplines*, pp. 225–250. Mahwah, NJ: Lawrence Erlbaum.

Sturm, T. (2007). The Self between Psychology and Philosophy: The Case of Self-Deception. In: M. G. Ash & T. Sturm (Eds.), *Psychology's Territories: Historical and Contemporary Perspectives from Different Disciplines*, pp. 169–193. Mahwah, NJ: Lawrence Erlbaum.

Thue, F. W. (2006). *In Quest of a Democratic Social Order. The Americanization of Norwegian Social Scholarship 1918–1970*. Doctoral dissertation, University of Oslo.

Tolman, E. C. (1948). Kurt Lewin (1890–1947). *Psychological Review*, 55, 1–4.

van Strien, P. J. (1997). The American "Colonization" of Northwest European Social Psychology after World War II. *Journal of the History of the Behavioral Sciences*, 33, 349–363.

3

Economics

Roger E. Backhouse

The Second World War

The Second World War and the events surrounding it – the rise of the Nazi regime and the economic trauma of the 1930s – were crucial for economics. In the 1920s, though American economics had grown rapidly since the turn of the century, European economics remained dominant. The generation that had shaped economics as it entered the twentieth century, many of whose members died in the 1920s, was overwhelmingly European. In the 1920s and 1930s, a high proportion of the most innovative work was still done in Europe – Alfred Marshall's Cambridge, the London School of Economics (LSE), Karl Menger's seminar in Vienna, Stockholm, and Lausanne.

By the end of the Second World War, the situation was completely different. Hundreds of European economists, many Jewish, had been forced to emigrate and, though some stopped in Britain, most ended up in the United States (Hagemann 2000), joining those who had left Russia and Eastern Europe after the 1917 revolution. Many rapidly achieved influential positions: Harvard had Joseph Schumpeter (from Austria) and Wassily Leontief (from Russia via Germany); Jacob Marschak (Ukrainian, via Germany and Britain) was at the Cowles Commission in Chicago, along with many other émigrés; Fritz Machlup (Austrian) was at Johns Hopkins. The extent of this migration is shown by the fact that in 1945, half the articles in the *American Economic Review* (*AER*), the journal of the American Economic Association (AEA), were written by economists born outside the United States, but holding positions in U.S.

This chapter draws on Backhouse 2008; see also Backhouse 2010. I am indebted to Philippe Fontaine and Robert Adcock for helpful comments on an earlier draft, as well as to the many people who commented on the earlier piece.

universities.[1] Earlier in the century, the corresponding proportion had been less than 5 per cent.

It was, however, the Second World War itself that propelled the United States and, with it, American economics, to its dominant position (at least outside the Soviet bloc). Germany, a major centre of economics up to the 1930s, had been destroyed; in any case, most economics chairs had been filled with Nazi party members, usually with no significant academic reputation. French economists were inward looking because of the peculiar economic problems confronting postwar France (Arena 2008).[2] Britain was in a different position, for it had not suffered in the same way as continental Europe, and there had been significant wartime collaboration between British economists and their American counterparts (e.g., James Meade and Richard Stone were highly influential in the emerging field of national accounting [Vanoli 2008]), but its economics profession remained small and lacking the resources or organization to challenge U.S. dominance.

In contrast, American economics emerged from the Second World War much stronger than at the beginning, and it grew rapidly during the late 1940s and 1950s. Mobilization created great opportunities for American economists, large numbers being recruited into government organizations such as the Office of Price Administration, the War Production Board, the Bureau of Agricultural Economics, and the Treasury, many of which were extensions of agencies established under the New Deal, working on the mobilization of the U.S. economy. Economists were also recruited by the Office of Strategic Services (OSS), forerunner of the Central Intelligence Agency (CIA), which employed around fifty economists under the Harvard economist, Edward Mason, in its Research and Analysis Division (Katz 1989; Leonard 1991). There, they were employed alongside physicists and other scientists in tasks where economics shaded imperceptibly into statistics and engineering. They became valued as general problem solvers, analysing intelligence and solving problems related to military tactics and strategy. Operations research, an idea dating from the 1930s, came to be seen as close to economics. Economics emerged from the war with its reputation greatly enhanced, both by its contribution to mobilizing the American economy and for what it had contributed to military activities.

The so-called GI Bill of 1944 provided financial support for ex-servicemen returning to education, with the result that by 1950, the number of degrees

---

[1] See Backhouse 1998. Other evidence of the importance of émigrés in U.S. economics is provided by Frey and Pommerehne (1988), cited in Hagemann (2000, p. 115).
[2] For discussion of other European countries, see the essays in Coats (2000).

being awarded was more than double the number a decade earlier.[3] Many of these veterans chose to study social science. This created a demand for the economists who were no longer required in government service and who, in the later 1940s, could fill the academic posts created in response to rising student demand for economics. There was similar growth in other countries, but the sheer size of the American profession, the resources available to it, and its strong starting point meant that no other country was in a position to challenge American dominance.

What made this expansion so significant is that, as it expanded, the U.S. economics profession was transformed, institutionally and intellectually. What many economists had learned during their wartime experience was that economists could play a more technical role, similar to that of engineers. Wartime experience had shown that, faced with clear goals, it was possible to transform an economy through planning. The development of new quantitative techniques – from national income accounting to linear programming – made it much easier to see economics as a technical discipline, dealing with resource allocation and the relationship between means and ends, than had been the case for previous generations. There was also the influence of Keynesian economics, for many of those who entered the economics profession in the 1940s, whether they had served as economists in government during the war or entered economics after military service, were acutely aware of the Great Depression. Economists such as James Tobin, a leading Keynesian, had entered the profession because they were motivated by a desire to understand the Depression and to make sure that it did not happen again.

The result was an intellectual transformation. Before the Second World War, U.S. economics had been pluralist (Morgan and Rutherford 1998). There were 'neoclassical' economists, who engaged in theory, drawing on the theory of utility-maximizing consumers and profit-maximizing firms that stemmed from the work of Alfred Marshall, Léon Walras, John Bates Clark, and their late-nineteenth-century contemporaries. There were others, such as Frank Taussig, Jacob Viner, or Allyn Young, who used much less abstract theory. There was also a large group, known as institutionalists, who sought to make economics more scientific by providing it with strong empirical foundations. They were generally sceptical about what they saw as the highly abstract theorizing of their neoclassical counterparts. It was this approach that underlay Wesley Mitchell's National Bureau of Economic Research (NBER), which undertook a mass of statistical investigations,

---

[3]   A similar bill was passed a few years later, in relation to the Korean War.

including early work on the national accounts, the New Deal studies on business pricing by economists such as Gardiner Means, and the legal investigations of John Commons at Wisconsin.

In contrast, the trend in postwar empirical work was to formalize the relationship between economic theory and statistical work. Institutionalists had not dismissed theory altogether but they had generally been sceptical about neoclassical economic theory: it was too abstract in the sense of being insufficiently empirical to be taken seriously as scientific economics. In contrast, after 1945, economists increasingly adopted the view that scientific rigour required that theories be formulated as mathematical models, so that their implications could be derived rigorously, which implied a higher level of abstraction.[4] It was only once theories had been precisely formulated, usually as algebraic models, that they could be tested against data.[5] Empirical work came to be seen not as working towards a detailed statistical description of the economic world, but as involving formal tests of precisely specified hypotheses using statistical methods grounded in probability theory.[6] 'Quantitative methods' came to mean the algebraic techniques needed to specify and analyse theoretical models, as well as the construction and analysis of economic statistics.[7]

This change, along with a view of economics as social engineering, was encouraged by economists' wartime experiences. The development of national income accounting was central to planning in both the United States and Britain. Estimates of national income were used not just to calculate the extent to which civilian demand had to be reduced if inflation were to be avoided, but also to estimate the levels of military hardware that could be produced. Economists developed techniques for making the best use of limited shipping capacity and, more generally, for working out how resources could optimally be used. They were also involved, in the OSS, in the calculation of enemy military capacity, from the effects of allied bombing to estimating German tank production from the serial numbers of those captured or destroyed in battle. In

---

[4] Weintraub (1998) explains that this reflected a change in the way rigour was conceived in mathematics.

[5] Widespread use of the term 'model' dates only from the 1940s.

[6] European émigrés played a major role in developing these new methods, which was clearly linked to the broader philosophical changes represented by the movement away from Deweyan pragmatism (linked to Institutionalism) to logical positivism.

[7] This change, though not necessarily its timing, is most dramatically illustrated by the change that took place in the NBER. See Rutherford (2008).

an environment where disciplinary borderlines were blurred, economists were also involved in seemingly non-economic activities, such as designing gun sights and coping with the problems arising from the fact that different batches of shells would travel different distances when fired. If there were a common feature to these varied problems, it was optimization. Thus, when these economists entered or returned to academia, it was natural for them to see economics in terms of resource allocation. Their experience contrasted with that of, for example, J. K. Galbraith, a representative 'New Dealer' who for a while ran the wartime Office of Price Administration: though well aware of resource allocation problems and the role of the price mechanism, he remained much more conscious of the political element in economics (Parker 2005). Whereas the profession at large remained more sceptical, it was these more technical economists who were most enthusiastic about Lionel Robbins's (1932) definition of economics as the science that studies the allocation of scarce resources between competing ends, the implications of which were very different from earlier definitions in terms of the production of wealth or the study of the business system (Backhouse and Medema 2009).

These intellectual changes were linked to significant institutional changes. The Econometric Society had been established in 1930 as 'an international society for the advancement of economic theory in its relation to statistics and mathematics' (Frisch 1933, p. 1). Attracting the support of a businessman named Alfred Cowles, the society became linked to the Cowles Commission, set up in 1933. In 1939 the Cowles Commission moved to Chicago where, under Jacob Marschak, Research Director from 1943–48, its members worked out the theories and econometric (statistical) techniques that were to dominate postwar economics. The period after 1945 saw the rise to prominence within the economics profession of universities such as MIT and Berkeley, and the decline of the strongholds of the institutionalist approach to economics such as the University of Wisconsin (Backhouse 1998). There were also changes within universities that retained their prewar positions. Harvard became, under Alvin Hansen, the center of American Keynesianism. Beginning around 1950, Chicago moved towards a new style of economics influenced by Milton Friedman. Elsewhere, economists with a technical approach to the subject, including European émigrés, those who had acquired a technical perspective through working in interdisciplinary environments such as the OSS, and others who had passed through the Cowles Commission, were increasingly in evidence. They were still in the minority but became increasingly influential in ensuing decades.

The Context of Postwar Economics

During the Second World War, the U.S. armed forces had learned the value of bringing together scientists and engineers to undertake scientific research relevant to the war effort. Seeing that there would be a continuing need for such activities in peacetime, a group headed by General H. H. Arnold, Commanding General of the U.S. Air Force, established the RAND Corporation. Initially this was a division of the Douglas Aircraft Company, but in 1948 it became established as a non-profit organization with the aim of engaging in scientific research 'for the public welfare and security of the U.S.A.'.[8] It was an interdisciplinary environment where economists worked alongside physicists, engineers, and other social scientists. Its output spanned aviation, space research, and information technology. Its economic outputs included Kenneth Arrow's *Social Choice and Individual Values* (1951) and *Linear Programming and Operations Analysis* by Robert Dorfman, Paul Samuelson, and Robert Solow (1958). However, though these were highly influential, its most important influence was probably on the theory of games, perceived as directly relevant to problems of military strategy in an age of nuclear weapons.[9] Prominent developers of game theory among RAND's consultants and staff members included John von Neumann and Oskar Morgenstern, authors of an influential book on game theory published in 1944 (see pp. 48–9), Lloyd Shapley, Martin Shubik, and John Williams.[10]

In 1949, after the Communist takeover of China, the ongoing fear of the Soviet Union developed into the Cold War. This clearly reinforced the perception that the U.S. armed forces needed the research that RAND, with its links to academia, could provide. This was true for economics as much as science, engineering, or psychology. In addition, the U.S. Navy sponsored research in economics. Though its Office of Naval Research (ONR) had a smaller impact on economics than RAND, it was still able to include Arrow and Herbert Simon in the list of Nobel Prize winners it had sponsored. The ONR underwrote Project Troy, a collaborative social science venture in 1950–51 involving the CIA and the Massachusetts Institute of Technology

---

[8] From the 1948 Article of incorporation, quoted at http://www.rand.org/about/history/.

[9] The theory of games has a longer history. However, for obvious reasons, RAND was more interested in the theory of non-cooperative games, going back to John Nash's work around 1950, than in the theory of cooperative games applied to economics by John von Neumann and Oskar Morgenstern in the 1940s. See Leonard 2008.

[10] Its 'official history' can be found at http://www.rand.org/publications/PAFbook.pdf. For other accounts see Jardini (1996) and Mirowski (2002).

(MIT) on the problem of how to influence populations behind the Iron Curtain. This fed directly into MIT's Center for International Studies (CENIS), funded by the CIA, in which economists, notably Max Millikan and Walt Rostow, worked alongside psychologists and political scientists (this volume, chap. 8). The Cold War, and with it CIA funding, was important in the development of Area Studies, focusing first on the Soviet Union and China and later on Asia and Africa.

There was also a change in the way economists were involved in the design of economic policy. The experience of the New Deal and the Second World War, when economists involved with government agencies had been the target of much public criticism, led to a new role for U.S. government economists as represented by the Council of Economic Advisers (CEA), established in the Employment Act of 1946. CEA members were aides providing advice to those who were making policy. The nature of that advice changed over time: at the outset, under President Truman, the CEA's role was confined to forecasting, whereas during the 1960s, under President Kennedy, it took a much bolder role in designing a Keynesian expansion of the economy through a tax cut (Goodwin 1998, pp. 62–3; Bernstein 2004). This provided a model for the role of economists in other U.S. government agencies.

In other countries there was also a marked increase in the practice of employing professional economists in government after the Second World War. In Britain, for example, apart from the employment of economists in the Ministry of Agriculture, the provision of economic advice from within government (as opposed to bringing in academics or outsiders on a more or less *ad hoc* basis) began with the establishment of the Economic Section of the War Cabinet Secretariat, headed for most of the war by Lionel Robbins. This was eventually transformed into the Government Economic Service. In Britain, as in many other countries, the number of economists grew rapidly from the 1940s to the 1970s. There was also growth in the demand for economists from the organizations established as part of the postwar international settlement: the International Monetary Fund (IMF); the International Bank for Reconstruction and Development, later known as the World Bank; the General Agreement on Tariffs and Trade, later the World Trade Organization; and various bodies linked to the United Nations.

The basis for this expansion of economics was the notion that professional economists were needed and could be trusted to provide advice necessary for the conduct of economic policy. The Great Depression had seen not only a massive fall in production, but also a virtual collapse of the system of international trade, creating a determination that this should not happen again. Although it opted out of the League of Nations, the United States was at the heart of the postwar system, which two prominent economists, Harry Dexter White and John Maynard Keynes, had played a crucial role in designing. The United States also became involved in the reconstruction of Europe. Planning of some sort was necessary: in some countries (Britain and France), such planning was sufficiently extensive to be described as socialism, whereas in countries such as the United States or Germany, it was better described as management rather than anything resembling socialism, even if business leaders found it useful to describe it that way. Nevertheless, in either case, there was an enhanced role for economists as technical advisers.

The need for macroeconomic management was a lesson drawn from the experience of the Great Depression. In 1937, after several years of recovery but still a long way from full employment, the U.S. economy began to move back into recession. A group of economists in the Roosevelt Administration noticed that there appeared to be a connection between government spending and the performance of the economy. On the basis of this, they argued for a deficit in the 1938 budget to turn the economy around.[11] In Germany, political constraints meant that the government had no choice but to implement policies that created government deficits. In Scandinavia, policies were based around theoretical ideas developed by Swedish economists. Governments discovered, in various ways, that deficit spending could create employment. This idea was later reinforced by the virtual elimination of unemployment, at least in Britain and the United States, during the Second World War.

Though these policies had varied origins, in the postwar period they came to be associated with the name of a British economist, John Maynard Keynes. His book *The General Theory of Employment, Interest and Money* (1936) was seen as providing the theoretical basis for policies of demand management: it provided, for many economists, an explanation of why the Great Depression had occurred and of how a repetition of this episode could be avoided. Although Keynes himself had not endorsed government deficits (except to fund investment projects), and although he had placed great emphasis on monetary policy, what came to be known as fiscal fine tuning (adjusting the budget to achieve continuous full employment) became known as Keynesian economic policy. Such policies became closely linked to the idea of the welfare state that emerged in the postwar period: not only was full employment itself a key component of welfare,

[11] This paragraph is based on Bateman (2006, pp. 282–3).

but without reasonably low levels of unemployment, it would be impossible to fund social security systems that would keep people out of poverty. Keynesianism came to be the name applied to the political philosophy that dominated what Jean Fourastié later called the thirty glorious years from the end of the Second World War to the mid-1970s (Bateman 2006).

In certain quarters, however, Keynesianism came to be portrayed not as providing the basis for social democracy, but as tantamount to communism. Paul Samuelson had claimed that despite the teaching of Keynesian economics, his textbook *Economics* (1948) survived only because it was written in a clearly scientific style. For members of the American business community who were hostile to government intervention, Keynesians presented a far more plausible target than the U.S. Communist Party. As McCarthyism took hold, attacks on left-wing economists intensified; their victims included Lawrence Klein who was denied tenure at Michigan in 1954, but later became an influential figure in the construction of large-scale Keynesian macroeconomic models (Schrecker 1986, pp. 253–5).[12]

Sponsorship of economics also came from the private sector. In the interwar period, the main sources of private funding were the charitable foundations associated with Carnegie, Sloan, Rockefeller, and Russell Sage. These foundations had funded the NBER (1919) and the Brookings Institution (1927) to conduct independent research into, respectively, economics and social science. In the 1920s and 1930s, the Rockefeller Foundation was heavily involved in supporting European social science, including economics, and focusing on building institutions. Oxford, Cambridge, and Manchester Universities, and LSE all were able to develop through Rockefeller grants, which also funded the National Institute of Economic and Social Research. After 1933, as well as mounting a programme to support scholars migrating from Europe, the foundation switched to problem-oriented research focusing on economics (Stapleton 2003; Crowther-Heyck 2006). This activity continued after 1945, but from 1951, the Rockefeller Foundation was dwarfed by the Ford Foundation. These foundations had always held to a position of scientific neutrality, though their funding served to represent and to promote values that were congenial to and represented the perceived interests of the United States.

In the era of the Cold War, the borderline between private- and government-sponsored support for economics would become blurred. Support for rational analysis of economic problems rather than ostensibly 'political'

---

[12] Lee (2004, p. 180) claims that at least twenty-seven economists were directly affected by McCarthyism.

analysis had a history going back at least to the Progressive Era, but during the Cold War 'rational choice' came to be linked to the struggle for democratic over totalitarian values. Rational choice represented individualism against collectivism, and acquired a stronger ideological dimension (Amadae 2003). This was represented by the links that developed between RAND and the Ford Foundation, represented by H. Rowan Gaither's position as Chairman of RAND's Board of Trustees and as President of the Ford Foundation. RAND produced 'systems analysis', a broad umbrella encompassing a range of mathematical work centred on rational choice. Game theory, developed at RAND and at Princeton University, the home of von Neumann and John Nash, and where economist Martin Shubik developed strong connections with the mathematics department, was applied by Thomas Schelling to bombing strategies in the Vietnam War, the conduct of which was directed by Robert MacNamara who had been at the Ford Motor Company before he became Secretary of Defense. At MIT, CENIS funding came from the CIA through Rockefeller and Ford (Simpson 1998, p. xxxiv, n. 18; Blackmer 2002).

One way in which foundation activity, involving primarily Carnegie and Ford, changed the institutional setting for economics was through its involvement in developing business schools. In the late 1950s and early 1960s, the Ford Foundation, following a strategy it often followed, invested massively in business schools by designating five 'centers of excellence'. These centres would adopt new standards, creating pressure on others to follow their lead. Although the Harvard Business School received the most funding, the first to receive a large grant was Carnegie-Tech's Graduate School of Industrial Administration (GSIA).[13] The significance of this was that, though the involvement of Harvard gave the project legitimacy in the business community, the GSIA represented the new approach that was being fostered. Its tone was set by the economist Lee Bach, Dean of GSIA. This emphasized disciplinary-based scholarship and the application of quantitative methods. He appointed political scientist Herbert Simon and economist William Cooper, both trained at Chicago, who helped him establish a curriculum involving economics alongside organizational behaviour and quantitative management techniques. Unlike traditional vocational models for business education, such as Harvard's case-study approach, advanced training in quantitative methods and a background in engineering were prerequisites (Khurana 2007, pp. 254–5).

---

[13] The others were the business schools at Chicago, Columbia, and Stanford. This account is drawn from Khurana (2007, chap. 6).

This development clearly had implications for business schools, where economics became the dominant discourse, but it also affected economics itself, for economists in business schools remained economists but now brought to economics a perspective that reflected their location in GSIA (see later).

The Growth of an International, Technical Economics

In the postwar period, as Solow (1997) has observed, economics became more technical.[14] Economists increasingly saw themselves as model builders. The most visible aspect of this change was the increasing use of mathematics but it was not confined to that, for it involved a different way of thinking in which economists consciously analysed structures that were abstracted from the world they were analysing. Such an attitude was consistent with the use of many types of mathematics ranging from basic algebra and geometry to much more-advanced techniques.

At one extreme lay Gérard Debreu, trained in the French Bourbaki school of mathematics, who introduced his *The Theory of Value* in 1959 by saying that he approached his subject with the degree of rigour associated with the contemporary formalist school of mathematics. Few economists shared Debreu's commitment to pursuing axiomatic methods with this degree of rigour,[15] but even where economists were less rigorous, there was a movement towards placing economic theory on a more formal foundation. In the 1950s, the most prominent instance of this trend was general-equilibrium (GE) analysis (the subject of Debreu's book), which involved searching for the most general assumptions under which it was possible to prove the existence, uniqueness, and stability of equilibrium in a system of perfectly competitive markets (markets in which no trader has any bargaining power) involving arbitrary numbers of consumers and producers (Ingrao and Israel 1990; Weintraub 2002).

Another very formal approach was game theory, whose most prominent exponents in the 1940s were the mathematician and polymath John von Neumann and economist Oskar Morgenstern, authors of *The Theory of Games and Economic Behavior* (1944). Though he was a critic of formalism as the term was understood in mathematics, von Neumann (with

---

[14] This section draws on the corresponding section of Backhouse (2008), from which some paragraphs are taken.

[15] For example, Kenneth Arrow, though he could collaborate with Debreu, also undertook much work that was, by the standards of formalist mathematics, much less rigorous.

Morgenstern) shared a commitment to axiomatic methods. However, his concern with artificial intelligence, as Mirowski (2002) has argued, differentiated his views sharply from those of economists concerned with general competitive equilibrium.

Probably the most influential exponent of mathematics in economics was Paul Samuelson, whose *Foundations of Economic Analysis* (1947), written at Harvard before he became the leading economist at MIT, amounted to a manifesto for mathematical economics. His work, which arose from a mathematical tradition very different from the European traditions influenced by von Neumann and Debreu, sought to be rigorous without being based on axiomatic methods. His emphasis was on deriving testable propositions, implying a very different attitude towards the role of mathematics. Solow, cited earlier, was closer to Samuelson, seeing mathematical methods as tools for analysing concrete problems, a far cry from the formalism of Debreu. Even further from formalism but equally influential was the Chicago School, which was dominated from the 1940s to the 1970s by Milton Friedman (see p. 59 below). Friedman favoured simpler models and was more sceptical about complex mathematical reasoning.[16]

What lay behind all such work was a more basic change: conceiving theory as something that stood apart from application (Backhouse 1998, pp. 105–6). Irrespective of whether theories were developed in tandem with applications or separately, economists increasingly distinguished between theoretical propositions and statements about the world, a distinction that, in the interwar period, was frequently blurred. This change is reflected in the language economists used when theorizing, talking increasingly in terms of 'models', a term now almost universal that was hardly used before the Second World War. The notion of modelling, whether theoretical or empirical, went along with the idea that economics should be technical and scientific.

As economics became more technical, economics education changed, a process in which the AEA became involved. During the 1940s, partly to work out how the profession could support the war effort and partly because of a sense of uncertainty about how economics should be taught, the AEA reviewed undergraduate economics education. Supported by the Rockefeller Foundation, a committee chaired by Harold Bowen then turned to the graduate curriculum (Bowen 1953). The result of extensive consultation, the Bowen Report argued for a 'common core' for graduate work. It

---

[16] See Hands and Mirowski (1998) on the differences between the approaches associated with Stanford, MIT, and Chicago.

should consist 'primarily of economic theory including value, distribution, money, employment, and at least a nodding acquaintance with some of the more esoteric subjects such as dynamics, theory of games and mathematical economics' (p. 3). No one, it was argued, had claim to an economics PhD without 'rigorous initiation' into these areas as well as economic history, history of economic thought, statistics, and research methods (p. 43). Mathematics was placed alongside Russian, German, and Chinese, in the sense that it was considered important to have some economists to have knowledge of it, but it was not necessary for all to do so.

In Bowen's report, the core was still very broad – a statement of the range of knowledge that those with a PhD in economics should be expected to have. Over the following two decades, the term came to be used more narrowly, referring to 'a common core of basic economic theory' (Ruggles 1962, p. 487) and the emphasis on mathematics increased. In the survey by Nancy Ruggles (1970), the subject was defined in the now-familiar way of a unifying core of micro and macro theory, quantitative methods (interestingly, econometrics, simulation, survey methods, and operations research), and a range of applied fields that did not include any history.

At the same time, microeconomics and macroeconomics were themselves becoming more technical, to the extent that by the end of the 1980s, some liberal arts professors claimed that a PhD from the leading graduate schools no longer equipped someone to teach at the undergraduate level: they know too little about either the literature on economics or the institutions of contemporary market economies. The AEA again commissioned a report, but little changed (Krueger 1991; Colander 1992).[17] A survey conducted in the late 1980s found evidence that PhD students had become sceptical about the value of the hurdles through which they were jumping (Colander and Klamer 1987, 1990). However, when the exercise was repeated a decade and a half later, it suggested that students had adjusted to the more technical syllabus and that disquiet was much less (Colander 2005). These changes in the discipline were linked to another dimension of postwar economics during this period: its internationalization. As long as economics was closely linked to politics, let alone to law, as was the case in much of Europe in the first half of the century, it remained linked to specific cultures. As it became more technical, it became easier for economics to cross boundaries. This process was inseparable from the position of the United States. There had long been transatlantic exchanges between American and European

---

[17] Coats (1992) makes a comparison with Bowen (1953).

economists,[18] and in the interwar period such exchanges had been assisted by the Rockefeller and other foundations. Such contacts increased after 1945, assisted by the close American involvement in European reconstruction and by the reduced cost of international travel and communication. Many foreign economists either undertook postgraduate study in the United States or spent sabbaticals in U.S. universities.[19] This was reflected in significant changes in European economics. Academic systems became more like their American counterpart, with increased emphasis on publication in journals as the criterion for advancement, as well as a trend towards publication in English. Internationalization based on technical economics was also fostered by international organizations such as the IMF and the World Bank.

The speed and extent of these changes varied greatly. For example, in the United Kingdom, the proportion of staff with a degree from an American university rose steadily from 1950 to the 1990s. The highest proportion was at the London School of Economics, where it reached 45 per cent by the mid-1990s, whereas in other universities it was only 5 per cent. In Belgium, CORE at the Université Catholique de Louvain, was an important centre for economists with strong U.S. connections. Similarly, there was variability in the speed with which PhD requirements changed, with some British universities adopting the American model in the 1950s and 1960s, while others did not require any coursework beyond undergraduate level as late as the 1990s. In Britain, emphasis on a doctorate took the place of a system where it was common to enter academic work without any postgraduate qualification. In contrast, in much of continental Europe, advancement required the equivalent of a Ph.D. degree followed some years later by an advanced doctorate. There was also the complication of language and, in many cases, academic systems that were much more rigid and less rapid to change, but many of these changes still took place, culminating in the Bologna declaration of 1999, which sought to harmonize higher education within the European Union along lines similar to those prevailing in the United States. The emergence of an international economics was also represented by the emergence of intercontinental commuters, with a way of life impossible before the Boeing 707. The outstanding example is Harry Johnson, a Canadian who for several years simultaneously held Chairs at LSE and Chicago, and was legendary both for his productivity and the extent of his international travel (Moggridge 2008).

---

[18] In the mid- to late nineteenth century it had been normal for Americans wanting post-graduate education to go to Germany.

[19] This and the following paragraph are based on the case studies in Coats (1997, 2000).

Outside Europe, there was the further factor of decolonization. At the end of the Second World War, many countries were still closely linked to former colonial powers, and the changes involved a switch from those to the United States.

As in Europe, these changes were partly a matter of emulation, though in some cases change was brought about through connections with U.S. universities. Chicago economists developed close links with Latin American countries, consciously exporting Chicago economics to Chile: Chilean students studied in Chicago, and Chicago staff taught at the Catholic University of Chile (Valdes 1995; Harberger 1997). Similar developments took place in Brazil, though involving a much wider range of universities: Chicago, Berkeley, Harvard, Yale, Michigan, Illinois, and Vanderbilt (Loureiro 1997). The U.S. Agency for International Development and the Ford Foundation provided a significant role in funding several of these interuniversity agreements.

The Age of Keynes and General Competitive Equilibrium

During the 1940s, Keynes came to be seen as having laid the foundations for what came to be known as 'macroeconomics', dealing with the economy as a whole.[20] It was distinguished from 'microeconomics', which dealt with individual firms, households, and markets for individual commodities, by the need to account for the fact that one agent's spending constituted another agent's income. The insight underlying Keynesian economics was that if, say, households increased their spending, aggregate income (wages and profits) would rise, enabling households to raise their spending even further, giving rise to what Keynes called the multiplier and the theory of income determination.

Keynesian economics made such a mark on economics for two reasons. The obvious reason is that it provided a new way to think about economic policy. If the theory was right, it demonstrated what many economists had long believed, namely that spending money on public works could raise the level of employment. It shifted attention from the business cycle to the level of employment. It also had a clear empirical counterpart in the national accounts. A less obvious, though equally important, reason was that Keynesian theory provided a set of mechanisms that could be analysed formally. It abounded in new concepts that could be analysed using the algebraic tools then available to economic theorists: it provided material for

---

[20] This was usually thought of as a nation, though this was not essential.

countless doctoral dissertations, crucial in a discipline that was expanding rapidly. The key relationship, the consumption function, which postulated a relationship between consumers' expenditure and aggregate income, could be estimated using statistics from the newly available national accounts. At the same time, Keynesian theory presented conceptual puzzles concerning its relationship to what Keynes called 'classical theory'. Keynes's *General Theory* was an exciting book, seen by many economists as providing an explanation of why unemployment could occur, but it was not understood: it contained many lines of argument and unfamiliar terms that were not clearly related to existing theory. As Harry Johnson (1971, p. 5) put it, the theory was at just the right level of difficulty that young economists could leave their elders behind, developing a new economics without having to learn the old.

The framework that was perceived to underlie economics as a whole was the theory of general competitive equilibrium, often referred to simply as general equilibrium (GE). Modern work on GE had three main sources. First, there was the reformulation by John Hicks and Roy Allen, both at LSE in the 1930s, of the late nineteenth-century theories of Léon Walras and Vilfredo Pareto. They offered a representation of the individual based on assumptions about preferences, shorn of any taint of hedonism. Hicks then provided an elegant statement of GE theory in a widely read book, *Value and Capital* (1939). Second, there was the work in the United States, represented by Paul Samuelson's *Foundations of Economic Analysis* (1947), published after the War but conceived in the 1930s. This argued the case for using mathematics and provided economists with a toolkit for deriving 'operationally meaningful' theorems from economic theory. As with Hicks and Allen, Samuelson's theory of individual behaviour, the theory of 'revealed preference', sought to rid economics of the unnecessary metaphysical baggage of utility. Finally, there was there was the work that stemmed from Karl Menger's mathematical seminar in Vienna in the late 1930s, notably by John von Neumann and Abraham Wald. Their work drew on a different type of mathematics involving set theory, topology, and fixed-point theorems. They took the equations describing a GE system and reformulated them so that they could prove rigorously, using fixed-point theorems, that a solution existed.

It is safe to say that in the 1950s, and possibly for much of the 1960s, GE theory was fully understood by only a small minority of economists. However, it came to be seen, in a way not true before the 1950s, as the foundation on which the whole of economics should rest. Several things could explain this. Economists saw themselves as modellers, and by the mid-1950s had come to accept that individuals should be modelled as maximizing agents and that markets should be modelled as perfectly competitive. It also seemed self-evident that it was more rigorous to model the economy as a whole, allowing for interactions among all markets, than to analyse only a part of the system. GE theory was a mathematical representation of the economy that met all of these requirements, holding out the prospect of a completely general economic theory.

Existence proofs were not proofs that equilibrium existed in the real world (indeed, as the theory was refined, it became ever-clearer that GE theory depicted a world that could not conceivably exist), merely proofs that models had solutions. The justification for this was that, as Kenneth Arrow and Gérard Debreu had proved in the early 1950s, a competitive equilibrium was efficient in the sense that it was not possible to make any-one better off without making someone else worse off. This meant that it was possible to read GE theory as showing how a competitive market econ-omy could allocate resources efficiently. Existence proofs could therefore be read as showing that this vision of the world was coherent. Workaday theorising might be conducted at a lower level, but GE encapsulated the economist's vision of how an ideal market economy worked.

Macroeconomics was different in that it was based on relationships that, though reflecting individual behaviour, were identified at an aggregate level. It thus responded to newly available statistics, such as the evidence collected by Simon Kuznets on the relationship between consumption and income over long periods of time. Macroeconomics was always directly linked to policy, beginning with the fear, widespread in the 1940s, that there would be long-term stagnation once the world had demobilized. Inflation became a problem during the Korean War, and during the 1950s and 1960s there was ongoing concern with stabilization policy. However, perhaps more importantly, macroeconomics was driven by a theoretical agenda. Aggregate behaviour is clearly the result of actions taken by many individu-als. Economists interpreted this as meaning that macroeconomic theory should be based on theories about the behaviour of individuals. This was what came to be called the search for microfoundations in the 1960s and 1970s. These microfoundations were, naturally, sought in the theory of gen-eral competitive equilibrium.

Keynes had not thought in terms of GE but in the 1940s models based on his theory came to be seen as miniature GE models, typically comprising only four markets: commodities, money, government bonds, and labour. In order to explain macroeconomic phenomena, these models made assumptions that bore little relation to the assumptions made in rigorous

GE models. Unemployment, for example, was taken to imply that the labour market, for a reason that needed to be explained, is not in equilibrium. The search for microfoundations thus involved both showing how the elements of the Keynesian model (consumption function, marginal efficiency of capital, and liquidity preference) could be derived from individual optimising behaviour, and how the system as a whole could be related to a properly specified GE model of individual agents. Thus, Don Patinkin's *Money Interest and Prices* (1956, pp. 2, 7), probably the leading graduate textbook of the period, could describe his task as being 'the rigorous development of the monetary theory of an exchange economy', in which 'of necessity, our viewpoint is that of general-equilibrium analysis'. Starting from a GE model in which money played a special role, he derived both 'classical' and Keynesian results.

The perceived relationship between microeconomics and macroeconomics, foreshadowed by Keynes in his general theory, was summed up by Samuelson in the third (1955) edition of *Economics* as 'the neoclassical synthesis'. At the level of theory, Keynesian problems arose because wages and prices did not adjust sufficiently quickly for markets to be in equilibrium; analysing this was the task of macroeconomics. The economy could be controlled using highly detailed forecasting models that, by the 1960s, were being run by large teams of economists. Though specified on Keynesian lines (centred on the components of aggregate demand), their theoretical foundations were perceived to rest on GE theory. This had clear political implications, for it provided the theoretical basis for a mixed economy. Demand-management policy, conducted by government, was needed to maintain a high level of employment, but once that was achieved, competitive markets would allocate resources in a way that was generally efficient. Problems might arise in individual markets (such as natural monopolies, where technological conditions made competition impossible), but microeconomic theory could be used to work out appropriate policy interventions to deal with them.

However, although GE was the foundation on which economics was seen to be based, there were problems. The first was that there were many problems that GE models could not handle: they were too simple. Their defence, clearly articulated by Tjalling Koopmans (1957), formerly Research Director of the Cowles Commission, was that existing models were prototypes of later, more realistic models. In the meantime, therefore, macroeconomics and other fields, including labour and industrial economics, and the economics of less-developed countries, were free to be different. The second was that, in the early 1960s, the GE research programme encountered theoretical problems. In the early 1960s, a highly technical result (the Sonnenschein-Debreu-Mantel theorem) showed that it would never be possible to derive general stability conditions.

There was also a theoretical challenge from the macroeconomic side. Robert Clower (1965) argued that, if Keynesian economics was to make sense, the theory of the consumer needed to be placed on a new theoretical foundation. Formally, his argument was similar to one used by Patinkin in the second edition of *Money, Interest and Prices* (1965) about how unemployment was to be conceptualized. Axel Leijonhufvud took up these ideas in a book, the message of which was clearly captured by its title, *On Keynesian Economics and the Economics of Keynes* (1968): what was called 'Keynesian economics' was significantly different from the theory Keynes had proposed in his *General Theory*. Though using the language of GE, he outlined a vision of Keynes's economics that challenged the neoclassical synthesis.

Thus, when, in the 1970s, macroeconomic events took centre-stage, they did so in a discipline facing fundamental challenges to its theoretical foundations. Ironically, however, the practical challenges faced by economic theory led to these theoretical challenges being largely swept aside.

Radicalism and Reaction in the 1970s

The United States turned explicitly to Keynesian demand-management policies only in the 1960s when, under Presidents Kennedy and Johnson, tax cuts were used to expand the economy and substantially reduce unemployment. This was planned by the avowedly Keynesian economists on the Council of Economic Advisers. Started under Kennedy, but implemented under Johnson, was also a raft of civil rights legislation and a package of reforms advertised by Johnson as a 'war on poverty', or the 'Great Society Program' (Bernstein 2004; Huret 2008). But despite or even because of this legislation, the mid-1960s was a period of unrest, with rioting in many American cities and the growth of radical movement. There was also the Vietnam War, the origins of which can be dated back to Kennedy, but which escalated under Johnson. These had diverse effects on economics both through encouraging radicalism within the economics profession and their effects on the world economy.

In economics, the most tangible sign of radicalism was the establishment, in December 1968, of the Union for Radical Political Economics (URPE) (Lee 2004, pp. 187–9; Mata 2009).[21] This was formed by groups

---

[21] For a broader view of radical challenges to the status quo during this period, see Lee (2009).

of young economists and graduate students concerned that economics, as then taught and practiced, failed to address issues of war, race, gender, justice, and poverty; indeed, many saw economics as complicit in the problems in American society that they were diagnosing. URPE organized chapters in a number of universities and created a series of programs, which were part of a much broader radical student movement focused above all on Vietnam. They included Marxists but also economists who rejected Marxian theory, seeing orthodox economics as providing tools they could use. They also achieved considerable visibility in the profession. The programme of the 1970 AEA meeting, organized by J. K. Galbraith, explored many radical themes, and 'radical economics' was the subject of an article in the AEA's abstracting journal, *Journal of Economic Literature* (Bronfenbrenner 1970).

However, radical movements were kept under control more effectively by the AEA than by other social science organizations (Coats 2001), the economists largely seeking to preserve academic neutrality. There were changes, however, such as the establishment of the Committee on the Status of Women in the Economics Profession. A number of prominent radical economists were denied tenure, notably at Harvard, as a result of which the University of Massachusetts was able to become a centre of radical economics (along with the New School and a small number of other universities). Most important, radicals felt that the journals, in particular the *AER*, were closed to them. They were not the only group to feel this way. A group, politically close to the radicals, that called themselves post-Keynesian economists, emerged in the mid-1970s following the AEA meeting that Galbraith had organized. At the other end of the political spectrum, 'Austrian economics', drawing on the ideas of Ludwig von Mises and Friedrich Hayek, emerged. 'Public choice', associated with James Buchanan and Gordon Tullock, concerned with the analysis of non-market decision making, was becoming institutionalized in Virginia (Medema 2000). Though public choice later became accepted into the mainstream, what these groups had in common was a belief (often justified) that the mainstream journals were closed to them. They identified themselves as heterodox economists, developing new paradigms.

This upsurge in radical challenges to the establishment was a widespread phenomenon within the social sciences. However, it can be argued that there were also reasons for radical discontent that were specific to the economics profession. Since the early 1960s, economists had started to theorize formally about situations where information was limited; game theory was increasingly used to model strategic behaviour, first in industrial economics, later in other fields; economics abandoned the search for ever-more general models, working instead with models that were simple enough to be tractable. In the late 1960s, in his Presidential Address to the AEA, Milton Friedman (1968) made expectations central to an argument about why macroeconomic stabilization policy would fail, and Edmund Phelps and a group of collaborators began to lay the foundations of a macroeconomics based on limited information (Phelps et al. 1970). The 1960s also saw the application of economists' methods to problems outside the traditional domain of the subject, exemplified by public choice theory and Gary Becker's work on social problems (Becker 1976). These developments broadened economic theory to encompass problems that, previously, had not been amenable to formal theorizing. One consequence of this was that it became much easier than it would have been a decade earlier to dismiss much of the work by radicals as not meeting required technical standards. Moreover, it was not just radical work that was thought inadequate. In the eyes of the theorists who came to dominate macroeconomics in the 1970s, even Keynesian economics, along with most postwar macroeconomics, was condemned as methodologically flawed. A crucial stimulus to this revolution in macroeconomic theory came from the crisis in the world economy. The escalation of expenditure on the Vietnam War, combined with Lyndon Johnson's Great Society Program, contributed to an expansion in the world economy. Worldwide shortages began to emerge around 1970, with wages and commodity prices fuelling inflation. Throughout the 1960s the price of oil had been static, falling in real terms. In 1970–72, fuelled by the U.S. expansion, the world economy grew rapidly, leading to a rise in oil prices. The main oil exporters managed to form a cartel and in 1973–74 the price of oil rose by over 300 per cent. This had three main effects. Combined with a high level of demand, it pushed up prices, with inflation in industrial countries rising to 13.3 per cent in 1974. At the same time, it immediately transferred purchasing power from oil importers to oil exporters. Oil importers faced balance of payments problems and were forced to cut back their spending, without any matching increase in demand from oil exporters. The result was a sudden reduction in world demand, causing unemployment. On top of this, the rise in energy prices caused firms to adopt more energy-efficient techniques; this rendered obsolete many older, less energy-efficient capital goods.

The significance of these developments was that they created a situation that existing Keynesian or neoclassical synthesis models were ill-equipped to analyse. Some Keynesian economists had warned that the expansion caused by U.S. fiscal policy would lead to inflation, but once the world faced a massive supply shock, models that focused on aggregate demand failed to give useful policy advice and were unsatisfactory as theory.

The most visible response was monetarism. Since the 1950s, Milton Friedman had been arguing that inflation was caused by expansion of the money supply, and that the optimal monetary policy was for governments to commit themselves to keeping the growth rate of the money supply constant (using legislation to take it out of the hands of politicians). The oil price rises could be seen as part of a worldwide inflation caused by increases in the money supply in the previous two and three years. Monetarists challenged the consensus, not just because they questioned the wisdom of recent policies, but because they challenged the very idea of managing the economy so as to maintain full employment. During the 1970s, faced with the need to reduce inflation, governments paid increasing attention to the money supply, some introducing monetary targets.

The response of economic theorists to the challenge posed by these events was different. Monetarism was primarily an empirical doctrine, based on evidence concerning the relationship between money and prices over long periods of time. For theorists committed to rigorous theoretical modelling, it was inadequate. In the 1970s, economists were increasingly convinced that Friedman, in his AEA Presidential Address, had been right to focus on the importance of inflationary expectations, but he did not provide a method that could be used to develop a theoretically satisfactory model of the economy as a whole. In contrast, a method could be found in the parallel work of Phelps and his collaborators, who were constructing models in which agents made choices in the face of limited information.

The economist whose work, more than anyone else's, set the agenda from the mid-1970s was Robert Lucas, one of those involved in the Phelps volume. In 1973–76 he outlined a theory based on two main assumptions: that markets were perfectly competitive (and hence efficient) and that expectations were 'rational'. The latter involved assuming that agents predicted everything that it was possible to predict – that they had learned as much as they could learn about the economy. The argument for both assumptions was that if they were not satisfied, agents would have an incentive to change their behaviour, either by undercutting rivals (if markets were not in equilibrium) or by changing the way they formed their expectations (if expectations were not rational). Using these assumptions, Lucas and others argued that effective stabilization policy was impossible: demand management could affect the economy only if it were unpredictable and hence destabilizing. Predictable policy interventions could affect prices but would have no affect on the level of economic activity.

This was not the only response to the crisis faced by macroeconomics in the 1970s. Another, most eloquently expressed by Edmond Malinvaud (1977), was that simultaneous high unemployment and high inflation (stagflation) showed that markets could not be efficient; there must be rigidities and market imperfections, otherwise there would not be high unemployment. Building on ideas drawn from Clower and Leijonhufvud, they developed what came to be known as 'disequilibrium macro-economics', which claimed to offer a microeconomic foundation for macroeconomics that could explain why persistent unemployment might occur. However, by the end of the decade, economists were increasingly attracted to Lucas's 'new classical' approach because of its apparently greater rigour and the persuasiveness of the assumption that behaviour was rational. Thus, when it became clear that the evidence contradicted Lucas's claim that the business cycle was driven by unanticipated monetary shocks, the theory that displaced it was 'real business cycle' (RBC) theory, adopting the Lucasian framework but with real (productivity) shocks causing the cycle.

In the same way as Lucas transformed the theory relating to demand-management policy, Franco Modigliani and Merton Miller laid the foundations for a transformation of the theory of finance. In articles written in the late 1950s and early 1960s, they advanced a series of propositions radically at variance with traditional ideas, such as that a firm's dividend policy would not affect the price of its stock. These were taken up by Fischer Black, Myron Scholes, and others who, in the 1970s, developed the theories of finance, such as option pricing, that opened up the transformation of financial markets in the 1980s and 1990s (Mehrling 2005; MacKenzie 2006). Though outwardly very different (and though Modigliani remained a vociferous Keynesian), the new theory of finance had much in common with the new classical macroeconomics: both rested on rigorous application of the notion of rational behaviour in a world characterized by competitive markets.

An interesting feature of these changes in macroeconomics is that their most influential exponents were based, at one time, at Carnegie-Mellon's GSIA (see p. 47), which developed strong links with the universities of Chicago and Rochester. They brought into macroeconomics and finance a view of firms and management, fostered by their institutional location, as information-processing systems (Fourcade and Khurana 2008). For a business school in a small, newly established institution with no prior reputation in economics, it was associated with a remarkable number of those involved in transforming the subject in the 1970s.[22]

A consequence of these changes in macroeconomics was that macroeconomics became closer to microeconomics. This was one aspect of a methodological shift that was pervasive in the 1970s. Industrial economics became more theoretical, using game theory as the main theoretical tool. Development economics ceased to be a separate field, as economists began to assume that people in developing countries must be rational and that their behaviour must be open to analysis using the same theories that described developed countries. International economics was changed by the development of models where agents had monopoly power. Labour economics became more technical, as formal modelling based on the notion of human capital displaced more institutional approaches to labour problems.

Reinventing Markets – the 1980s and After

Friedman's opposition to Keynesian demand-management policies went along with a broader critique of government involvement in the economy that formed part of an ideological battle against socialism and collectivism.[23] This battle was fought both inside and outside academia by a network centred on the Mont Pèlerin Society (MPS). The MPS was formed in 1947 by Friedrich Hayek, Keynes's main rival as a macroeconomic theorist in the early 1930s, but whose ideas fell into obscurity after publication of the *General Theory*. During the 1940s, his academic work moved into political philosophy – *The Road to Serfdom* (1944), and later *The Constitution of Liberty* (1960) – and psychology. Concerned at the success of collectivist ideas and the threat to liberty (as he perceived it), Hayek brought together a group of like-minded individuals, including many economists, to embark on a long-term strategy to change public opinion. Though the group contained academics, including four from Chicago, it also included businessmen and, crucially in Hayek's view, 'second-hand dealers in ideas', such as Leonard Read from the Foundation for Economic Education, a free-market think tank established in 1946.

One branch of the network that developed around the MPS involved think tanks, such as the Institute of Economic Affairs, established in Britain in

---

[22] http://www.tepper.cmu.edu/about-tepper/history/the-b-school-change-agents/carnegie-connections/index.aspx. Last accessed date 1 March 2010.

[23] This section draws heavily on Backhouse (2005), which contains more extensive references to support the claims made.

1957, the Heritage Foundation, set up in the United States in 1973, and the Canadian Fraser Institute, set up in 1974. The purpose of these organizations was explained in the advice Hayek gave to Antony Fisher before he founded the IEA: 'I would join with others in forming a scholarly research organization to supply intellectuals in universities, schools, journalism and broadcasting with authoritative studies of the economic theory of markets and its application to practical affairs' (quoted in Cockett 1994, p. 124). These 'advocacy' think tanks were, for the most part, not engaging in basic academic research but were proposing free-market solutions for economic problems and offering critiques of government activities, in a style that was readily accessible to journalists and politicians. By the end of the century, the Atlas Foundation (also set up by Fisher) was in touch with over 150 such organizations in a large number of countries. In Britain the IEA developed close links with members of Margaret Thatcher's government, and in the United States, Ronald Reagan's administration turned to ideas from the Heritage Foundation.

MPS was also linked with academic economics in Europe and the United States. Four of its founding members were from the University of Chicago, among whom Friedman became most prominent. MPS was a key part of the network linking libertarian economists with each other, policy makers, and funding organizations. The last of these included businessmen and charitable foundations with a clear conservative agenda. Though tiny compared with foundations such as Ford, Carnegie, and Rockefeller, they targeted resources into successfully building academic departments and programs where a free-market agenda was being pursued. Public choice and law and economics received significant support. Such funding, though only a small part of their overall budgets, was important at certain universities, of which Chicago was the most important.

During the 1950s and 1960s, Friedman was the dominant influence, along with George Stigler (another MPS member) on what came to be known as the Chicago School. This questioned the role of government intervention in industry, as well as at the macroeconomic level. However, the reason why Chicago economics became so influential was because it was perceived, even by many who did not share Friedman's or Stigler's political views, to be 'good economics'. The Chicago style was highly problem-centred, involving the rigorous application of basic price theory, based on maximizing behaviour.

From the 1970s onward, market-oriented solutions to economic problems became much more widely accepted by academic economists. Ideas such as privatization, deregulation, education vouchers, and a negative attitude towards welfare benefits, once entertained only by a small minority, became widely supported. Though only a small minority adopted the free-market position associated with the MPS, most economists accepted the need for significant government intervention in the economy, and that markets needed to be appropriately designed if they were to work properly, and the belief spread that the government was inherently inefficient compared with the private sector. The reasons for this change are not well understood, but several factors are no doubt relevant. It is hard not to believe that the changed political climate represented by Thatcher and Reagan was not a factor. The economic turbulence of the 1970s and, at least in Europe, structural problems that persisted into the 1980s were certainly important. Public choice theory, with its theories about how self-interested politicians and bureaucrats would be unlikely to implement policies designed to maximize social welfare, no doubt also played a part. This, however, was related to a deeper factor: that economics, possibly for purely intellectual reasons, came to be based on a set of assumptions (notably rational behaviour) that made it easy to generate results that supported free-markets. Very loosely, if private agents have foresight that is as good as it is possible to be, and if markets are assumed to be completely efficient, whereas governments are assumed to be controlled by self-interested individuals whose interests rarely coincide with those of the public, it is comparatively easy to produce theories where markets perform better than state intervention. Models of market failure increasingly looked *ad hoc*, requiring monopoly power, frictions, or non-rational behaviour.

This combination of factors caused economists to explore market-based solutions to an increasing range of problems: using marketable permits to control pollution; trading in carbon emissions; auctioning rights to use parts of the radio frequency spectrum for telecommunications; auctioning franchises for transport; contracting out services provided by local authorities; and many others. They 'reinvented the bazaar' (Macmillan 2002), not in the sense of having government opt out, but in the sense that government used market mechanisms to achieve its objectives. This change was possible only because economists had abandoned the search for general theories, represented by GE theory. GE might be used to tackle certain problems but it was no longer the organizing framework for economics. If such a framework existed, it was game theory, a much more flexible framework that, because it was so flexible and compatible with so many outcomes, could never give completely general results.

Towards the end of the twentieth century, economists turned to new methods. Economists had long been very sceptical about the possibility of using experiments in their subject (it was routinely described as non-experimental), but in the 1990s experimental economics became much more widely accepted as a way to analyse individual behaviour and how markets might work (Fontaine and Leonard 2005). Supporters of such work argued that, because their subjects were making choices that determined the money they could take home, they were conducting real experiments. Some of this work questioned whether behaviour followed the canons of rationality that dominated economic theory, leading some economists to advocate 'behavioural' economics, in which psychological factors played a significant role. One application was finance, where it was hoped to explain seemingly irrational behaviour, such as stock-market bubbles. Other economics have turned to psychological measures of happiness based on questionnaire responses. A related, more recent, development has been 'neuroeconomics', in which attempts are made to measure well-being using technologies such as MRI scans, seeing the consequences of certain activities in brain activity.

These recent developments have significantly broadened economics. The range of methods used by economists has become significantly broader than in the 1960s. On top of those listed here, developments in information technology have opened up new sources of data and new methods for analysing those data. The switch to computerised trading in stock markets means that it is possible to analyse datasets that list every single transaction made during the day, or minute-by-minute prices, not simply close-of-business prices. This makes it possible to study the way markets work in much more detail than was possible a generation ago. And as data collection has expanded, so too has the computing power available to process those data, resulting in the development of estimation techniques and statistical tests that would have been impossible to implement in the 1970s.

Concluding Remarks

Since 1945, economics has been transformed. The discipline has expanded enormously, both inside academia and outside, in government, business, and international organizations; it has become much larger; and it has become highly technical, requiring proficiency in the use of ever more-advanced mathematical techniques. Economic theorizing has become both narrower (in that it is based on a narrower range of assumptions) and broader (in that theory can be applied to problems about which it was previously silent). This change in economic theory has been paralleled by an equally dramatic change in the statistical tools used and in the range and availability of economic data.[24]

---

[24] This has not been discussed here. For accounts of some of these developments, see Bodkin, Klein, and Marwah (1991); Qin (1997); and Geweke, Horowitz, and Pesaran (2008).

Should this transformation be seen as an Americanization of economics? It is clear that the discipline is dominated by American economics, perhaps more so than other social sciences in which local institutions are seen as important. Yet, though they were arguably Americanized when they entered the United States, the theoretical ideas that dominated the period's economics had significant if not predominantly European origins. Keynesian economics goes back to a British economist, writing in the 1930s. Work on existence and stability of GE originated in the mathematical community of Vienna in the 1930s, as did game theory. Similarly, the econometric techniques that became the workhorse of academic empirical work from the 1950s were developed mostly by Europeans, either before the Second World War, or as short- or long-term residents of the United States during wartime. The dominant position of the United States has been due largely to its size, reinforced by the migrations of the Nazi era.

Economic ideas have developed in response to outside events and problems, from the goal of avoiding a repeat of the Great Depression, the challenge of economic development and world poverty, Cold War rivalry with the Soviet Union, and the macroeconomic turmoil of the 1970s, to the implications of the collapse of the Soviet Union, global climate change, and the transformation of world financial markets. Yet underlying that has been a conceptual framework that, though it has been modified in ways that brought about substantial change, would in essence have been familiar to most economists in the 1930s, even if they would not have agreed with it. The definition of economics outlined by Robbins fitted the discipline just as well, and arguably much better, at the end of the century as when it was first published in 1932.[25] Changes in the tools at their disposal have enabled economists to tackle new problems, though the success with which they have done so remains controversial.

An important unanswered question concerns the relationship between economics and political ideology. As this chapter has explained, economics developed in the shadows of the Second World War and the Cold War, and later against the background of a society where economics has increasingly become the dominant discourse.[26] However, while it is possible to place ideas in relation to the institutions in which they were developed, causal inferences remain far more speculative. The period opened with a profession

[25] No claim is made that the definition is a good description of what economists do or of what they should be doing.

[26] Though the main instance of this is the pervasiveness of economic discourse in politics, it also extends to intellectual life, as in the use of economic metaphors in sociology and science studies.

that was, both in the United States and Europe, more favourable towards planning than it is now. It is impossible to believe that economists, even in academia, have been isolated from political events, and that their work did not reflect these broader developments. In the same way, it would no doubt be going too far to claim that economists caused society to change – it is hard to believe that they were so influential – yet it is impossible to believe that academic work did not at least lend legitimacy to changes in society at large.

REFERENCES

Amadae, S. M. 2003. *Rationalizing Capitalist Democracy: The Cold War Origins of Rational Choice Liberalism*. Chicago, IL: Chicago University Press.

Arena, R. 2008. *French forms of Keynesianism*. Paper presented to HISRECO Conference, Lisbon, June 5–7, 2008.

Arrow, K. J. 1951. *Social Choice and Individual Values*. New York: Wiley.

Backhouse, R. E. 1998. The transformation of US economics, 1920–1960: viewed through a survey of journal articles. In *From Interwar Pluralism to Postwar Neoclassicism*, ed. M. S. Morgan and M. Rutherford, 85–107. Durham, NC: Duke University Press. Annual Supplement to *History of Political Economy* Volume 30.

  2005. The rise of free-market economics: economists and the role of the state since 1970. In *The Role of Government in the History of Economic Thought*, ed. S. G. Medema and P. Boettke, 355–92. Durham, NC: Duke University Press. Annual Supplement to *History of Political Economy*, Volume 37.

  2008. Economics in the United States, 1945 to the present. In *New Palgrave Dictionary of Economics*. second edition, ed. L. Blume and S. Durlauf, 522–33. London: Palgrave.

  2010. *The Puzzle of Modern Economics: Science or Ideology?* Cambridge: Cambridge University Press.

Backhouse, R. E., and Medema, S. G. 2009. Defining economics: the long road to acceptance of the Robbins definition. *Economica* 76 (special issue):805–20.

Bateman, B. W. 2006. Keynes and Keynesianism. In *The Cambridge Companion to Keynes*, ed. R. E. Backhouse and B. W. Bateman, 271–90. Cambridge: Cambridge University Press.

Becker, G. S. 1976. *The Economic Approach to Human Behavior*. Chicago, IL: Chicago University Press.

Bernstein, M. A. 2004. *A Perilous Progress: Economists and the Public Purpose in Twentieth-Century America*. Princeton, NJ: Princeton University Press.

Blackmer, D. L. M. 2002. *The MIT Center for International Studies: The Founding Years, 1951–1969*. Cambridge, MA: MIT Center for International Studies.

Bodkin, R. G., L. R. Klein and K. Marwah. 1991. *A History of Macroeconometric Model-Building*. Cheltenham: Edward Elgar.

Bowen, H. R. 1953. Graduate education in economics. *American Economic Review* 43(4 (Part 2)):1–223.

Bronfenbrenner, M. 1970. Radical economics in America: a 1970 survey. *Journal of Economic Literature* 8(3):747–66.

Clower, R. W. 1965. The Keynesian counterrevolution: a theoretical appraisal. In *The Theory of Interest Rates*, ed. F. H. Hahn and F. P. R. Brechling, 103–25. London: Macmillan.

Coats, A. W. 1992. Changing perceptions of American graduate education in economics, 1953–1991. *Journal of Economic Education* 23(4):341–52.

——— ed. 1997. *The Post-1945 Internationalization of Economics*. Durham, NC: Duke University Press. Annual Supplement to *History of Political Economy*, Volume 28.

——— ed. 2000. *The Development of Economics in Western Europe since 1945*. London: Routledge.

——— 2001. The AEA and the radical challenge to social science. In *Economics Broadly Considered: Essays in Honor of Warren J. Samuels*, ed. J. E. Biddle , J. B. Davis, and S. G. Medema, 144–58. London: Routledge.

Cockett, R. 1994. *Thinking the Unthinkable: Think Tanks and the Economic Counter-Revolution, 1931–1983*. London: Harper Collins.

Colander, D. 1990. *The Making of an Economist*. Boulder, CO: Westview Press.

——— 1992. The sounds of silence: the profession's response to the COGEE report. *American Journal of Agricultural Economics* 80(3):600–607.

——— 2005. The making of an economist redux. *Journal of Economic Perspectives* 19(1):175–98.

Colander, D., and A. Klamer. 1987. The making of an economist. *Journal of Economic Perspectives* 12(3):95–111.

Crowther-Heyck, H. 2006. Patrons of the revolution: ideals and institutions in postwar behavioral science. *Isis* 97(3):420–46.

Dorfman, R., P. A. Samuelson, and R. M. Solow. 1958. *Linear Programming and Economic Analysis*. New York: McGraw Hill.

Fontaine, P., and R. Leonard. 2005. *The Experiment in the History of Economics*. London: Routledge.

Fourcade, M., and R. Khurana. 2008. *Scientific and merchant professionalism in American economics*. Paper presented to History of Economics as History of Science Workshop, Cachan, 20 June, 2008.

Frey, B., and R. Eichenberger. 1993. American and European economics and economists. *Journal of Economic Perspectives* 7(4):185–93.

Frey, B., and W. W. Pommerehne. 1988. The American domination among eminent economists. *Scientometrics* 14(1–2):97–110.

Friedman, M. 1968. The role of monetary policy. *American Economic Review* 58(1):1–17.

Frisch, R. 1933. Editor's note. *Econometrica* 1(1):1–4.

Geweke, J., J. L. Horowitz, and H. Pesaran. 2008. Econometrics. In *The New Palgrave Dictionary of Economics*. Second edition, ed. S. N. Durlauf and L. E. Blume. London: Palgrave Macmillan. Online at www.dictionaryofeconomics.com.

Goodwin, C. D. W. 1998. The patrons of economics in a time of transformation. In *From Interwar Pluralism to Postwar Neoclassicism*, ed. M. S. Morgan and M. Rutherford, 53–81. Durham, NC: Duke University Press. Annual Supplement to *History of Political Economy*, Volume 30.

Gordon, R. 1965. The role of the history of economic thought in the understanding of modern economic theory. *American Economic Review* 55(1):119–27.

Hagemann, H. 2000. The post-1945 development of economics in Germany. In *The Development of Economics in Western Europe since 1945*, ed. A. W. Coats, 113–28. London: Routledge.

Hands, D. W., and P. Mirowski. 1998. A paradox of budgets: the postwar stabilization of American neoclassical demand theory. In *From Interwar Pluralism to Postwar Neoclassicism*, ed. M. S. Morgan and M. Rutherford, 260–92. Durham, NC: Duke University Press. Annual Supplement to *History of Political Economy*, Volume 30.

Harberger, A. 1997. Good economics comes to Latin America. In *The Post-1945 Internationalization of Economics*, ed. A. W. B. Coats, 301–11. Durham, NC: Duke University Press. Annual Supplement to *History of Political Economy*, Volume 28.

Hayek, F. A. 1944. *The Road to Serfdom*. London: Routledge.

    1960. *The Constitution of Liberty*. Chicago, IL: University of Chicago Press.

Hicks, J. R. 1939. *Value and Capital*. Oxford: Clarendon Press.

Huret, R. 2008. *La fin de la pauvreté? Les experts sociaux en guerre contre la pauvreté aux Etats-Unis (1945–1974)*. Paris: EHESS.

Ingrao, B., and G. Israel. 1990. *The Invisible Hand: Economic Equilibrium in the History of Science*. Cambridge, MA: MIT Press.

Jardini, D. R. 1996. *Out of the Blue Yonder: The RAND Corporation's Diversification into Social Welfare Research, 1946–1968*. Doctoral thesis, Carnegie-Mellon University.

Johnson, H. G. 1971. The Keynesian revolution and the monetarist counter-revolution. *American Economic Review* 61(2):1–14.

Katz, B. 1989. *Foreign Intelligence: Research and Analysis in the Office of Strategic Services, 1942–1945*. Cambridge, MA: Harvard University Press.

Keynes, J. M. 1936. *The General Theory of Employment, Interest and Money*. London: Macmillan.

Khurana, R. 2007. *From Higher Aims to Hired Hands: The Social Transformation of American Business Schools and the Unfulfilled Promise of Management as a Profession*. Princeton, NJ: Princeton University Press.

Koopmans, T. C. 1957. *Three Essays on the State of Economic Science*. New York: McGraw Hill.

Krueger, A. O. 1991. Report of the commission on graduate education in economics. *Journal of Economic Literature* 29(3):1035–53.

Lee, F. S. 2004. To be a heterodox economist: the contested landscape of American economics, 1960s and 1970s. *Journal of Economic Issues* 38(3):747–63.

    2009. *A History of Heterodox Economics: Challenging the Mainstream in the Twentieth Century*. London: Routledge.

Leijonhufvud, A. 1968. *On Keynesian Economics and the Economics of Keynes*. Oxford: Oxford University Press.

Leonard, R. J. 1991. War as a 'simple economic problem': the rise of an economics of defense. In *Economics and National Security*, ed. C. D. Goodwin, 261–84. Durham, NC: Duke University Press. Annual Supplement to *History of Political Economy*, Volume 23.

    2008. Game theory in economics, origins of. In *The New Palgrave Dictionary of Economics*, Second edition, ed. L. Blume and S. Durlauf. London: Palgrave Macmillan. Online at www.dictionaryofeconomics.com.

Loureiro, M. R. 1997. The professional and political impacts of the internationalization of economics in Brazil. In *The Post-1945 Internationalization of Economics*, ed. A. W. Coats, 184–207. Durham, NC: Duke University Press. Annual Supplement to *History of Political Economy*, Volume 28.

MacKenzie, D. 2006. *An Engine, Not a Camera: How Financial Models Shape Markets*. Cambridge, MA: MIT Press.

Macmillan, J. 2002. *Reinventing the Bazaar: A Natural History of Markets*. New York: WW Norton.

Malinvaud, E. 1977. *The Theory of Unemployment Reconsidered*. Oxford: Basil Blackwell.

Mata, T. 2009. Migrations and boundary work: Harvard, radical economists, and the Committee on Political Discrimination. *Science in Context* 22(1):115–143.

Medema, S. G. 2000. Related disciplines: the professionalization of public choice analysis. In *Toward a History of Applied Economics*, ed. R. E. Backhouse and J. Biddle. Durham, NC: Duke University Press. Annual Supplement to *History of Political Economy*, Volume 32.

Mehrling, P. 2005. *Fischer Black and the Revolutionary Theory of Finance*. Hoboken, NJ: Wiley.

Mirowski, P. 2002. *Machine Dreams: Economics Becomes a Cyborg Science*. Cambridge: Cambridge University Press.

Moggridge, D. 2008. *Harry Johnson: A Life in Economics*. Cambridge: Cambridge University Press.

Morgan, M. S., and M. Rutherford, eds. 1998. *From Interwar Pluralism to Postwar Neoclassicism*. Durham, NC: Duke University Press. Annual Supplement to *History of Political Economy*, Volume 30.

Neumann, J. von, and O. Morgenstern. 1944. *Theory of Games and Economic Behavior*. Princeton, NJ: Princeton University Press.

Parker, R. 2005. *John Kenneth Galbraith: His Life, His Politics, His Economics*. New York: Farrar, Strauss and Giroux.

Patinkin, D. 1956. *Money, Interest and Prices*. Evanston, IL: Row, Peterson.

1965. *Money, Interest and Prices,* Second edition. New York: Harper and Row.

Phelps, E. S. et al. 1970. *Microeconomic Foundations of Employment and Inflation Theory*. London: Macmillan.

Portes, R. 1987. Economics in Europe. *European Economic Review* 31(6):1329–40.

Qin, D. 1997. *The Formation of Econometrics: A Historical Perspective*. Oxford: Clarendon Press.

Robbins, L. C. 1932. *An Essay on the Nature and Significance of Economic Science*. London: Macmillan.

Ruggles, N., ed. 1970. *The Behavioral and Social Sciences Survey: Economics Panel*. Englewood Cliffs, NJ: Prentice Hall.

Ruggles, R. 1962. Relation of the undergraduate major to graduate economics. *American Economic Review* 52(2):483–89.

Rutherford, M. 2008. National Bureau of Economic Research. In *The New Palgrave Dictionary of Economics*, Second edition, ed. Steven N. Durlauf and Lawrence E. Blume. London: Palgrave Macmillan. Online at http://www.dictionaryofeconomics.com.

Samuelson, P. A. 1947. *Foundations of Economic Analysis*. Cambridge, MA: Harvard University Press.

1948. *Economics.* New York: McGraw Hill.

Samuelson, P. A.1955. *Economics.* New York: McGraw Hill.

Schrecker, E. 1986. *No Ivory Tower: McCarthyism and the Universities.* Oxford: Oxford University Press.

Simpson, C., ed. 1998. *Universities and Empire: Money and Politics in the Social Sciences during the Cold War.* New York: The New Press.

Solow, R. M. 1997. How did economics get that way, and what way did it get? *Daedalus* 126:39–58.

Stapleton, D. H. 2003. Joseph Willits and the Rockefeller's European programme in the social sciences. *Minerva* 41(2):101–114.

Valdes, J. G. 1995. *Pinochet's Economists: The Chicago School in Chile.* Cambridge: Cambridge University Press.

Vanoli, A. 2008. National accounting, history of. In *The New Palgrave Dictionary of Economics*, Second edition, ed. L. Blume and S. Durlauf, Volume 5: 838–43. London: Palgrave Macmillan. Online at www.dictionaryofeconomics.com.

Weintraub, E. R. 1998. Axiomatisches mißverständnis. *Economic Journal* 108(451):1837–47.

2002. *How Economics Became a Mathematical Science.* Durham, NC: Duke University Press.

4

Political Science

Robert Adcock and Mark Bevir

Introduction

Many histories can be told of political science. Some start in classical Athens (Almond 1995); others start in the Scottish Enlightenment (Farr 1988). But if we are specifically interested in political science as one of the set of institutionally differentiated disciplines that together make up contemporary academic social science, it was born in America early in the twentieth century (Ross 1991, chaps. 3 and 8; Adcock 2003). The prominence of America then and now might suggest a narrative of Americanization. However, we will argue that this narrative needs tempering with recognition of the influence of Europe on America and the way different traditions modify ideas adopted from elsewhere. The history of political science is one of the contingent transnational exchanges in which ideas are appropriated, modified, and transformed.

The direction and extent of the transnational exchanges vary across different aspects of political science. If the Americanization narrative appears most plausible with regard to the institutions of political science as an autonomous discipline, it becomes harder to sustain once our focus shifts to intellectual history. When we look at the British case, for example, we will argue that new empirical topics in political science arose from exchanges in which British figures played as great an initiating role as Americans; that new quantitative techniques were indeed more commonly developed in America and then adopted in Britain, but they were modified in the process of adoption; and that the postwar history of American political science has been dominated by new theories – from the positivist theories of behavioralism to rational choice theory – that had little impact on British political science.

The Institutions of Political Science

American scholars pioneered the institutions of political science as an autonomous discipline. In 1903, they founded the world's first national political science association, the American Political Science Association (APSA), and in 1906, the young association began a journal, the *American Political Science Review* (*APSR*). The association had rapid and noteworthy success in attracting members. An initial growth spurt took it from a membership of 204 in 1904 to 1,462 just over a decade later in 1915; membership subsequently doubled during the interwar decades to cross the 3,000 mark by the early 1940s (Somit and Tanenhaus 1967, pp. 55, 91). In their home universities and colleges, members of the APSA took the lead in forging departments devoted to political science, which became understood as a field apart from history, philosophy, law, sociology, and economics.

Whether we retrospectively celebrate or bemoan these institutional developments, we should not think them obvious or inevitable. The prior generation of scholars who, during the 1870s and 1880s, had given shape to America's first research universities – Johns Hopkins and Columbia – had not approached the study of politics as a freestanding field (Adcock 2003). Moreover, with the sole exception of Canada where a national political science association was founded in 1913, scholars in other countries were in no rush to imitate the path of institutional differentiation pioneered in America. For almost half a century, the existence of an autonomous discipline of political science was a North American anomaly.

The disciplinary path blazed by American scholars exemplified their growing independence from the academic metropoles of Germany, France, and Britain. But trans-Atlantic exchange did not abruptly end. While it ebbed somewhat, the flow of intellectual trade continued principally westward until the Second World War. As we will see, for example, early American forms of proto-behavioralism and pluralism drew inspiration from the British scholars Graham Wallas and Harold Laski. The American discipline also received European scholars directly into its ranks. Earlier transplants – like Carl Friedrich, a student of Alfred Weber, who joined the Harvard faculty as its department was rising to disciplinary pre-eminence in the 1920s – were followed by émigrés from the Nazi regime, such as Leo Strauss, Hans Morgenthau, and Karl Deutsch. Much of mid-century American political science cannot be understood without attending to such trans-Atlantic migrations of ideas and individuals (Gunnell 1993; Lowenberg 2006). The general lesson here is that the *institutional* trajectory of political science's development need not correspond to the *intellectual* trajectory of the traditions and debates in which political scientists participate.

America's institutionally differentiated political science went from an anomaly to an international model in the years around 1950. In the aftermath of World War II, America enjoyed heightened prestige because of its military ascendance, and its role in creating new international organizations and in aiding European reconstruction. Against this backdrop, the recently founded UNESCO set out in the late 1940s to promote political science. Its initiative spurred the founding of the International Political Science Association in 1949, as well as national-level associations in France in 1949, Britain in 1950, and West Germany in 1951. Just as APSA had founded a journal some half a century before, so did each new national association: the Association Française de Science Politique began *La Revue Française de Science Politique* in 1951, the British Political Studies Association began *Political Studies* in 1953, and the Deutsche Vereinigung Politische Wissenschaft began *Politische Vierteljahresschrift* in 1960.

Of course, the creation of national associations and journals did not give immediate birth to full-fledged disciplines. It took decades for the institutions and ethos of an autonomous political science to diffuse across varied levels and aspects of the academy in France, Britain, and Germany (Hayward 1991; Kastendiek 1991; Roux 2004). But this had also been true in America, where various ties between political scientists and historians persisted for a quarter of a century after the 1903 differentiation of the APSA from the American Historical Association (Farr 2007, pp. 90–2). Thus, the institutional development of political science in postwar Europe may plausibly be narrated as a process of "Americanization." It was influenced by the American model, and its stages and tempo corresponded to the earlier American experience: the founding of a national association and journal pointed toward a disciplinary autonomy that took several decades to be realized in the form of differentiated institutions and instruction across a range of academic settings.

The emergence of political science disciplines in Europe frames, but cannot answer, a common question and anxiety: did Americanization characterize not only institutional but also intellectual trajectories in political science? Rather than hazard continent-wide claims, we will address this question in the more limited setting of Britain. A shared language and other ties might suggest that Britain was especially permeable to American intellectual influences. Yet even here, the Americanization narrative obscures more than it illuminates. British scholarship did adopt ideas and practices from America, especially certain empirical topics and techniques. But this element of Americanization should not overshadow two equally, or indeed more, significant intellectual dynamics. First, exchanges after 1950 built on trends that began earlier, and initially took shape as much, if not more, from British influence on American scholars as vice versa. Second, there were and are trans-Atlantic divergences, with ideas being modified by local traditions rather than simply adopted wholesale, and with some ideas from one country barely registering in the other. All aggregate narratives simplify, but the Americanization narrative becomes outright misleading if pushed too far beyond the institutional into the intellectual history of postwar political science.

New Empirical Topics

The years around 1950 mark not one but two turning points in the history of political science. At the same time as new political science associations were being founded in Europe, the American discipline was experiencing a wave of self-criticism. The curtains were rising on what has come to be known as the "behavioral revolution," in which a movement of scholars set out to make political science more "systematic" by transforming both its methods and its theories. When explicating behavioralism in American political science, we should, however, not take its own revolutionary self-characterization for granted. To clarify how this multifaceted movement of the 1950s and 1960s stood in relation to previous intellectual trends, we need a sense of what those trends were. A sense of prior trends is especially significant for a comparative study of political science in Britain and America, because the principal trends in both countries in the first half of the century were often common ones in which the British played a pioneering role.

Political science arose as an autonomous discipline as part of a broad epistemic shift in the late nineteenth and early twentieth centuries (Bevir 2006). This shift was one from developmental historicism to modernist empiricism as the dominant mode of knowing human life. The developmental historicism that dominated the nineteenth century located actions, norms, institutions, and even states in broad temporal narratives governed by largely fixed principles, such as those of nation, liberty, and reason. Examples of this developmental historicism include not only Hegelian idealism but also Comtean positivism, Whig historiography, and early evolutionary theories. All such developmental historicism was challenged by the rise of new forms of logic initially, and only slightly later by the crisis of faith in reason and progress associated with World War I. These challenges facilitated the rise of modernist empiricism. Modernist empiricists

typically turned away from historical forms of explanation toward formal classifications, correlations, and appeals to synchronic systems and
structures and the formal location and function of units in them. One
notable manifestation of modernist empiricism in the study of politics was
the crafting of new analytic frameworks for cross-national comparison by
Herman Finer, who left the London School of Economics for the University
of Chicago in the 1930s, and by Carl Friedrich at Harvard. Finer (1932) and
Friedrich (1937) abstracted from nation-by-nation presentations and proposed frameworks of general categories to guide comparative analyses of
institutions and politics across modern nations.

The rise of modernist empiricist modes of explanation occurred alongside a shift in the topics of interest to political scientists. Although the two
trends tended over time to mutually reinforce one another, each had its
own roots, and participation in one did not necessitate participation in
the other. By the turn of the twentieth century, developmental histori-
cists as well as modernist empiricists had begun to look beyond topics
associated with institutional history, constitutional law, and the philosophical theory of the state. They believed that these older agendas reflected
a predemocratic Europe and were insufficient to the mass-based politics
that had developed with the extension of the suffrage. Students of politics
championed a new range of topics, reflecting the belief that the distinctive
politics of modern democratic societies could be understood only if the
dynamics of mass-based political parties and public opinion were studied
alongside formal government structures and decisions. They hence began
to investigate how parties and public opinion actually worked. The most
important study inaugurating this investigation was the British scholar-
politician James Bryce's *The American Commonwealth* (1888), which cur-
tailed historical and legal pursuits to devote hundreds of pages to parties
and public opinion. Many American scholars were influenced by Bryce's
seminal book, including most notably Harvard's A. Lawrence Lowell, who
later repaid the trans-Atlantic debt with *The Government of England* (1908).
In addition to writing books on each other's countries, Bryce and Lowell
also undertook pioneering comparative studies of contemporary politics
in continental Europe and the British-settler colonies (Lowell 1896; Lowell
1913, esp. chap. XII–XIV, appendix A; Bryce 1921).

The interwar decades witnessed further developments in the study of
politics. Bryce and Lowell had introduced new empirical topics associated
with mass-suffrage societies, but they continued to conceive of democracy
in terms of the sovereignty of a collective will. Such concepts of democracy
and the state began to lose ground to pluralist alternatives only after World

War I. Once again, the new intellectual departure involved trans-Atlantic exchanges, for while American discussions of pluralism later developed a distinctive hue, their rise owed much to British scholars, especially Harold Laski, who spent several years lecturing at Harvard and then Yale. Laski brought the term "pluralism" and British debates about sovereignty into the American academy. Equally, his time in America made it central to his democratic theory (Gunnell 2007).

A final development in political science prior to the Second World War was specific initially to America. Here the rising current of empirical research into the workings of mass democratic societies was extended in its scope by a series of studies of pressure groups. A string of future APSA presidents – Peter Odegard, Pendleton Herring, and E. E. Schattschneider – built their careers on such empirical studies (Odegard 1928; Herring 1929; Schattschneider 1935). By the end of the interwar period, empirical research on public opinion, parties, and pressure groups was already coming to be known collectively as the study of "political behavior." This research was not the province of any one department. Odegard and Schattschneider were introduced to it as doctoral students at Columbia, and Herring at Hopkins; the tradition established earlier by Lowell was extended at Harvard by Arthur Holcombe (1924, 1933), and at Chicago by Charles Merriam (1922) and his students Harold Gosnell (Merriam and Gosnell 1929) and V.O. Key Jr. (1942). The state of the discipline volume put together by the APSA in the 1940s went so far as to hold that "political behavior has largely replaced legal structures as the cardinal point of emphasis among political scientists" (Griffith 1948, p. 224). If this claim was perhaps an overstatement, it still makes clear that the study of political behavior was prominent in American political science *before* the onset of the "behavioral revolution" of the 1950s and 1960s.

It is telling that the one intellectual trend missing from interwar Britain involved empirical work. Research into British pressure groups would eventually take flight but only in the 1950s, some thirty years after the topic was taken up in American political science. Moreover, its inaugurators at that time would include the recent Harvard PhDs Samuel Beer (1956; 1963a) and Harry Eckstein (1960), alongside W. J. M. Mackenzie (1955) – one of the British scholars most attentive to American political science – and Herman Finer's younger brother S. E. Finer (1958). Empirical work on British political parties was also somewhat lacking in the interwar decades: the classic study of the subject, Robert McKenzie's *British Political Parties*, did not appear until the 1950s (McKenzie 1955). Thus, while the British Bryce stands at the very fountainhead of inquiry into new empirical topics, such inquiry had been subsequently taken up and extended far more fully in America than Britain. This contrast might be seen in light of the much smaller number, and different institutional home, of British scholars. When the British Political Studies Association was founded in 1950, it had only around one hundred members. The APSA, by contrast, had already surpassed 4,000 members during the 1940s. As well as being fewer in number, British scholars of politics remained intellectual generalists, trained and housed in fields such as history, law, and classics (Kavanagh 2007). The prerequisites and incentives for an extensive and expanding body of empirical scholarship on contemporary political behavior scarcely existed in Britain during the first half of the century.

The growth of empirical work that distinguishes interwar American political science provides a starting point for understanding the later behavioral revolution. Empirical work had developed at some remove from contemporary theoretical innovation. The empirical study of pressure groups, for example, largely developed less as an illumination of the new pluralist theory of democracy than as a critical exposition of the obstacles to realizing democracy conceived in older terms as the expression of a collective will.[1] By the 1940s, the gap between empirical work and theory was becoming a locus of anxiety within the American discipline. Benjamin Lippincott (1940), in particular, charged his fellow political scientists with atheoretical empiricism. When Lippincott reiterated this complaint in UNESCO's 1950 worldwide review of political science, his was far from a lonely voice: the same worry was voiced by most American contributors (UNESCO 1950: Lippincott, Bernstein, Cook, and Fainsod chapters). Thus, when David Easton's behavioralist manifesto *The Political System* (1953) diagnosed American political science with "hyperfactualism," it offered an evocative reformulation of a criticism that had been gaining adherents for some time.

Growing dissatisfaction and overlapping perceptions of what ailed the American discipline did not dictate a single prescription for the road ahead. While the 1940s saw increasing calls for "the creative thinker, who must give meaning to the painstaking research that, while indispensable, is still not enough" (Griffith 1948, p. 237), by the early 1950s it was evident that there were profound disagreements about the kind of theoretical pursuit needed, and what other intellectual departures with which it ought to be combined.

---

[1] The older theory of democracy still infused, for example, the proposal for reforming the American political system drawn up under APSA auspices in the 1940s (APSA Committee on Political Parties 1950).

The behavioral movement set out to make political science more rigorously "scientific." Its vision stood in contrast, not only to that of political scientists happy with things as they were, but also to that of émigrés such as Hans Morgenthau and Leo Strauss, who offered alternative prescriptions for the discipline. Ironically Morgenthau and Strauss were housed in the Chicago political science department, where many behavioralists had earned their doctorates during the interwar decades, but which had its character changed dramatically in the 1940s (Heaney and Hansen 2006).

To specify what was revolutionary about the behavioral movement, we must remember that new empirical topics had long been on the rise. Many behavioralists had substantive interests in public opinion, pressure groups, and other phenomena outside formal government structures, but these interests simply extended an intellectual trend evident across leading departments and dating from the turn of the century. The movement's consolidation was crystallized by the efforts and money of the Social Science Research Council (SSRC) Committee on Political Behavior (CPB), established in late 1949 under the chairmanship of the Chicago graduate V. O. Key Jr. The main objective of this committee, despite its name, was *not* to promote the study of political behavior topics *per se*. Rather, if we look at the earliest articles growing out of the CPB's efforts, the common theme was instead the call to make political science "systematic" (Garceau 1951; Leiserson 1951; Truman 1951; Eldersveld et al. 1952). Their overlapping aspirations had more to do with *how* to study politics than *what* topics to study.

The transformative aspirations of behavioralism lay in the departures it prescribed to make political science systematic. The behavioralists believed that systematic science depended on the cumulative interplay between theoretical innovation and empirical research, and they set out to remake both sides of this interplay. The CPB thus had two declared goals: the "development of theory" and "improvement in methods" (SSRC CPB 1950, p. 20). Behavioralism is generally remembered for the second goal, and in the next section we review its success in bringing quantitative and statistical methods into political science. But behavioralism was about more than changing techniques, and in the subsequent section we consider its theoretical agenda. The specific theories advanced by behavioralists in the 1950s and 1960s failed to win lasting support, but this should not obscure the revolutionary impact of behavioralism upon conceptions of the character and role of theory. The impact of behavioralism's theoretical agenda still lingers in intellectual cleavages that continue to characterize American political science today. Equally, the relative weakness of behavioral theory in

Britain helps to explain many of the ways in which British political science differs from its American counterpart.

Quantitative Techniques

American scholars of politics have, for the most part, always viewed their discipline as a science. But up into the 1940s they did so with little anxiety or, for that matter, self-reflection. A low-key empiricist notion of science as fact gathering and objective reporting prevailed, and it gave little reason to prefer quantitative over qualitative techniques. The behavioralists challenged the status quo dramatically. Their vision of a systematic political science was based on a more demanding conception of science. They exhorted political scientists critically to examine and improve their methods, meaning, whenever possible, taking up techniques that produced quantitative data and analyzed it statistically. Quantification is not a necessary companion of heightened methodological self-consciousness, but behavioralists bound them tightly together.

The association of quantitative method with scientific advance was not born with behavioralism. We find it previously in Graham Wallas's *Human Nature in Politics* (1908, chap. V). Although Wallas's move was largely ignored or rejected in Britain, his methodological call was taken up in America by Charles Merriam, who inspired students and colleagues at the interwar University of Chicago to explore new methods (Heaney and Hansen 2006). Under Merriam's leadership, the interwar Chicago department surpassed the previously dominant Columbia department in both the number of doctoral students produced and prestige in the discipline. Merriam trained, and then hired, the methodologically and substantively innovative Harold Gosnell and Harold Lasswell, who in turn trained such leading figures of the future behavioral movement as V. O. Key Jr. and Gabriel Almond.

But the "Chicago school" forged by Merriam was the exception not the norm in the interwar discipline. While it surpassed Columbia, Chicago was itself surpassed by Harvard as the most prolific and prestigious producer of political science doctorates (Somit and Tanenhaus 1967, pp. 102–8). Harvard won this position by the mid-1920s and has held it ever since. The skepticism of Harvard's Friedrich (1929) toward incipient quantitative analyses was much more expressive of norms in the interwar discipline than the work of the Chicago school. When we recall that the American discipline was, by the 1940s, already widely committed to new empirical topics, we should bear in mind that it was, at the same time, also common to recall Merriam's advocacy of quantification as, at best, a distraction that had mercifully little impact (Griffith 1948, p. 213).

The methodological state of play was notably different elsewhere in the interwar social sciences. Psychologists and sociologists had pioneered the use of a rich array of quantitative methods. When the behavioralists introduced new techniques to political science in the 1950s and 1960s, they relied heavily on transfers from these other disciplines. The long-term future of quantitative techniques in American political science depended on training a new generation to understand and apply them. But in the meantime, there was an immediate need for exemplary studies to show that such techniques could produce engaging results in political research. Many of these exemplary studies were either produced by political scientists trained at the interwar Chicago school, as were V. O. Key Jr. and Gabriel Almond, or by scholars trained and sometimes housed in psychology or sociology, as respectively were Philip Converse and S. M. Lipset.

The diffusion of survey research into political science has long been taken as the paradigmatic example of behavioralism's success. As early as 1961, Robert Dahl's influential overview of the "behavioral approach" anointed the development of survey research – from *The People's Choice* (Lazarsfeld et al. 1944) study of the 1940 election led by Columbia sociologist Paul Lazarsfeld to *The American Voter* (Campbell et al. 1960), produced by psychologically oriented scholars at the University of Michigan's Survey Research Center – as the "oldest and best example of the modern scientific outlook at work" (Dahl 1961, p. 768). Political scientists were, however, not just passive recipients in this development. Under V. O. Key Jr.'s leadership, the CPB actively aided the development of surveys on political topics. After some of the scholars at Michigan's recently founded center – which was refining techniques of sampling, interviewing, and data analysis for survey research more broadly – conducted a small nationwide survey during the 1948 election, the CPB stepped in to nurse the incipient agenda by securing Carnegie Corporation support for a full-scale survey during the 1952 election, and using it to fund the Michigan centre carrying out the survey. When Carnegie (along with the Rockefeller Foundation) supported another national survey in 1956, the funding went directly to Michigan. The data from the 1956 survey, together with the center surveys conducted since 1948, provided the basis for *The American Voter*.

The American Voter marks a milestone in the diffusion of survey research into the mainstream of American political science. The book acquired the status of a disciplinary classic. Two of its four authors – Warren Miller and Philip Converse – went on to become APSA presidents. The work of the

Michigan center in forging national sample survey techniques also set the stage for extending such research beyond America. A pioneer here was Gabriel Almond, the chair of the SSRC Committee on Comparative Politics (CCP), which was founded in 1954. While teaching at Yale in the late 1940s, Almond had been one of the first political scientists to exploit the potential of national surveys when he used some of the Michigan center's earliest data in *The American People and Foreign Policy* (1950). In the late 1950s, while at Princeton, Almond began working with Sidney Verba to organize sample surveys of citizen attitudes and socialization across five different nations, and these surveys provided the basis for their classic *The Civic Culture* (1963).

The American Voter and *The Civic Culture* illustrate a seismic shift in American political science toward the use of quantitative techniques. The extent of this shift is evident in the discipline's flagship journal (Sigelman 2006). Between 1950 and 1970, the percentage of articles in the *APSR* based on surveys went from 0 to almost 50 percent. After this dramatic rise, survey research stabilized, making up on average about one-third of the journal through the 1980s, 1990s, and onward until today. Moreover, the evolving content of the *APSR* also reminds us that the behavioral revolution in techniques encompassed more than surveys. If we group all species of quantitative analysis together, we find a pattern of surge and stabilization, the periodization of which is identical to that for specifically survey-based work, but the absolute level is significantly higher. Since the 1970s, about two-thirds of *APSR* articles have been quantitative studies of one sort or another.

What made up the rest of the quantitative turn in postwar American political science? At least three major types of social science work produce and/or analyze quantitative data: surveys, experiments, and secondary analyses of aggregate data culled from census, election, and other records created by governments and other organizations. Of these three, experiments were the last to gain traction in political science. Scattered earlier examples can be found, such as the field experiments of Gosnell (1927) and Eldersveld (1956) that tested factors affecting voter turnout. But only in the 1980s did mainstream disciplinary skepticism about the utility of experiments begin to weaken in the face of exemplary studies such as Iyengar, Peters, and Kinder's (1982) laboratory experiments investigating the effects of television news on issue opinions. A tradition of experimental research has, since then, been developing in American political science, but it remains the least widespread type of quantitative work (Druckman et al. 2006).

It was analyses of aggregate data that accompanied surveys as the second major strand of the behavioral revolution in techniques during the postwar decades. We previously saw how V. O. Key Jr. aided the Michigan SRC in his role as CPB chairman, but Key's own scholarship exemplified the potential of aggregate analysis. Indeed, Key's *Southern Politics* (1949) and his articles on critical elections (1955) and secular realignment (1959) should stand beside survey works in any pantheon of the classics that opened the study of American politics to quantitative techniques. Aggregate analysis also played a major role in the behavioral revolution in other subfields of the discipline. In comparative politics, the sociologist and later APSA president, Seymour Martin Lipset relied on aggregate statistics when he conducted (with CCP funding) his influential cross-national study of the "social requisites of democracy" (Lipset 1959). Another pioneer was émigré political scientist Karl Deutsch, whose classic *APSR* article "Social Mobilization and Political Science" (1961) explored how to combine indicators of various aspects of modernization into a general index for use in cross-national comparisons. Deutsch went on to win National Science Foundation support for the Yale Political Data Program, which gathered political, economic, and social information from diverse sources, then organized and coded this information to score as many countries as possible on a large number of variables. Other similarly ambitious projects included the Polity and Correlates of War datasets. All three projects were launched in the early 1960s as attempts to make aggregate data with broad cross-national, temporal, and topical range easily available to scholars in a standard format.[2] The building of such datasets has continued ever since. Today, a wide variety of aggregate-level datasets, together with the individual-level datasets created by survey research, and the advances in statistical tools and computer technology, provide political scientists with ever-increasing opportunities to conduct quantitative analyses with an ease, speed, and complexity that would have astounded their predecessors.

While following the methodological transformation of postwar American political science, it is easy to get carried away. We should now step back to emphasize three points. First, the surge of quantitative analyses gave way to stabilization in the 1970s. Subsequent decades have seen a ratcheting up in the technical complexity of quantitative work, but the proportion of the American discipline doing such work has not increased. Indeed, if there were any subsequent shift, discernible in the *APSR* at least, it was

---

[2] For a historically informed overview of the output of the first decade or so of these projects, see Flora (1974).

a slight decline in the 1980s paralleled by a surge in the kind of formal models we will consider later when we turn to rational choice (Sigelman 2006, pp. 469–70). Second, the tide of quantitative work stabilized at different levels in different subfields. If we look at the major American journals, we find that since the 1970s, quantitative research has averaged about 85 percent of articles on American politics, 60 percent on comparative politics, and 40 percent on international relations (Bennett et al. 2003). While the behavioral revolution pushed qualitative work to the periphery in studies of American politics, such work thus retains a major role elsewhere in the discipline. Finally, behavioralism's general preference for quantification left room for sometimes tense debates about the relative merits of aggregate (macro) versus survey-based (micro) methods. The character and legacy of the behavioral revolution in techniques do not lie solely in either aggregate studies or surveys, but rather in the competition and cooperation between the two. Their interplay remains to this day a driving force of quantitative political science in America.

Quantitative techniques have not all fared equally well in Britain. At one extreme, experiments have never gotten much support outside of policy analysis, and even there had only a minor and transient presence. At the other extreme, survey research became an integral part of British political science. Of course, surveys in Britain long predated American behavioralism. At the end of the nineteenth century, Charles Booth, Henry Mayhew, and Seebohm Rowntree conducted surveys of urban poverty (Englander and O'Day 1995). Moreover, one of Booth's assistants was Beatrice Webb, the leading Fabian socialist. In the early twentieth century, socialist and radical groups, including the New Fabian Research Bureau, conducted surveys into a vast array of social issues, inaugurating a style of activist research that was itself a major influence on the beginning of survey work among American progressives.[3]

Within the institutional space of British political science, however, survey research has largely meant election studies. The Nuffield election studies were started in 1945 by R. B. McCallum and Alison Readman (McCallum and Readman 1947), and continue to this day, with a Nuffield study appearing on each general election. The Nuffield studies generally include a brief history of the previous parliament, accounts of the campaigns, analysis of the backgrounds of candidates, and reproductions of opinion polls,

---

[3] On exchanges between European social researchers and American progressives, see Rodgers (1998) and Kloppenberg (1986), and even more generally, Bevir and Trentmann (2002).

together with a statistical appendix. The evolution of election studies in Britain shows a clear debt to American behavioralism. Before long, David Butler came to dominate the Nuffield studies, and his approach owed much to his collaboration with Donald Stokes – an American scholar who worked at the University of Michigan from 1958 to 1974 and was for a long time also an associate member of Nuffield College, Oxford (Butler and Stokes 1969). In this way, British electoral studies developed as a fusion of the distinctly British approach of McCallum and the Michigan school. Butler and others adopted the Michigan school's concern with rigorous assessments of the relative weight of various causal factors based on statistical analysis. But large chunks of the Nuffield studies also continued to be written in a kind of high-table, insider style, with a suggestion of privileged information as the basis for informed accounts of the strategies and personalities involved in the campaigns.

A more aggressive form of behavioralism reached Britain in the 1960s and 1970s when Richard Rose and Jean Blondel, respectively, brought it to the Universities of Strathclyde and Essex. Rose was American and Blondel was French, but both got their doctorates from the University of Oxford.[4] Their brand of behavioralism inspired three important developments in the use of quantitative techniques in British political science. First, Essex and, to a lesser extent, Strathclyde began to rival, and arguably surpass, Nuffield and Oxford more generally as centers for such research: it is significant, for example, that the Economic and Social Research Council (ESRC) established its data archive in Essex. Second, the use of surveys and statistical analysis spread – as it had in America – beyond election studies, to cover political culture, socialization, and then yet other areas such as race and politics (e.g., Rose 1965). Third, British political scientists became increasingly engaged with the creation and use of cross-national studies and initiatives. The data archive at Essex is a major source of data sets leading to comparative work by scholars such as Kenneth Newton and Elinor Scarbrough. More generally, Blondel was an important figure in the creation of the European Consortium for Political Research (ECPR), and the ECPR began running a ten-week summer school on statistical analysis at Essex in the late 1960s (cf. Barry 1999, pp. 455–65). These institutional developments followed rather rapidly upon precursors in America, where the Inter-University Consortium for Political and Social Research was founded in 1962 and began a summer methods school at the University of Michigan in 1963.

---

[4]   Rose's first book was one of the Nuffield studies co-authored with Butler (Butler and Rose 1960).

Today, U.K. political science includes a large institutional and intellectual space for quantitative analyses. Institutionally, the Specialist Group on Elections, Parties, and Public Opinion (EPOP) is the largest one in the Political Studies Association (PSA), while the ESRC requires all Ph.D. candidates to do a methods course as part of their masters degree if they are to be eligible for a scholarship. Intellectually, a recent benchmarking exercise conducted by the ESRC and PSA found electoral studies to be a particular strength of British political science. Nonetheless, the benchmarking exercise found that the strength of electoral studies went along, at least in comparison with America, with a weakness in methods including not only the kind of formal modeling we discuss later but also statistical techniques and basic research design (ESRC 2007).

Positivist Theory

To grasp the character of behavioralism in America and its ramifications for the comparative character of political science in Britain, we must consider not only topics and techniques but also new theories. The behavioralists' transformative vision of a more systematic discipline gave an equally central role to theoretical innovation as it did to new techniques. If the impact of behavioral theories is now less widely recognized than the quantitative techniques also associated with the movement, their impact on American political science was no less revolutionary.

Up into the 1940s there was little contention about what theory was or should be. Political scientists on both sides of the Atlantic understood "theory" principally to mean scholarship in the historical ideas and institutions tradition that had crystallized during the late nineteenth century. Theorists characteristically spent more time studying, teaching, and writing about texts from earlier times than attempting to produce novel theories. The ideas to institutions tradition arose out of earlier forms of moral philosophy, theory of the state, and constitutional history. From moral philosophy, it inherited the idea of training young elites to take their places in the world by teaching them a canon of great texts. From the theory of the state, it inherited a concern with classifications of types of governments and institutions. From constitutional history, it inherited a concern to study law, authority, and institutions through the study of legal documents. Together these currents gave shape to a tradition of studies on the history of political thought infused with a sense of close connections between changes in ideas and in institutions.

The gravitation of American political science toward empirical studies of contemporary politics in the first half of the twentieth century did not presume or promulgate hostility to the ideas and institutions tradition. The prevailing view of science as fact gathering and objective reporting gave no reason to question the standing of historical research. While fewer and fewer American political scientists outside the theory field did such work, they did not see their theory colleagues as obstacles to a scientific discipline. Indeed, political theory complemented the rest of political science. Political theory gave students, first, a historical survey of political ideas framed in relation to the evolution of institutions, and, second, an introduction to the concepts used by contemporary scholars. These two pedagogical goals blended into one another, because political scientists at the time tended to understand their own concepts as a reflexive outgrowth of ideas that developed alongside the historical evolution of institutions. Moreover, while tendencies to specialization were growing in the American discipline, the generalist ideas and institutions scholar, as exemplified by Ernest Barker in Britain, still found parallels in America. Harvard's Carl Friedrich, like Barker, produced comparative historical institutional studies, histories of ideas, translations of canonical texts, and many other works (Barker 1915, 1944, 1946; Friedrich 1941, 1949, 1952). There was, in sum, little sign of the theoretical departures and cleavages to come within the American discipline.

Debates about the nature of theory arose in America, not out of an empiricist suspicion of theory, but out of the 1940s complaint that American political science had an impoverished theoretical imagination. Both behavioralists (Easton 1951) and the émigré Leo Strauss (1949), in a curious alliance between future antagonists, advanced this complaint and laid blame on the historicism of the ideas and institutions tradition. But where Strauss criticized historicism as part of a sweeping challenge to all varieties of modern thought, behavioralism's criticism reflected a faith in novelty infused with an instrumentalist concept of theory akin to that of logical positivism. When the CPB heralded the development of theory as one of its core concerns (SSRC Committee on Political Behavior 1950, p. 20), what it specifically had in mind was, as SSRC President Pendleton Herring later put it in his APSA presidential address: "theory as a conceptual scheme for the analysis and ordering of empirical data on political behavior" (Herring 1953, p. 968). The positivist aspiration of such theory was to systematically synthesize existing findings and to strategically highlight empirical questions that needed to be addressed to advance further theoretical refinement. The behavioralists vision of a systematic political science thus revolved around a cumulative interplay between theoretical innovation and empirical research.

The promotion of positivist theory was not the American discipline's first or only call for new theoretical work. But it stands out for its radical re-imagining of what theory should be, or at least what it should not be. While behavioralists provided only sketchy accounts of criteria by which to judge the instrumental scientific payoff of theories, they were clear about what they did not consider relevant. They had little sympathy for criteria that reflected the lingering philosophical idealism of the ideas and institutions tradition, such as a theory's relation to past ideas or everyday concepts and practices. They believed that new abstract theoretical vocabularies were essential if political science was to become a cumulative science. Similarly, behavioralists broke with the reformist pragmatism widespread in American political science during the first half of the century. Their vision of a systematic discipline firmly separated the scientific merit of a theory from its ability to promote normatively favored beliefs and outcomes. They aspired to build a new positivist type of theory that would be empirically oriented and ethically neutral.

Positivist theory took different forms in different subfields of political science. In the study of American politics, the most famous theoretical product of behavioralism was a new variant of pluralism, best illustrated by Robert Dahl's classic *A Preface to Democratic Theory* (1956), and more broadly associated with the Yale department (Merelman 2003), which in the 1960s rivaled Harvard for pre-eminence in the discipline (Somit and Tanenhaus 1967, pp. 162–7). But it was in the subfield of comparative politics that positivist theoretical aspirations were most ambitious. This subfield underwent dramatic expansion in size, scope, prestige, and funding as America became a superpower competing for the allegiance of the "new nations" emerging from decolonization in Africa and Asia. When Friedrich and Finer crafted new analytic frameworks for comparative political science back in the interwar decades, they had grounded their categories in the historical experiences of Europe and America, and saw these categories as having a consequently restricted scope of application. In contrast, when the SSRC's CCP brought young scholars together in the 1950s in a bid to remake the subfield, their positivist theoretical aspiration was to take abstraction to a whole new level by forging a general conceptual scheme to bring comparative studies of all countries within a single framework. This quest for a general theory was pitched at the macro-societal level and drew together functionalism with systems theory. It found its fullest expression in work by the CCP's chairman Almond

(1960). Although the sociological theorist Talcott Parsons (1951) was an influence here, other influences, such as David Easton (1953) within the American discipline, and earlier works by British social anthropologists (Fortes and Evans-Pritchard 1940), led comparative political scientists to adopt the "political system," rather than Parsons' "social system," as their core concept. Similarly, when Almond (1965) and other CCP-affiliated scholars later set out to craft a general theoretical scheme for analyzing change in political systems (Adcock 2007, pp. 202–5), they made "political development" their key concept, rather than the sociologically reductionist "modernization."

The universalizing theoretical aspiration of the CCP was not without critics. Leading scholars of the elder generation voiced early concerns. Harvard's Friedrich (1953) in particular responded to an early CCP report by arguing that comparative politics should concentrate on problems specific to certain countries at certain points in time, and that the field would lose contact with such historically grounded problems if it pursued "excessive abstraction." The initial excitement about general theory among young scholars also gave way, for some, to disenchantment. A good example is Samuel Beer, Harvard's leading scholar of British politics. In the late 1950s Beer (1958) extolled the "structural-functional" theory of the "political system" as the polestar guiding the way to a general comparative political science. But in the early 1960s, he changed his mind and began to take aim at the "dogma of universality" and the "utopia of a universal theory" (Beer 1963b, pp. 8, 13).

Beer's shift was part of a broader upswing, particularly notable at Harvard, of discontent with the most positivist theoretical elements of behavioralism. This discontent inspired a return to a less-ambitious modernist empiricism, established earlier at Harvard by Lowell and Friedrich, which promoted empirical study and analytical comparisons, while expecting (or assuming) that theory and generalizations would be contextually limited in reach. The possibility of reviving modernist empiricism in a form more open to quantification but suspicious of general theory was charted in the 1958 APSA presidential address of V. O. Key Jr., who had been at Harvard since 1951. While Key extolled "systematic analysis" in line with his Chicago training and prominent role in the behavioral movement, he also distanced himself from the positivist ideal of discovering general laws and abstract theories that transcend the ebb and flow of historically delimited phenomena. He argued that whatever beguiling "psychic satisfactions" the pursuit of "grand hypotheses" offers, they fail to come to terms with the "incorrigibility" of political data, and he urged political scientists instead to seek "modest general propositions" and to remember that the "verified general proposition of one era may not hold at a later time" (Key 1958, p. 961). This call for theoretical modesty put Key in line with the modernist empiricism of his older colleague Friedrich, to which his younger colleague Beer soon thereafter similarly swore allegiance.

The revival of modernist empiricism as a discontented reaction to positivist theoretical ambitions was far from a wholesale rejection of behavioralism. The new cleavage that emerged around this issue should be seen against the backdrop of behavioralism's broad success in propagating its vision of political science. Thus, even as the revived modernist empiricists challenged more positivist concepts of theory, they accepted the vision of a systematic science advancing through the cumulative interplay of empirical research and theory, with theory instrumentally framed as a tool of scientific advance to be judged by non-normative criteria. Behavioralism made this vision part of the self-understanding of American political science, and even today this vision arguably delimits the boundary of the discipline's mainstream.

The success of behavioralism redefined relations between the subfield of political theory and the rest of political science. While the new instrumentalist conception of theory made rapid gains in American political science in the 1950s and 1960s, nearly all those who promoted and adopted it worked outside the subfield of political theory, with its traditional focus on the history of Western political thought. The most prominent new theoretical development within the subfield itself came from Strauss, whose attack on both historicism and positivism revitalized the moralizing study of canonical philosophical texts. In contrast, while behavioralists stressed the importance of theory, their conception of what theory should (and should not) be in a scientific discipline led them increasingly to contrast the theory they sought against "normative theory" – an amorphous category encompassing varied forms of theorizing that they saw as irrelevant or hostile. The compartmentalizing of normative concerns within the theory subfield made it particularly prone to influence from the increasingly charged political debates of the 1960s. As the American left turned upon itself over the Vietnam War, left-leaning theorists engaged (or enthralled) by these events came increasingly into conflict with behavioralist colleagues. When, by the late 1960s, leaders of the political theory subfield, such as Berkeley's Sheldon Wolin, embraced the notion that they did indeed pursue a "vocation" fundamentally different from that favored elsewhere in the discipline (Wolin 1969), the incipient division between camps was complete. The study of political theory had once been the nearest thing to a common core in the American discipline. Now it was reconstituted as the locus of hostility – whether conservative, radical, or some curious blend of them – to the scientific aspirations of the discipline's new mainstream.

The situation was very different on the other side of the Atlantic. Behavioral theory, especially in its most aggressively positivist forms, barely appeared in Britain. To the contrary, even when British political scientists adopted techniques such as survey research or cross-national aggregate analysis, they generally remain tied to the elder modernist empiricism that inspired the work of McCullum and later Butler. There were arguably a few political scientists who believed in something akin to the positivist theoretical agenda outlined by Americans such as Easton – perhaps Rose, perhaps Blondel. But they concentrated on empirical work, writing little about theory; when they did write about it, they often made concessions to the modernist empiricism dominant in the British discipline. Such concessions are apparent, for example, throughout the work of Blondel. On the one hand, he defined his approach to comparative government as a "general and analytical" investigation of the "conditions which lead to the development of types of political systems," a type of investigation that elsewhere he suggested required quantification to distinguish it from mere journalism (Blondel 1969, pp. ix–x; 1981, p. 109). On the other hand, however, Blondel (1981) also qualified positivist ambitions, suggesting that politics was messy and unscientific, that general or universal theories were thus too ambitious, and so concluding that mid-range theories and partial systems comparisons are the best way of tackling political science.[5] In accepting empirical topics, quantitative techniques, and paying lip-service to theory while insisting on mid-range studies, Blondel can look rather like some of the so-called "new institutionalists" (on the multiple meanings of this contentious phrase within the American discipline, see Adcock, Bevir, and Stimson 2007) in more recent American political science. No wonder many British political scientists (e.g., Rhodes 1997, pp. 78–9) later responded to this new institutionalism by suggesting it was what they had been doing all along – the commonality is modernist empiricism after a dose of behavioralism.

Ironically, then, the main impact of positivist theory on British political scientists was that they began to define themselves against it. The biggest clichés about British political science define it in contrast to American positivism. This contrast enabled British scholars to forget the modernist

---

[5] It is arguable that this vacillation in Blondel involves disenchantment over time. There is certainly a retreat from high claims for positive theory apparent in successive editions of his *Comparative Government*.

empiricist inheritances they shared with American political scientists from Friedrich to Key and Beer. It enabled them to forget the extent to which their search for formal explanations based on classifications or correlations among types of institutions embodied a modernist revolt against developmental historicist approaches to the study of politics. British political scientists were able instead to define themselves as, purportedly unlike American positivists, peculiarly sensitive to history, context, and agency. As Vernon Bogdanor (1999, p. 150) wrote, typically unaware of the historical context of the contrast he was making, "if there is a central tendency to the discipline as it has developed in Britain in the twentieth century, it lies in aversion to positivism." Such a pose does not distinguish British political science – it instead aligns the mainstream of the British discipline with one wing of the mainstream of the American discipline, which is internally characterized by the contained contention between its positivist and modernist empiricist wings.

Rational Choice Theory

In the postwar decades, American political scientists explored a dizzying array of theoretical vocabularies and frameworks. Group theory, systems theory, structural–functional theory, the theory of action, and decision theory all entered political science from other disciplines during the 1950s and 1960s (Easton 1966). The most telling division among these theories was, as Brian Barry (1970) suggested, between "sociological" and "economic" ones. The behavioral movement drew primary attention to sociological theories pitched at the macrolevel of systems. But by the 1970s, a reversal in fortunes was underway. American political science exhibited two divergent reactions against sociological theorizing. First, as we saw earlier, some scholars turned to a modified modernist empiricism, diagnosing an illness of excessive positivist abstraction and prescribing a regime of more modest theorizing. This revival of modernist empiricism, with its mid-range institutionalist orientation, paralleled the dominant reaction of British political science to behavioralism. In contrast, the second reaction against sociological theorizing was missing in Britain, and this largely remains the case to this day; it is the rise of economic theorizing, specifically rational choice theory. As applied in political science, rational choice theory analyzes political outcomes as the products of choices by individuals rationally seeking to maximize their expected utility, where expected utility itself is analyzed in terms of axiomatic preference theory and probability theory.

Rational choice theory first developed during the 1950s and 1960s but – with the exception of William Riker and the Rochester department he led – it had little impact upon political science during the heyday of the behavioral movement.[6] The broader reception of rational choice theory in American political science had to wait for a growing disappointment with the sociological theorizing of the behavioral era. As sociological theories lost favor, so rational choice theory arose to offer both an appealing account of why they had failed and a proposed way forward. While rational choice was similar enough in its instrumental conception of theory to inherit the mantle of science from behavioralism, the substance of its theory was different enough for it to escape the sense of theoretical failure around behavioralism, and thus to point to a new road to the scientific paradise.

Two key differences set rational choice theory apart. First, it grounded itself on positive axioms stated in a formal language that made it possible to use deductive techniques to logically prove what conclusions followed from those axioms. While sociological theorists such as Parsons had extolled deductive reasoning, they had not made their arguments "positive" or "formal" in the sense that rational choice theorists would give to these terms and, as a result, their reasoning could be criticized as loose and indeterminate. The second difference setting rational choice apart was its basis in explicit microlevel assumptions about individuals. Rational choice theorists complained that the macrolevel claims of sociological theories were divorced from an account of individual choices and their often unintended collective consequences.

Rational choice, with its rigorous deductive logic and formal modeling techniques, proved especially attractive within what had become the most technically complex subfield of political science, the study of American politics. The use of formal models here dates back to the 1960s. However, modeling really took off after the late 1970s when the concept of structure-induced equilibrium facilitated the inclusion of institutional arrangements in models (Shepsle 1979; Shepsle and Weingast 1981),[7] and later when Barry Weingast and others expanded the repertoire of modeling concepts and techniques by drawing on the new economics of organization associated with economists such as Oliver Williamson (Moe 1984). By the mid-1980s, articles using formal techniques came to constitute about one-fifth of the *APSR*, a level they have maintained ever since (Sigelman

---

[6]   On the earlier history of rational choice theory, see Amadae (2003), and on Riker in relation to theoretical agenda of Easton and other behavioralists, see Hauptmann (2005).

[7]   For Shepsle's own account of the institutional turn in rational choice, see Shepsle (1995).

2006, p. 469). Early critics of the rise of rational choice sometimes suggested that formal modeling was limited in applicability to the study of contemporary American institutions. But this charge always ignored the fact that a significant portion of the *APSR*'s modeling articles were in the subfield of international relations, and it became even more implausible by the end of the 1980s, as Weingast and others began collaborating with the leading economic historian Douglass C. North on historical topics (North and Weingast 1989; Milgrom, North, and Weingast 1990).

We should, however, not identify rational choice too closely with formal modeling. Modeling has no intrinsic tie to an economic perspective in which the axioms are specifically about rational choices of individuals. In principle, all kinds of theoretical perspectives could state axioms in a formal language and apply deductive logic to them. What is more, one major strand of rational choice theory developed independently of the technical appeal of formal modeling. In the 1970s, some younger scholars of comparative politics, who believed that sociological theorizing failed to fit what they saw in their countries of study, found a more compelling alternative in the analysis of individual choices and collective consequences advanced by the economist Mancur Olson. The pioneering works here were Samuel Popkin's *The Rational Peasant* (1979) and Robert Bates's *Markets and States in Tropical Africa* (1981). Popkin's and Bates's "collective-choice school of political economy" used the Olsonian conception of the "collective action" problems of large groups in a largely informal manner to interpret and explain outcomes in their respective areas of field research – Vietnam and Africa.

The rise of rational choice theory in contemporary American political science can thus be traced back both to technically sophisticated formal modelers of institutions and the fieldwork-based Olsonian scholars of comparative politics. Indeed, the shape of rational choice today owes much to the exchange and cooperation between these groups that developed in the 1980s. Rational choice scholars of comparative politics were quick to make common ground with the formal modelers studying American politics and even to describe these commonalities as a shared rational choice approach to institutions (Bates 1983, pp. 134–47). Rational choice institutionalism thus has a good claim to be the first and foremost of the multiple "new institutionalisms" that have contended within the American discipline since the late 1980s (Adcock, Bevir, and Stimson 2007). Yet this rational choice institutionalism, like rational choice theory more generally, has found little echo in Britain. In Britain, the earlier skepticism toward behavioralism and its more positivist pretensions has largely been extended to rational choice. As a result, when British political scientists have looked across the Atlantic, they have generally identified with two other varieties of "new institutionalism" – the historical and sociological institutionalisms – which are infused with modernist empiricism.[8]

Conclusion

Political science emerged and developed out of a wide range of transnational exchanges in which ideas were less straightforwardly adopted than continually overpowered, dominated, adjusted, and reinterpreted, with their former meanings and purposes being obscured or obliterated. Any simple narrative of Americanization domesticates the contingency and contests involved in this process. American political science itself has been characterized by warring factions who are inspired by different ideas but who often forget the history of those ideas even as they forge them anew in the heat of a different battle. At least as importantly, ideas have not simply flowed from America to Britain and Europe. Rather, intellectual inspiration and support have travelled back and forth across the Atlantic, with alliances being forged, or merely claimed, on both sides of the ocean, often as ways of boosting weaponry or morale in a local conflict. More often than not, the alliances have been ones of partial convenience. At times, they have even been based on mutual incomprehension. The history of political science, as of so much else, is messy – far too messy to be captured by the narrative of Americanization.

The general lesson of the messiness of history may serve as a counter to the danger of a purely internal disciplinary history that fails to recognize not only the impact of social factors on intellectual life, but also the impact of social science on public affairs. The Americanization narrative is, after all, one that appears in much of European society, from simple jibes about McDonald's to more complex worries about the changing nature of politics and, especially, political campaigning. To conclude, therefore, we want briefly to suggest how our argument may extend from political science to cover the impact of techniques derived from the social sciences on public life.

In Britain, political scientists and journalists alike regularly discuss – and generally bewail – the Americanization of politics, especially the spread of media and electoral strategies based on polling, focus groups, and related techniques. They describe – and generally denounce – the rise of

---

[8] The exchanges that have occurred here are explored in Bevir (2007).

a presidential style of politics in which the party leader and image become more important than public policies (Foley 1993).[9]

Superficially, the Americanization narrative can seem compelling. Opinion polling took off earlier in America, quickly becoming an established part of the political landscape. Whereas in America opinion polls have been used extensively since the 1930s, they did not become a feature of political life in Britain until the 1950s or even 1960s. Thus, while the UK Parliament blocked tentative moves to bring polling under the Wartime Social Survey during the Second World War, in America the government conducted literally hundreds of wartime polls (though doing so spurred congressional ire that eventually killed the enterprise of government-run polling).[10] It is possible, moreover, to highlight direct American influences on the introduction of polling in Britain. For example, the British Institute of Public Opinion (BIPO) arose as an offshoot of the American Institute of Public Opinion which was founded by George Gallup in 1935.

On closer inspection, however, the Americanization narrative obscures more than it illuminates. For a start, the rise of surveys and polls is not a story native to American political science but an international story based on all kinds of trans-Atlantic and other flows. Surveys of populations date back to European mercantilism in the seventeenth and eighteenth centuries.[11] One well-known example followed the Great Plague of 1665. John Graunt then made a systematic analysis of birth and death records, thereby recording the faster rate of recovery in London than the rest of Britain. As we saw earlier, the humanitarian concerns of the late nineteenth century led Booth, Mayhew, and others to conduct door-to-door and other surveys of urban life and poverty. Of course, these surveys were conceived as akin to total censuses. Yet, the idea of sampling can also be traced among British and European scholars. So, in 1912 Arthur Bowley, a statistician and economist, undertook a survey of urban laborers in Reading, to the west of London (Darnell 1981). The limited funds available to him precluded the kind of censuses undertaken by Booth and others. Thus, he turned instead to the use of representative techniques developed by statisticians across Europe in the late nineteenth century.

Another problem with the Americanization narrative is that even after the founding of the BIPO, polling in Britain long continued to be influenced

---

[9] For a critical discussion, see Bevir and Rhodes (2006).

[10] On this history in the United Kingdom, see Worcester (1991), and in the United States, see Converse (1987).

[11] Compare the provocative comments in Foucault (1977).

by a progressive ethos and to exhibit sympathy for qualitative methods that provided richer insight into the lived experience that lay behind mere numbers. The mass observation movement produced numerous surveys of public opinion, including by-election polls for the Labour Party and other polls for the Ministry of Information, and it made extensive use of qualitative methods as well as quantitative ones. Indeed, mass observation was conceived as a type of human anthropology in which researchers kept diaries and even listening in on others' conversations (Hubble 2006).

Clearly, American political scientists have indeed generated a number of technologies that have transformed the conduct of politics. Equally clearly, they have done so against the backdrop of a complex array of international and interdisciplinary exchanges, and different cultures have picked up and deployed different sets of technologies to very different degrees.

REFERENCES

Adcock, Robert. 2003. "The Emergence of Political Science as a Discipline: History and the Study of Politics in America, 1875–1910." *History of Political Thought* 24: 481–508.

2007. "Interpreting Behavioralism," in Adcock, Bevir, and Stimson (eds.), *Modern Political Science: Anglo-American Exchanges Since 1880*, pp. 180–208. Princeton, NJ: Princeton University Press.

Adcock, Robert, Mark Bevir, and Shannon C. Stimson. 2007. "Historicizing the New Institutionalism(s)," in Adcock, Bevir, and Stimson (eds.) *Modern Political Science: Anglo-American Exchanges Since 1880*, pp. 259–89. Princeton, NJ: Princeton University Press.

(eds.). 2007. *Modern Political Science: Anglo-American Exchanges Since 1880*. Princeton, NJ: Princeton University Press.

Almond, Gabriel A. 1950. *The American People and Foreign Policy*. New York: Harcourt Brace.

1960. "A Functional Approach to Comparative Politics," in Gabriel A. Almond and James S. Coleman (eds.), *The Politics of the Developing Areas*. Princeton, NJ: Princeton University Press.

1965. "A Developmental Approach to Political Systems." *World Politics* 17: 183–214.

1995. "Political Science: The History of the Discipline," in Robert E. Goodin and Hans-Dieter Klingemann (eds.), *A New Handbook of Political Science*, pp. 50–96. Oxford: Oxford University Press.

Almond, Gabriel A., and Sidney Verba. 1963. *The Civic Culture: Political Attitudes and Democracy in Five Nations*. Princeton, NJ: Princeton University Press.

Amadae, S. M. 2003. *Rationalizing Capitalist Democracy: The Cold War Origins of Rational Choice Liberalism*. Chicago, IL: University of Chicago Press.

APSA Committee on Political Parties. 1950. "Toward a More Responsible Two-Party System." *American Political Science Review* 44, suppl.

Barker, Ernest. 1915. *Political Thought in England from Herbert Spencer to Present Day.* New York: Holt.

1944. *The Development of Public Services in Europe, 1660–1930.* New York: Oxford University Press.

ed. 1946. *The Politics,* by Aristotle, trans. E. Barker. Oxford: Clarendon Press.

Barry, Brian. 1970. *Sociologists, Economists, and Democracy.* London: Collier-Macmillan.

1999. "The Study of Politics as a Vocation," in Hayward, Barry, and Brown (eds.), *The British Study of Politics in the Twentieth Century,* pp. 455–65. Oxford: Oxford University Press.

Bates, Robert H. 1981. *Markets and States in Tropical Africa: The Political Basis of Agricultural Policies.* Berkeley, CA: University of California Press.

1983. *Essays on the Political Economy of Rural Africa.* Cambridge: Cambridge University Press.

Beer, Samuel H. 1956. "Pressure Groups and Parties in Britain." *American Political Science Review* 50: 1–23.

1958. "The Analysis of Political Systems," in Samuel H. Beer and Adam B. Ulam (eds.), *Patterns of Government: The Major Political Systems of Europe.* New York: Random House.

1963a. *Modern British Politics: A Study of Parties and Pressure Groups.* London: Faber.

1963b. "Causal Explanation and Imaginative Re-enactment." *History and Theory* 3: 6–29.

Bennett, Andrew, Aharon Barth, and Kenneth R. Rutherford. 2003. "Do We Preach What We Practice? A Survey of Methods in Political Science Journals and Curricula." *PS: Political Science and Politics* 36: 373–78.

Bevir, Mark. 2006. "Political Studies as Narrative and Science, 1880–2000." *Political Studies* 54: 583–606.

2007. "Institutionalism and the Third Way," in Adcock, Bevir, and Stimson (eds.), *Modern Political Science: Anglo-American Exchanges Since 1880,* pp. 290–312. Princeton, NJ: Princeton University Press.

Bevir, Mark and Frank Trentmann (eds.) 2002. *Critiques of Capital in Modern Britain and America: Transatlantic Exchanges 1800 to the Present Day.* Basingstoke: Palgrave.

Bevir, Mark and R. A. W. Rhodes. 2006. "Prime Ministers, Presidentialism, and Westminster Smokescreens." *Political Studies* 54: 671–90.

Blondel, Jean. 1969. *Comparative Government.* London: Weidenfeld and Nicolson.

1981. *The Discipline of Politics.* London: Butterworth.

Bogdanor, Vernon. 1999. "Comparative Politics," in Hayward, Barry, and Brown (eds.) *The British Study of Politics in the Twentieth Century.* Oxford: Oxford University Press.

Bryce, James. 1888. *The American Commonwealth,* 3 vols. London: Macmillan.

1921. *Modern Democracies,* 2 vols. London: Macmillan.

Butler, David, and Donald Stokes. 1969. *Political Change in Britain: Forces Shaping Electoral Choice.* New York: St. Martin's Press.

Butler, David, and Richard Rose. 1960. *The British General Election of 1959.* London: Macmillan.

Campbell, Angus, Philip E. Converse, Warren E. Miller, and Donald Stokes. 1960. *The American Voter.* New York: Wiley.

Converse, Jean. 1987. *Survey Research in the United States: Roots and Emergence 1890–1960*. Berkeley, CA: University of California Press.

Dahl, Robert A. 1961. "The Behavioral Approach in Political Science: Epitaph to a Monument to a Successful Protest." *American Political Science Review* 55: 763–72.

Darnell, A. 1981. "A. L. Bowley, 1869–1957," in D. O 'Brien and J. Presley (eds.), *Pioneers of Modern Economics in Britain*, pp. 140–74. Basingstoke: Macmillan.

Deutsch, Karl W. 1961. "Social Mobilization and Political Development." *American Political Science Review* 55: 634–47.

Druckman, James N., Donald P. Green, James H. Kuklinski, and Arthur Lupia. 2006. "The Growth and Development of Experimental Research in Political Science." *American Political Science Review* 100: 627–35.

Easton, David. 1951. "The Decline of Modern Political Theory." *Journal of Politics* 13: 36–58.

1953. *The Political System: An Inquiry into the State of Political Science*. New York: Knopf.

(ed.). 1966. *Varieties of Political Theory*. Englewood Cliffs, NJ: Prentice-Hall.

Easton, David, John G. Gunnell, and Luigi Graziano (eds.). 1991. *The Development of Political Science: A Comparative Survey*. London: Routledge.

Eckstein, Harry. 1960. *Pressure Group Politics*. Stanford, CA: Stanford University Press.

Eldersveld, Samuel J. 1956. "Experimental Propaganda Techniques and Voting Behavior." *American Political Science Review* 50 (March): 154–65.

Eldersveld, Samuel J., Alexander Heard, Samuel P. Huntington, Morris Janowitz, Avery Leiserson, Dayton D. McKean, and David B. Truman. 1952. "Research in Political Behavior." *American Political Science Review* 46: 1003–45.

Englander, David, and Rosemary O'Day (eds.). 1995. *Retrieved Riches: Social Investigation in Britain, 1880–1914*. Aldershot, UK: Ashgate.

ESRC. 2007. *International Benchmarking Review of UK Politics and International Studies*. http://www.esrcsocietytoday.ac.uk/ESRCInfoCentre/Images/P_IBR-Final_Report_tcm6-23426.pdf. Last accessed February 22, 2010.

Farr, James. 1988. "Political Science and the Enlightenment of Enthusiasm." *American Political Science Review* 82: 51–69.

2007. "The Historical Sciences of Politics: The Principles, Association, and Fate of an American Discipline," in Adcock, Bevir, and Stimson (eds.), *Modern Political Science: Anglo-American Exchanges Since 1880*, pp. 66–96. Princeton, NJ: Princeton University Press.

Finer, Herman. 1932. *Theory and Practice of Modern Government*, 2 vols. London: Methuen.

Finer, S. E. 1958. *Anonymous Empire: A Study of the Lobby in Great Britain*. London: Pall Mall Press.

Flora, Peter. 1974. "A New Stage of Political Arithmetic." *Journal of Conflict Resolution* 18: 143–65.

Foley, Michael. 1993. *The Rise of the British Presidency*. Manchester: Manchester University Press.

Fortes, Meyer, and E. E. Evans-Pritchard. 1940. *African Political Systems*. London: Oxford University Press.

Foucault, Michel. 1977. *Discipline and Punish: The Birth of the Prison*, trans. A. S. Smith. London: Tavistock Publishers.

Friedrich, Carl J. 1929. "Review of Quantitative Methods in Politics." *American Political Science Review* 23: 1022–27.

1937. *Constitutional Government and Politics*. New York: Harper.

1941. *Constitutional Government and Democracy*. Boston, MA: Little, Brown.

Friedrich, Carl J., (ed.). 1949. *The Philosophy of Kant*. New York: Modern Library.

Friedrich, Carl J. 1952. *The Age of the Baroque, 1610–1660*. New York: Harper.

1953. "Comments on the Seminar Report." *American Political Science Review* 47: 658–61.

Garceau, Oliver. 1951. "Research in the Political Process." *American Political Science Review* 45: 69–85.

Gosnell, Harold F. 1927. *Getting Out the Vote: An Experiment in the Stimulation of Voting*. Chicago, IL: Chicago University Press.

Griffith, Ernest S. (ed.). 1948. *Research in Political Science*. Chapel Hill, NC: University of North Carolina Press.

Gunnell, John G. 1993. *The Descent of Political Theory: The Genealogy of an American Vocation*. Chicago, IL: University of Chicago Press.

2007. "Making Democracy Safe for the World: Political Science between the Wars," in Adcock, Bevir, Stimson (eds.), *Modern Political Science: Anglo-American Exchanges Since 1880*, pp. 137–57. Princeton, NJ: Princeton University Press.

Hauptmann, Emily. 2005. "Defining 'Theory' in Postwar Political Science," in George Steinmetz (ed.), *The Politics of Method in the Human Sciences: Positivism and its Epistemological Others*. Chapel Hill, NC: Duke University Press.

Hayward, Jack. 1991. "Political Science in Britain." *European Journal of Political Research* 20: 301–21.

Hayward, Jack, Brian Barry, and Archie Brown (eds.). 1999. *The British Study of Politics in the Twentieth Century*. Oxford: Oxford University Press.

Heaney, Michael T., and J. M. Hansen. 2006. "Building the Chicago School." *American Political Science Review* 100: 589–96.

Herring, Pendleton. 1929. *Group Representation before Congress*. Baltimore, MD: Johns Hopkins University Press.

1953. "On the Study of Government." *American Political Science Review* 47: 961–74.

Hubble, Nick. 2006. *Mass Observation and Everyday Life: Culture, History, and Theory*. Basingstoke: Palgrave Macmillan.

Iyengar, Shanto, Mark D. Peters, and Donald M. Kinder. 1982. "Experimental Demonstrations of the 'Not-So-Minimal' Consequences of Television News Programs." *American Political Science Review* 65: 991–1017.

Kastendiek, Hans. 1991. "Political Science in West Germany," in Easton, Gunnell, and Graziano (eds.). *The Development of Political Science: A Comparative Survey*. London: Pioutledge

Kavanagh, Dennis. 2007. "The Emergence of an Embryonic Discipline: British Politics without Political Scientists," in Adcock, Bevir, Stimson (eds.), *Modern Political Science: Anglo-American Exchanges Since 1880,* pp. 97–117. Princeton, NJ: Princeton University Press.

Key, V. O., Jr. 1949. *Southern Politics in State and Nation*. New York: Knopf.

1955. "A Theory of Critical Elections." *Journal of Politics* 17: 3–18.

1958. "The State of the Discipline." *American Political Science Review* 52: 961–71.

1959. "Secular Realignment and the Party System." *Journal of Politics* 21: 198–210.

Kloppenberg, James T. 1986. *Uncertain Victory: Social Democracy and Progressivism in European and American Thought, 1870–1920.* Oxford: Oxford University Press.

Lazarsfeld, Paul F., Bernard Berelson, and Hazel Gaudet. 1944. *The People's Choice.* New York: Knopf.

Leiserson, Avery. 1951. "Systematic Research in Political Behavior." *Social Science Research Council Items* 5: 29–32.

Lippincott, Benjamin E. 1940. "The Bias of American Political Science." *Journal of Politics* 2: 125–39.

Lipset, Seymour Martin. 1959. "Some Social Requisites of Democracy." *American Political Science Review* 53: 69–105.

Lowell, A. L. 1896. *Governments and Parties in Continental Europe,* 2 vols. Boston, MA: Houghton, Mifflin.

   1908. *The Government of England,* 2 vols. New York: Macmillan.

   1913. *Public Opinion and Popular Government.* New York: Longmans.

Lowenberg, Gerhard. 2006. "The Influence of European Émigré Scholars on Comparative Politics, 1925–65." *American Political Science Review* 100: 597–604.

Mackenzie, W. J. M. 1955. "Pressure Groups in British Government." *British Journal of Sociology* 6: 133–48.

McCallum, Ronald B., and Alison Readman. 1947. *The British General Election of 1945.* London: Oxford University Press.

McKenzie, R. T. 1955. *British Political Parties.* London: Mercury Books.

Merelman, Richard M. 2003. *Pluralism at Yale: The Culture of Political Science in America.* Madison, WI: University of Wisconsin Press.

Moe, Terry M. 1984. "The New Economics of Organization." *American Journal of Political Science* 28: 739–77.

Milgrom, Paul R., Douglass C. North, and Barry R. Weingast. 1990. "The Role of Institutions in the Revival of Trade: The Law Merchant, Private Judges, and the Champagne Fairs." *Economics and Politics* 2: 1–23.

North, Douglass C., and Barry R. Weingast. 1989. "Constitutions and Commitment: The Evolution of Institutions Governing Public Choice in Seventeenth-Century England." *The Journal of Economic History* 49: 803–32.

Odegard, Peter H. 1928. *Pressure Politics: The Story of the Anti-Saloon League.* New York: Columbia University Press.

Parsons, Talcott. 1951. *The Social System.* Glencoe, IL: Free Press.

Popkin, Samuel L. 1979. *The Rational Peasant: The Political Economy of Rural Society in Vietnam.* Berkeley, CA: University of California Press.

Rhodes, R. W. A. 1997. *Understanding Governance: Policy Networks, Governance, Reflexivity and Accountability.* Buckingham: Open University Press.

Rodgers, Daniel T. 1998. *Atlantic Crossings: Social Politics in a Progressive Age.* Cambridge, MA: Harvard University Press.

Rose, Richard. 1965. *Politics in England: An Interpretation.* London: Faber.

Ross, Dorothy. 1991. *The Origins of American Social Science.* Cambridge: Cambridge University Press.

Roux, Christophe. 2004. "Half a Century of French Political Science: Interview with Jean Leca." *European Political Science* 3: 25–30.

Schattschneider, E. E. 1935. *Politics, Pressures, and the Tariff.* New York: Prentice-Hall.

Shepsle, Kenneth A. 1979. "Institutional Arrangements and Equilibrium in Multidimensional Voting Models." *American Journal of Political Science* 23: 27–60.

1995. "Studying Institutions: Some Lessons from the Rational Choice Approach," in James Farr, John S. Dryzek, and Stephen T. Leonard (eds.), *Political Science in History*, pp. 276–95. Cambridge: Cambridge University Press.

Shepsle, Kenneth A., and Barry R. Weingast. 1981. "Structure-Induced Equilibria and Legislative Choice." *Public Choice* 37: 503–19.

Sigelman, Lee. 2006. "The Coevolution of American Political Science and the *American Political Science Review.*" *American Political Science Review* 100: 463–78.

Somit, Albert, and Joseph Tanenhaus. 1967. *The Development of Political Science: From Burgess to Behavioralism*. Boston, MA: Allyn and Bacon.

SSRC Committee on Political Behavior. 1950. "Committee Briefs: Political Behavior." *Social Science Research Council Items* 4: 20.

Strauss, Leo. 1949. "Political Philosophy and History." *Journal of the History of Ideas* 10: 30–50.

Truman, David B. 1951. "The Implications of Political Behavior Research." *Social Science Research Council Items* 5: 37–39.

UNESCO. 1950. *Contemporary Political Science: A Survey of Methods, Research and Teaching*. Paris: UNESCO.

Wallas, Graham. 1908. *Human Nature in Politics*. London: Constable.

Wolin, Sheldon S. 1969. "Political Theory as a Vocation." *American Political Science Review* 63: 1062–82.

Worcester, Robert. 1991. *British Public Opinion: A Guide to the History and Methodology of Political Opinion Polling*. Oxford: Blackwell.

5

Sociology

Jennifer Platt

Historical Background

Work in the history of sociology has concentrated on the thoughts and biographies of great men, commonly theorists; this is in curious contrast to sociology's defining concern with social structure and typical social patterns. A common version, a sequence of theories from the mainstream of Western sociology, creates a coherent account by leaving out other societies and most empirical work and the societal differences it deals with. This chapter attempts to tell a story more concerned with empirical work and disciplinary institutions than great theorists, not entirely centred on Europe and the anglophone world, and treating as problematic the extent to which there has been one sociology with a shared history. First, the prewar background, and some of the postwar changes and demographic flows that affected later developments are outlined. Then data are presented on various aspects of sociological activity since then. In conclusion, the threads are drawn together to sketch the pattern of historical change.

To the extent that sociology was institutionalized under that name in universities before World War II, its significant presence was in France, Germany, and the United States. There was, however, a less-known presence in Japan, Latin America, and Poland, for instance, in addition to the smaller contributions of Italy and Britain, and several countries had sociological journals. But sociology did not always have a clear identity distinct from that of other social science. For some prewar sociologists, it was the master social science that synthesized the materials provided by the special

This chapter draws on material collected as part of a project 'Intellectual and social structures of international sociology' funded by the British Academy, whose support is acknowledged with gratitude; that project is joint with Charles Crothers, who has contributed to the material used.

sciences, perhaps in a grand comparative historical sweep. Sociologists thus needed to be familiar with anthropological and historical material, did not necessarily need to carry out their own empirical work, and were certainly not confined to their own society. On the other hand, there was also a marked strand, outside academia as much as inside, where 'sociology' was not clearly distinguished from social reform and social work, and was strongly associated with the collection of empirical data on one's own society to inspire and support those; here, women played a much more prominent role. By the 1930s, an academic tradition of empirical research had been established in America, but the Depression led to job cutbacks and other social sciences came to the fore under the New Deal (Camic 2007).

The war and its aftermath created a major discontinuity that changed everything. The grand synthetic function gave way to a more limited identity and to a social rapprochement between theorizing and data collection. In U.S. sociology, the recruitment of a cohort from graduate school into the intense experience of the social research of the war effort created a break, and made an opening for new methods and more concern with empirical research. The shortage of new jobs in the 1930s meant that the relatively young men who got them could now assume leadership (Turner and Turner 1990, pp. 85–7). The sample survey, whose modern form emerged from the wartime work, was not merely an important methodological novelty for sociology, but seemed intrinsically democratic. The United States became globally dominant, and saw sociology as contributing to its political goal of spreading democracy, as well as offering data useful to policy; its prestige and its networks ensured wider diffusion of sociology American style. Fulbright and other grants offered many opportunities for study in the United States, eagerly taken by Europeans, and U.S. 'Counterpart Fund' money was available for social research in Europe relevant to postwar reconstruction, which helped to account for the emphasis of the period on industrial research. The Ford Foundation took up the role, played before the war by the Rockefeller Foundation, of funding social science and encouraging empirical research worldwide, if often in tacit cooperation with U.S. foreign policy. In the interwar period, U.S. graduate students and professors often visited Germany. After the war this ceased to be popular, given the state of the German sociology that remained and the general devastation of the country. However U.S. social scientists held key posts at newly established UNESCO in Paris, and had roles in occupied Germany and Japan as part of denazification. The Soviet bloc in Eastern Europe was established, and sociology was soon suppressed in favour of Marxism–Leninism and dialectical materialism, though in Poland, at least, it survived through vicissitudes of local politics (Kwasniewicz 1994, pp. 25–30). Communication through the Iron Curtain was limited, though each side had strong political motives to learn more about the other; some dissidents found refuge in the West and made careers in Soviet studies. Many important European social scientists had fled from fascism to the United States or Britain, while some from Italy and Spain went to Latin America. Some of those stayed and, with varying levels of assimilation, contributed to local social science, while others returned home bearing either new influences or greater knowledge of tendencies from which they dissociated themselves.

Higher education has certainly not been the only location for sociology, especially for empirical research, which has often been carried out within government departments, whether census or statistical units or those responsible for areas such as education, health, or law enforcement. In addition both commercial and non-commercial research agencies sprang up to carry out political polling and market research. Survey units were created for the first time within U.S. universities; they and fully commercial bodies both worked on academic projects, blurring the borderline between academia and business.

UNESCO created a set of international social-scientific bodies, including the International Sociological Association (ISA). Since 1893 there had been an international association, the Institut International de Sociologie (IIS), which held congresses; members of a small international elite were in touch with each other. But now some German and Italian sociologists were suspect because they had been associated with fascism. These included key figures among those who aimed to revive the pre-existing IIS, which then brought it into disrepute, and therefore it was not made the base for the new body. Unlike the IIS, which started with individual members elected in limited numbers from each country, the ISA's initial members were national associations, not individuals. (Individual membership was introduced in 1970.) Few such associations existed earlier, but this led to the creation in the 1950s of a large number of national associations, even where there were still few sociologists to join them (Platt 1998, pp. 15–21). The location of UNESCO in Paris reflected the traditional international prominence of France, but it saw with resentment its leading role reduced under American hegemony, and its language yielding to English as the *lingua franca* of international contacts. In response, the Association Internationale des Sociologues de Langue Française (AISLF) was founded in 1958. However, France drew on the largesse of U.S. funding to help reconstruct a sociology where the Durkheimian tradition had already been weakened (Pollak 1993).

As combatant countries recovered from the war, higher education expanded enormously, and sociology was one of the fields prominent in this expansion, peaking in the late 1960s to early 1970s. In the United States, the number of first degrees per year rose from around 7,600 in 1960 to 15,203 in 1966 and 35,915 in 1974. [Data on posts have not been found, but American Sociological Association (ASA) membership rose over the same period from 6,875 to 14,654.] In Britain, sociology posts rose from 109 in 1964 to 502 in 1976, while over the same period first degrees per year rose from 185 to 1,253. In France, 20 posts in 1958 became 100 in 1968 and around 300 in 1978 (Chenu 2002, p. 49). In anglophone Canada, the number of posts grew from 21 in 1960 to 474 in 1975 (Fisher 2002, p. 9). Given such rates of expansion it was inevitable, at least outside the United States, that many of the new staff recruited had formal qualifications in other fields, started teaching with only a first degree, or gained key qualifications abroad; the transmission of earlier traditions, where those existed, was thus disrupted. The great expansion, followed in some cases by cutbacks, meant that different intakes to academia worked under very different circumstances, and led to movements of people which have been important to the movement of ideas.

There was often a poor local fit between demand and supply to fill university posts. This created some distinct cohorts, rather than a steady flow in and out with retirements replaced by fresh recruits. In the United States, graduate courses expanded considerably; the demand for courses in sociology rose, fed initially by college funding for veterans. Both junior posts and the people to fill them came from local sources. But the demand from veterans could not last, so the job situation became tighter,[1] encouraging U.S. graduate students to look abroad, while many graduate students continued to come from elsewhere and returned home with American training and contacts. Sociology expanded in Canada later, starting from a lower base; initially most students had to go to the United States for doctoral work. (But some francophone students went to France, or – especially if, as was quite common in the earliest stages, they were priests – to Catholic universities in Belgium or the United States.) Thus Canadians often had U.S. qualifications, and U.S. graduates were interested in Canadian jobs before there were enough Canadians to fill them. Draft avoidance and political hostility to the Vietnam War also sent young Americans to Canada. Soon, many more

---

[1] Finsterbusch (1973), reporting on the U.S. and Canadian job market in 1973, estimates that the situation had changed from one where, in 1971, there were 1600 academic openings for 495 new Ph.D.s, while by 1973 there were only 338 for 594 new Ph.D.s.

home-grown doctorates were produced, and this cohort found jobs scarce at home because they had already been filled. In reaction, a strong movement for 'Canadianization' and against U.S. jobholders, graduates, and teaching material developed in the early 1970s. In Britain, expansion somewhat earlier created a demand that was somewhat hard to satisfy earlier, although it helped that at that stage a doctorate was by no means a prerequisite for a university post; some were filled by refugees from Nazism or the Soviet bloc, or people with uncompleted or no higher degree in sociology. Many young Britons went to America for an M.A. or Ph.D., originally available at home only at the London School of Economics (LSE). Those with early doctorates from LSE soon became professors heading new departments, while the youth and limited socialization of junior staff encouraged intellectual effervescence and competition among conflicting theories.

Such short-term patterns of supply and demand should be distinguished from centre-periphery relations, where degrees from the centre are preferred even if local numbers and programmes could meet the demand. There has been much circulation independent of job availability. In particular, many opportunities were created for study visits to the United States after the war. Halsey (1996, pp. 59–72) described how important this was to his British cohort. Sulek (2007) shows the importance for postwar Polish empirical sociology of U.S. contacts, transmitted through both visits to the United States funded by the Ford Foundation and visits to Poland by Lazarsfeld and others. Even French students and researchers took advantage of these opportunities and were influenced by American developments (Vannier 2003; Masson 2008). America has actively recruited distinguished foreigners at later career stages, such as Gino Germani (Italy/Argentina) and Manuel Castells (Spain), some of whom have become intermediaries between their country of origin and U.S. sociology. Of the British contingent, some appear to have been recruited by the pull of the search for leading figures in fields where Britain had a strong reputation – social theory and science studies – while others look drawn by the push of elective affinity to the original home of intellectual novelties with which they identified – black studies, ethnomethodology – that were more institutionalized there.

Sociopolitical links help to channel migration flows, and the United States has not been the only centre to a periphery.[2] France has served

---

[2]   UNESCO (2006) data show that by 2004 the main receiving countries for students studying abroad (all subjects) are the United States, the United Kingdom, Germany, France, Australia, and Japan. The influences of language and geography are clear. Although the United States leads for them, many from China and Korea go to Japan, while for Indonesia, Singapore, and Hong Kong Australia leads; in Europe, the United States leads only for

francophones everywhere but also East European countries with which it has traditionally had links; Britain has served the Commonwealth, and politically self-exiled white South Africans have, for instance, played a real if relatively unremarked role in Britain, while refugees from Thatcherism (Beilharz and Hogan 2005, p. 409) or in search of promotion, went from Britain to Australia or New Zealand. There have been many movements between Spain, France, and Italy, and Latin America, with patterns changing as regimes have fluctuated. Decolonization from 1945 to 1960 left essentially unchanged the pattern where sociologists and anthropologists of the colonial power studied their own colonies, and students from them took higher qualifications in the metropole before perhaps returning home. (Other immigrants from the colonies created new communities with problems to be studied under the rubric of 'race relations,' and eventually provided young sociologists of Asian and African origins who have made distinctive local contributions, and have been attracted to such fields as black studies and postcolonial theory.) New Zealand and Singapore offer examples of patterns following from such flows. New Zealand has had one-third of its university sociologists with wholly foreign qualifications, and a further fifth with either a B.A. or a Ph.D. from abroad; by nationality, the major contribution has been from Britain, followed by Canada and the United States, South Africa, and India. The National University of Singapore now has twenty-seven staff; of their highest degrees, fourteen come from the United States, ten from Commonwealth countries (Britain, Australia, Canada, and New Zealand), and only two from Singapore, though a majority are probably of local origin.

The demography of gender has been of special importance. It is hard to overemphasize the role played since the 1960s by the women's movement, started in the United States, in redefining issues and topics of research and theorizing, and the growing feminization of higher education and the discipline has both reflected and supported this. In America since 1966, women's share of M.A.s has increased from around one-third to about two-thirds, and of Ph.D.s from 15 per cent to 58 per cent (Ferree et al. 2007); in McFalls et al.'s sample (1999, p. 97) women were 57 per cent of sociologists aged twenty-five to thirty-nine. In Britain and Canada, the same general pattern appears (Warren and Gingras 2007, pp. 13–16). The presence of women teaching in universities has changed more slowly because of low rates of turnover. In Britain, for instance, when the effects of the women's

U.K. students, while those from Ireland, Germany, Sweden, and France go to the United Kingdom, and those from Russia and Poland to Germany.

movement started to be felt most posts were already filled by young men, and in the 1980s, university cuts meant there were few new posts. Since then a majority of vacancies have probably been filled by women, though they remain outnumbered at older ages (Platt 2004). But by about 2000, from a quarter to a third of tenured faculty positions in those countries were held by women, and with new recruits the shift in balance continued. This is reflected in a marked shift in the gender composition of association memberships, officers, editors, etc., and a wider political sensitivity to gender issues (Platt 2003, pp. 38–9, 89–99). Similar patterns can be found elsewhere. Some intellectual consequences are mentioned later.

Associations and Journals

Learned societies are a key component of the social structure of the discipline, and much of its intellectual life is conducted through them. National associations have proliferated; in 2007 there were fifty-six affiliated to the ISA, as compared with twenty-five in 1953, and this certainly underestimates the total. There have also been a number of regional associations, some reflecting internal social divisions (Canada has a francophone association in addition to the 'national' one), dealing with a situation where there were not yet the resources for a national single-discipline one (there was a joint one for Australia and New Zealand until it divided in 1988, and Canada started jointly with anthropology), or, like the European Sociological Association, providing a forum for more local concerns and making participation for those with limited funds easier. The existence of the ISA, despite the fact that its World Congresses are held only every four years, has certainly encouraged cross-national intellectual contacts.

Some associations have been elite bodies or open only to those with doctorates in sociology, while others admit interested parties irrespective of qualifications or disciplinary affiliation; some have been truly voluntary associations, while others were a façade under state control. Some countries have had two parallel associations, one for academic sociologists and another for those outside academia, while others have only one (many of whose members may still come from outside academia).[3] The chequered history of some countries' associations (e.g., Argentina, India, Turkey) has also reflected local rivalries and political constraints. Large associations in rich countries typically have a wide range of activities, smaller and poorer

---

[3]   For some details, see the 2002 (17.2) special issue on national associations of *International Sociology*.

associations cannot do so much. It is not to be expected that national associations from such diverse settings, where the age, size, and levels of institutionalization of sociology vary considerably, will follow identical patterns, but globalization appears to have encouraged increasing similarity in their organization.

Many narrower associations exist for more specialized groups, sometimes representing divergence of views or intellectual style: the (U.S.) Society for the Study of Social Problems was founded by members dissatisfied with the ASA, while the much newer European Consortium for Sociological Research, responding to the trend for more 'qualitative' research, is clearly aimed only at those involved in large-scale quantitative empirical work; there is a complex pattern of relations between sociology and history (mainly in the United States), partially manifested in the existence of hardly overlapping subgroups to represent different networks and intellectual tendencies across this borderline (Abbott 2001, p. 91–120). There are also cross-disciplinary bodies such as the World Association for Public Opinion Research, representing an intellectual community that has cut across the academic/commercial line, bringing together those involved in the development of the survey methods which have been central to sociology (Converse 1987).

Most general associations have developed subgroups for members with shared special interests (all here called 'sections'), some of which have actively promoted joint research.[4] The pattern of such groups conveys something about sociological concerns, and the extent to which they are shared cross-nationally. The basis of intellectual solidarity may be theoretical, methodological, political, or substantive; it may be essentially technical or strongly ideological. The feminist movement has left its mark here, with groups emerging around the early 1970s both working on women and existing to share their identity politics. By 1995, the ASA's section on Sex and Gender had, with more than a thousand members, become its largest (with a narrow lead over medical); the ISA group has also been very large.

Section titles for fifteen associations on which data were found[5] have been classified into roughly homogeneous categories, and on that basis there are some areas where most associations studied now have sections. Those

---

[4] A strong example of the latter is given by the ISA's group for Social Stratification, which has since the 1950s brought together those working on stratification and mobility and encouraged additional studies, offered informed collegial discussion, and provided the framework within which comparability of data collected in different countries has been planned, sometimes leading to collective works (Hout and DiPrete 2006; Shavit and Blossfeld 1993).

[5] International – ISA, ESA, AISLF; national – those of Argentina, Australia, Brazil, Britain, China, France, Germany, India, Italy, South Africa, Spain, United States. In some fields

that appear in more than half, most on substantive fields, are, with their frequencies: health and medicine (12); communication/media, religion, environment, theory (11); women/gender, family, aging, education, arts/ culture, methods (10); economic, children/youth, science/technology (9); work/organizations, political, stratification (8).

Associations from Western Europe have an average of thirty sections, while those from the rest of the world, apart from the United States, average only thirteen; this probably reflects membership size – as local sociologies have grown, there has been sufficient support for more specialized groupings. Where there are fewer sections, the tendency is for the most widely shared fields – those with ten or more cases – to account for a higher proportion of the associations' totals, which suggests that those areas are seen as most fundamental. Many of them have some general public/political interest, but that does not seem enough to account for their appearance when we consider that crime/deviance, sport, sexualities, and race/ethnic relations appear rather less often; however, titles of more technical disciplinary interest such as alienation theory and research (1), mathematical sociology (1), realism and social research (1), have been uncommon. Some topics specific to one association follow obviously from local situations, as in the ASA's 'Latino/a sociology', the Deutsche Gesellschaft für Soziologie's 'Ost- und Ostmittel- europa- Soziologie', or the Indian Sociological Society's 'Dalits and Backward Classes', though other more idiosyncratic ones have arisen from the enthu- siasms of small groups. Changes over time represent intellectual change in the discipline. In the whole list, one can see new areas of work emerg- ing – aging, consumption, HIV/AIDs, disasters and international tourism, which respond to wider social change, while animals, autobiography, and the human body arise from the internal development of the discipline.

Associations have also played a key role in the production of journals, though others have been run by departments, groups of individuals, or com- mercial publishers. Impressionistically, there is now a striking uniformity of format among the main Western journals; reading through the years, one sees shared conventions emerging: abstracts, methods sections, notes, references, author biographical details, etc. (cf. Vannier 2003). Some homogenization has probably arisen through the growing dominance of journals by large publishers such as Sage and Springer. There has been increasing pressure from cross-national publishing conglomerates for internationalism in such matters as editorial board membership because that potentially increases

(e.g., health and medicine, religion, sport) half or more of the members may not be for- mally sociologists, or even members of the sponsoring association, so in that sense one cannot be sure what story this list tells.

the market, but non-commercial journals, too, are interested in their market range and have also increased their boards' international membership.

Crothers' (2007) analysis of sociological journals at five-year intervals shows a huge increase in the number of both journals and articles between 1960 and 2005, with a special peak in 1970, after which growth continues but its rate slows; this corresponds to what we know about the general growth of the discipline.[6] Ninety-three journals are now listed for sociology in the ISI's *Journal Citation Reports* for 2006.[7] Nearly a-quarter (22 per cent) of the total are sponsored by international, national, or regional associations, and over a-quarter (29 per cent) by specialist associations; 11 per cent are from university departments, and the rest have no clear affiliation other than a commercial publisher. All the listed journals of national associations define themselves as specifically sociological, while those from specialist bodies are commonly defined by substantive topic rather than discipline. Analysis of a yet wider list of 'sociological' journals used by Sociofile shows how widely the boundaries can be drawn of the far-from-wholly sociological; it makes clear that, in practice, many authors are working at edges of the purely disciplinary field related to history, anthropology, politics, philosophy, etc. The number of new journals created rose from eighteen in the 1950s (with the highest proportion of those being general sociological ones) to 39 to 49 per decade in the 1970–90s (with a majority claiming to be interdisciplinary across a specialist field), with more specialists within sociology later in that period. This pattern of expansion shows how growth has allowed and has led to increasing diversity and specialization.

Table 5.1 looks more closely at the top ten for citations among the specifically sociological, which we may take to be the most influential among those covered; six come from associations, all in America or Britain. Citation rates for the journals claiming a specifically sociological identity have a sharp gradient; even within the top ten, the first had more than ten times as many citations as the tenth, and there is reason to believe that this pattern has held for some time. We may speculate why those have been the most cited. Five are general sociological journals, and two are in the substantively topic-neutral field of methods, which also presumably gives them a broad constituency; five are available to association members (and ASA

[6] He used the ISI's *Social Science Citation Index*. This has become the standard source for quantitative data on journals, but its selection criteria for them have a strong bias towards English.

[7] However, less than half of those claim on their web sites to be distinctively sociological, though many more mention sociology as one of the disciplines represented. Others commonly regarded as sociological, such as the ASA's *Journal of Health and Social Behavior* (3,526 citations) appear only under other headings.

Table 5.1 *Top ten 'sociological' journals for citations*

Journal	National base	Sponsorship	Publisher[a]	Circulation, 2006[b]	Total citations
American Sociological Review (ASR)	U.S.	ASA	Association	11,500	7,927
American Journal of Sociology (AJS)	U.S.	Dept	UP	4,000	6,730
Annual Review of Sociology (ARS	U.S.	Publisher	Non-profit	?	2,687
Social Problems (SP)	U.S.	SSSP	UP	3,695	1,520
Sociology of Health & Illness (SHI)	U.K.	BSA[c]	Commercial	4,800+	1,283
Sociology (Soc)	U.K.	BSA	Commercial	3,700	1,050
Sociology of Education (SocEd)	U.S.	ASA	Association	2,500	1,007
Sociological Methods & Research (SMR)	U.S.	Dept	Commercial	1,562	808
Sociological Methodology (SM)	U.S.	ASA	Association	2,200	806
British Journal of Sociology (BJS)	U.K.	Dept	Commercial	2,700	772

[a] In some cases the type of publisher has changed over time.
[b] Some of these figures come from Ulrich (2004), others from journal sources. Round numbers are unlikely to be exact, and institutional subscriptions, now often bought as part of a package, confer wider access than do individual ones. Thus these figures need to be treated with caution.
[c] Not formally listed as a BSA journal, but produced by the relevant section of the BSA.

membership is very large) free or at a discount; and three (*SP, SHI, SocEd*) have obvious relevance to constituencies outside sociology.[8] In addition, in 2005 the *AJS* and *ASR* published an estimated 3,339 pages of articles (4,659 if *SF* is included), as compared with the British three's 2,526; more articles

---

[8] *Social Forces* is generally regarded as one of the leading general sociology journals, but here it is, for consistency, classified as interdisciplinary because of what its web site states. If it were included it would be at 3 with 2,935 citations. It might seem appropriate to substitute it for *SP* in the list.

means both more sources to cite, and more places to make citations. All those factors have some face plausibility in accounting for their ranking. It might have been expected that one of the two ISA general journals would lead, because their remit and circulation are formally worldwide, but their impact factors are relatively modest; ISA individual members are fewer than those of ASA – and more likely to make their citations in journals not scanned by the ISI.

Topics and Specialisms

But what have the topics of the journal articles been? Several analyses have shown that theory is prominent everywhere, while other main areas have been education, family, and work and organizations; politics, social stratification, and social welfare/policy also figure.[9] Gender only becomes prominent relatively late, and then less so than the level of interest in it might suggest; health/medicine also is, surprisingly, not high here; these may publish more in specialist journals, which they are large enough to support. U.S. sociology has been distinguished by the salience of 'social psychology', its relatively low concern with theory, and the prominence in 1965–66 of crime/deviance, which we may take to flag the lively discussion around Merton's anomie theory (Cole 1975, pp. 198–204). Abbott and Sparrow (2007) identify social mobility, bureaucracy, and community studies as new areas of work emerging in the United States after the war in response to changing circumstances. Some shifts could, arguably, be imputed to the subdivision of broad areas, which the increasing size of the discipline makes possible and attractive: figurational sociology, not theory; childhood, not family. Others (food, the body, internet methods) represent real novelty.

Textbooks throw light on the areas taken for granted as the defining content of sociology, rather than those at the research front. For British textbooks, up to the end of the 1970s class, family, education, politics, and work were almost universal, followed by religion/beliefs, and only a sprinkling of other topics (Platt 2008a). In the 1980s the pattern was more mixed, with first appearances for gender, media, globalization, and health; by the 1990s, almost all those areas, plus race and deviance, were covered by most books. Turner and Turner (1990, p. 164) list the commonplace

---

[9] Nakao (1998) on Japan 1965–94, Collison and Webber (1971) on Britain 1950–70, Brown and Gilmartin (1969) on the United States 1940–41 and 1965–66, de Miguel et al. on Spain 1995–2005, Crothers on the United Kingdom, and the United States 1965–2005. Most use data from a limited range of leading journals; Crothers uses Sociofile.

topics of modern U.S. textbooks: family, crime and deviance, organizations, socialization, small groups, ethnic relations, religion, education, medicine, science – and see, as other authors do, a strong tendency to work in terms of such substantive fields rather than the 'principles' of prewar texts. This is explained by the market pressure to offer content that can be used in teaching, often of non-specialists, however the course is structured, rather than by a consensus on the 'core' of sociology (Platt 2008b). Small countries, and ones where sociology is not yet fully established, may not have the market to support local textbooks or the research to provide locally relevant data; the cases of New Zealand (Crothers 2008) and Sweden (Larsson 2008) illustrate how this may make their textbooks socially less representative. International conglomerates increasingly dominate academic publishing, with a concomitant tendency for American textbooks to dominate; books of American origin are modified only as much as necessary to meet the local situation in different markets without basic change, while trouble is not generally taken to modify ones of foreign origin for the American market (Thompson 2005).[10] This reflects the sheer size of the U.S. market, but of course it has wider intellectual consequences. French introductory textbooks have shown important differences of style from British and American ones, ranging from their more philosophical and theoretical approach to the absence of examples from everyday life or humorous drawings (Schrecker 2008).

Another way of identifying leading topics is to look at sociologists' declared interests.[11] In the United States, social psychology has had continuing salience; theory, methodology, and marriage and family (the last presumably because of the tradition of undergraduate courses in the area), follow. Race/ethnicity is in the top ten for them, but not for Britain. Education has been particularly prominent in Britain, which probably follows from the practice (ended with the closure of separate teacher training colleges) of teaching educational sociology to future school-teachers. Feminism/gender is prominent everywhere from the 1980s, and health/medicine also comes to the fore at the end of the periods covered. These patterns do not have an obvious relation to high intellectual fashions, partly because the categories used are so broad, but they include the interests of people for whom teaching is salient, and/or whose research is

---

[10] However, Giddens' *Sociology* (several editions) as Giddens and Duneier, *Introduction to Sociology* (2000) is an exception to this rule, perhaps because of Giddens' prominence.

[11] Germov and McGee (2005) on Australia; Carter (1968) and BSA *Registers* for 1977 and 1988 on Britain; Riley (1960), Stehr and Larson (1972), and Ennis (1992) on ASA members in 1959, 1970, and 1989.

funded from social-policy sources, governmental or private. Only a small minority can have articles in leading journals; data on interests, therefore, give a more accurate representation of the state of thinking in the whole discipline at one point in time, if saying less about the direction in which it is moving.

One can look more deeply into declared areas of specialization to throw light on the structures of thought represented. Ennis (1992) found that, for 1990 ASA members, specialisms at the centre had substantive and applied orientations (stratification and work, social psychology/gender/medical), while the theoretical and quantitative-method clusters pulled in opposite directions from that, and there were clearly distinguished macro and micro orientation clusters. [Cappell and Guterbock (1992) found some similar linkages among ASA 1980–86 section memberships.] Inference beyond U.S. sociology would be speculative, if plausible; certainly the divisions between theoretical and empirical work, and between quantitative and qualitative styles, are impressionistically familiar.

How have specialisms emerged as such? In varying ways; they have not always started within sociology, and may – like urban sociology in relation to geography – remain on the boundaries with other disciplines. There have been marked shifts in fashion over time. The emergence of at least the British sociology of science owed a lot to a movement that started among natural scientists, some of whom moved over. Claus (1983) points out that medical sociology has sometimes started in a medical rather than a sociological context. (In Britain, a professor of midwifery who made epidemiological studies played a key role.) In Europe, its growth responded to systems for the provision of medical care within a new welfare-state framework, which created a demand both for training in social medicine for doctors and for policy-relevant research. Some sociologists have been in rather isolated positions within medical schools, expected to work on sociology *in* medicine rather than the more critical sociology *of* medicine preferred in sociology departments.

Gender or women's studies has been very different. It emerged in the 1970s from the broader women's movement, in no way specific to sociology, and has often become a distinct cross-disciplinary programme or department, if one with which many sociologists have affiliated. There can be no doubt that it has been responsible for the growth in study of domestic and workplace division of labour, the understanding of housework as work, and the establishment of gender as a key theoretical dimension of inequality, appearing in introductory textbooks alongside race (also put in place as a by-product of an American social movement) and class. The ambitious attempt to establish a feminist epistemology has been less widely successful, but still important.

'Social theory' (not exclusively sociological) has emerged recently as a distinct field. For some years there has been an International Social Theory Consortium, which brings together Euro-American groups (with titles from 'Comparative Cultural and Literary Studies' to 'Social and Political Thought') strong in graduate teaching in this area, not all within sociology departments. This has a normative and political slant, and is not the kind of theory that is tested with data, even if it sometimes draws on data. A strongly contrasted movement has been that for rational-choice theory, used very much as the kind that is tested with data by proponents such as Goldthorpe (2000, 2007). The idea of rational choice originated in economics, and there have certainly been contacts with economists working on topics related to traditional sociological interests. Swedberg (1991, p. 267) saw a 'new economic sociology' emerging in the United States after the 1960s, much later than in France and Germany, from the meeting of 'new institutional economics' and 'new sociology of economic life'. Gary Becker, a Nobel Prize–winning economist who worked on such topics as marriage and crime, was recruited in 1983 to the famous sociology department of the University of Chicago, where he joined rational-choice theorist James Coleman[12] in running a successful interdisciplinary social-science faculty seminar on rational choice. The web site of the journal *Rationality and Society* (founded 1989) declares that the rational action paradigm has emerged as 'the inter-lingua of the social sciences', and 'offers the promise of bringing greater theoretical unity across disciplines such as economics, sociology, political science, cognitive psychology, moral philosophy and law'. That seems rather optimistic in relation to whole disciplines. Indeed, Goldthorpe belongs to a clearly distinct European group of sophisticated quantitative sociological researchers, many concerned with class, social mobility, and educational opportunity, working within a paradigm that they regard as importantly different even from that of the American sociological rational-choice theorists. The general approach has also had many critics, and more within sociology who simply disregard it; in particular, it has had little attention in discussions of 'theory'.[13]

---

[12] His *Foundations of Social Theory* (1990) has been hugely influential – and much criticized. For exposition and discussion of Coleman's work, see Marsden (2005).

[13] Zald (1995) provides useful short accounts of the intellectual communities of several other specialisms.

Sociologists' concerns have often been influenced by their extra-academic political positions, perhaps most obviously shown in the various marxisms and in second-wave feminism but by no means confined to them. (Numbers of smaller journals offer ideological agendas.) In the earlier part of our period, sociology, at least in Britain and France, looked remarkably like the study of the working class. In Britain this could be seen as a continuation of an older model of philanthropic concern as much as current leftist politics, while in France it owed a lot to the interests of the communist party to which many of the early empirical researchers belonged, despite the party's coolness towards empirical sociology. Some sociologists have put their own lives on the (assembly) line; workplace ethnographies offer several cases where the author joined a factory to find out by direct experience what factory work under capitalism was like, and more than one was fired for union activity (e.g., Cavendish 1982; Devinatz 1999; Pfeffer 1979).

In the American and European upheavals of the late 1960s, sociology students were very prominent (Blackstone et al. 1970; Lipset and Ladd 1972), though it cannot be assumed that it was studying sociology which formed their political views; certainly for some it was their political views that led them to sociology, though when there many of them put forward strong critiques of their elders. This experience has remained important for its cohort as they approach retirement; shared nostalgia is represented in such work as *The Disobedient Generation* (Sica and Turner 2005). Distinct but overlapping is, at least in Britain and the United States, the founding cohort of second-wave feminists, some now holding posts in women's studies.

Even in American sociology, often criticized from the left for its supposed positivistic scientism and claims to intellectual neutrality, it is clear that some ASA presidents have been elected on leftist political grounds as much as for their intellectual distinction or organizational skills, and no one who has attended ASA conferences could miss the salience of plenary speakers with leftist politics. It is not by chance, either, that Wright Mills, an icon of the left, has for many years been among the authors most cited. It has been shown in various contexts (Lipset and Ladd 1972) that sociologists have tended to hold views to the left of other academics, and this is perhaps exemplified in the taken-for-granted demonstration and critique of inequality (treated as such even when subcultural difference might be an equally valid description) as a theme in teaching and research, which over our period has added race and gender to class. Sanderson and Ellis (1992) and McFalls et al. (1999) found that political views of samples of U.S. sociologists not only inclined markedly to the left, but were also strongly related to their theoretical perspectives. The distribution of ASA section memberships has suggested that 'The ideological and philosophical divisions created by differing orientations toward politics and positivism … are institutionalised in [the discipline's] professional structure' (Cappell and Guterbock 1992, pp. 271–2). Burawoy's recent call for a 'public sociology' has had extraordinary reverberations, leading to worldwide discussions in journals and conferences; every sociologist has not agreed with him, but clearly his case for political participation struck a disciplinary nerve.[14]

But external political factors have also influenced sociology. For example, U.S. criminology has shifted over time in ways that corresponded to shifts in policy thinking – and consequent research funding. As policy in the 1970s and 1980s moved away from agendas of rehabilitation and reform towards crime control, criminology became more detached from general sociology, and the proportion of its articles based on politically funded work and concerned with formal control increased (Savelsberg et al. 2004). Masson (2008) has noted how the areas of research in France have been affected by changing opportunities for employment on governmental contracts; the European Union's funding requirement of cross-national cooperation must have affected the amount of comparative work. State control of funding is, of course, not necessary for research themes to change as social realities change, as exemplified, for instance, by the considerable body of 1980s work in Western sociology on Japanese management practices, or on women's work and the domestic division of labour. Lim (2007, p. 149) describes how in South Korea before the 1980s Marxist books were banned, and Marx could not be taught in the universities – so Weber was emphasized; modernization theory was taught, and dependency theory not mentioned. Park and Chang (1999, p. 151) add to this how, when democracy arrived in 1992, 'The role of sociology as a dissident doctrine against right-wing dictatorship gave way to a more practical role of providing perspectives on or explanations of social policy issues.' Similarly in South Africa, the end of 'the struggle' redirected many sociologists to practical policy work.

Theories and Canons

In principle the movements of general theory are important. Those will be dealt with only briefly here, both because they have been prominent

---

[14] His personal statement when standing (successfully) for president of the ASA urged that 'As mirror and conscience of society, sociology must define, promote and inform public debate about deepening class and racial inequalities, new gender regimes, environmental degradation, market fundamentalism, state, and nonstate violence … the world needs public sociology-a sociology that transcends the academy' (Burawoy 2002).

in many other historical accounts (e.g., Baert 1998; Kilminster 1998; May 1995), and because of scepticism about the extent to which explicit theoretical stances have had real consequences in practice, as they are meant to do in principle, for the work of other parts of sociology. Menzies (1982) found, in a large sample of articles in U.S., Canadian, and British journals, that theory in use in research did not correspond to theoreticians' theory (cf. Sica 1989). It is evident that uses made of the names of leading thinkers often show little interest in what they really meant, using citations as a diffuse means of claiming legitimacy, or as labels for such crude distinctions as quantitative (Durkheim, *Suicide*) versus qualitative (Weber, *verstehen*). The translations used of work by foreign authors have not always done them justice (Baehr 2002, pp. 185–204; Simeoni 2000), and lack of background knowledge about their social and intellectual settings can make for serious misunderstandings (Roth 1971) – even if such misuse is also a form of influence. Camic and Gross (1998) analyse the 'projects' evident in the range of recent anglophone work described as 'theory' and find the field incoherent, with a range of inconsistent aims and limited success in achieving them. It seems likely that the more limited theories associated with empirical specialisms, such as 'regulation theory' or 'new assimilation theory', have more practical import for those whose specialism is not general theory.

Disciplinary traditions are shown in canon formation; to what extent has there been a shared canon, and what does that show? It is generally agreed that there was a notable canon change from the 1950s in the United States, where émigrés, especially those from Germany with the primarily theoretical interests dominant there, made a significant contribution to this. The diffusion of U.S. influence then led, paradoxically, to the export, and re-export to France and Germany, of those choices. Durkheim, Weber, and Marx became the 'holy trinity', supplemented by varying local heroes and supported by a second team with members such as Simmel.[15] [Connell (1997) argues persuasively that this represented an epistemological break, in which the focus changed, in response to global social and political developments, from the difference between the metropole and its primitive 'other' to differences within the metropole.] The change was striking in the United States, where authors of local origin – such as Ward ('the American Aristotle'), Cooley, and Ross – were supplanted, which was quite misleading about historical forefathers, given the character of the attention previously

---

[15] Some of the names on these lists have been 'appropriated' for sociology from other identities (Baehr 2002, p. 22).

paid to these authors.[16] One may speculate how long the discipline can continue to use the same set of theoretical landmarks to think with as their origins vanish further into the past, and whether their persistence so far does not owe something to the career span, now ending, of the cohort of the great expansion. Their status is also made problematic by other factors; Alatas and Sinha (2001) have written interestingly about the difficulties of teaching 'classical' theory from prewar Europe in the radically different society of contemporary Singapore – though they do so, because it is seen as defining disciplinary identity.

To the canon of prewar authors was added a postwar, all-American set including Talcott Parsons, Robert K. Merton, and C. Wright Mills, although the first two then reached the stage of critique and rejection.[17] ISA members were asked in 1998 to list the five twentieth-century books most influential in their work. Weber came out well in the lead, with the most frequently mentioned single book, and more than twice as many total mentions as Mills in second place, who was followed at a distance by Durkheim and Marx. It is not clear what real intellectual meaning such statements show. Recently there has been, for political reasons, a movement in the United States to include representatives of women (Harriet Martineau, Jane Addams) and blacks (W. E. B. DuBois) in the ancestral pantheon. It is clear that these candidates have been chosen to inspire now, and to remedy past neglect, and the movement is as much concerned with the personnel of sociology as with the content of its intellectual work.

There has been a standard historical recital of recognized postwar general theoretical positions in anglophone introductory textbooks, starting with U.S. functionalism, in Britain often contrasted with 'conflict theory', which developed as a critique of that. In the United States, functionalism became a key element of 'mainstream' sociology. There it had strong critics such as Mills and Gouldner, as well as practitioners of what others called 'symbolic interactionism' who simply did different sorts of work. The student unrest of the late 1960s was associated with versions of Marxism; the ASA section on Marxist sociology was founded in 1977, and work in that tendency, represented most prominently by Immanuel Wallerstein's world systems theory, Erik Olin Wright's work on class, and Michael Burawoy's work on work, has continued as one grouping among others.

---

[16] For prewar, see Levine et al. (1976, p. 842); in a sample of textbooks from 1924 to 1933 no references at all to Weber were found.

[17] Some examples of studies bearing on this: Oromaner (1968 and 1980) on references in U.S. textbooks and articles; Harley (2008) on twenty-four textbooks in the United States, Britain and Australia; de Miguel et al. (2007) on citations in the main Spanish journal.

(In France and Germany, versions of Marxism were, of course, salient much earlier.) In Britain, there was in the 1970s a baroque flowering of alternative approaches, ranging from Garfinkel's ethnomethodology (American) to Althusserian Marxism (French) and 'critical sociology' of the Frankfurt school (German). What counted as 'theory' was often not specifically sociological; philosophical issues, whether social philosophy or the philosophy of science, were salient, as were ideological commitments, associated with what Giddens (1987, p. 42) later called 'the grand questions.' The civil rights movement and the Vietnam War, as elsewhere, encouraged a general political hostility to the Untied States – although this entailed support for internal U.S. oppositional trends. Attention then turned to European rather than American theorists, often introduced by the *New Left Review*. Recent, well-established, anglophone trends have come from Europe, particularly in the form of the 'French theory' of writers such as Foucault and Derrida; this is treated by the French as puzzling, because these are mostly not sociologists and have not had the same prominence in French sociology (Cusset 2005). This has been developed as the elusively defined 'postmodern' position, concerned with culture as much as structure. Analysis by date of the theoretical positions listed by British introductory textbooks shows that Marxism, feminism, and postmodernism are seen as emerging in turn, but old friends functionalism and symbolic interactionism are not forgotten. This expresses a commonly remarked trend: there is no longer a dominant paradigm, but many alternative possibilities coexist and are offered to students as possible choices.

More recent theoretical work remains to be fitted into a standard historical pattern. Bourdieu (French) has had great acclaim inside and outside France, and his influence has been extended because he was also active in empirical research to exemplify his approach. Britain has offered the world Giddens and his concept of 'structuration', with some success, and Beck's (German) ideas on the 'risk society' have had wide appeal. Recent developments include work, such as Runciman's (1998) neo-evolutionary theory and Dickens' (2004) environmental sociology, which apply biological ideas to social theory. Alongside these, sects committed to Elias's figurational sociology (mainly in the Netherlands and Britain), to rational choice theory with a concentration in northern Europe, to 'ethnomethodology' transatlantically, and to world systems theory based in the United States, continue. There are, of course, stories to be told from other national bases, which mention many other authors and historical trajectories (see, for instance, Delanty 2006).

Research Methods

Methods tend to develop as part of the paradigm package in intellectual communities working in particular substantive areas, sometimes for good substantive reasons (citation analysis in the sociology of science), sometimes by what looks more like historical accident (qualitative methods in nursing research). Easily observable and recorded behaviour lends itself to formalization and is more likely to be formalized. But methods have also affected the substance of what is studied. Boudon (1986, p. 207) and Coleman (1986, p. 1316) have pointed out that methodological individualism and mathematical approaches have had a compatibility that has discouraged the growth of techniques for dealing with compositional effects and system-level outcomes.

American sociology has been especially concerned with research methods (some drawn from contacts with other disciplines). It can probably claim the invention of the sociological methods textbook, supports specialized journals in the field, has had substantial membership of sections on method, etc. In the 1950s, the survey was dominant and enormously influential at home and abroad, though small-group laboratory studies and Moreno's 'sociometry' (Marineau 2007) were also in vogue. But from the late 1960s there was a surge of writing on qualitative methods (e.g., Glaser and Strauss 1967; Lofland 1971), in parallel with an autobiographical and reflexive literature (e.g., Hammond 1964; Sjoberg 1967). This novel genre showed how research decisions arose in practice, and treated the researcher as person as of methodological interest. The relativization that this approach suggested chimed with many of the themes of the late 1960s and early 1970s. That literature was very separate from the quantitative work seen as adequately represented in the journal *Sociological Methodology*, with 'an overwhelming emphasis on statistical models of covariance structures' (Burt 1982, p. 96), but despite its existence U.S. sociology has maintained a tradition of more heavily quantitative methods than even such culturally close comparators as Canada and Britain. In Britain, Canada, and France several observers have noted the more recent trend for a high proportion of articles to rest on data from small samples of semistructured interviews, raising scepticism among quantitative workers about the value of the data. The division between the worlds inhabited by quantitative and qualitative methodologists has continued even as a rich textbook literature on qualitative method has elaborated and diversified the range of its possibilities, introducing much more systematic analytical techniques, while quantitative work has applied its techniques to novel kinds of data. The *Bulletin de Méthodologie*

Sociologique, edited from Paris, is now full of highly sophisticated technical analyses of textual data.

A theme that crosscuts the purely methodological discussion is the ideological argument by some feminists that only 'qualitative' methods are appropriate to study women, and are consistent with feminist principles. It has indeed been the case that in some countries such methods have been used more by, and/or on, women, and seem particularly prevalent in fields traditionally dominated by women such as education and nursing (Clemens et al. 1995; Grant et al. 1987; Platt 2006, pp. 217–9; 2007). This has probably been a stronger tendency where feminist influence has been very salient and the traditional commitment to quantitative method less, but its currency has helped legitimize qualitative approaches more widely.

American methodological influence has been great,[18] but that does not mean that other countries have followed it slavishly. France provides an interesting example. Participant observation there has had a somewhat different history from that in the United States. Many of the earliest studies did not think of it as a 'method', but were undertaken with religious or political motives, associated with social Catholicism and leftist politics (Chapoulie 2001, p. 18; Peneff 1996, pp. 39–40). More recently, participant observation has been taken more seriously, and related to a lively interest in the Chicago School, whose myth is also related to the tremendous vogue for 'biographical method' or oral history since the mid-1970s (Peneff 1990).[19] A movement for life histories within sociology started with a group led by Bertaux, which treated autobiography as a special method. For him this was a reaction to the events of 1968, seen as giving a voice to those excluded from history, and an attack on 'positivistic imperialism'. Flynn (1991) provides a detailed account of the reception of ethnomethodology and the associated technique of conversation analysis, showing how it was in France associated with surrealism, and enthusiastically received in the 1980s – but not before – for reasons having a lot to do with local developments. In the quantitative field, American-style surveys became common as a mode of collecting data,

---

[18] Berthelot (1991, pp. 112–3) sketches a usual chronology from the mid-1950s in each country subject to American influence: first quantitative methods, then an attack on those and favour of the qualitative and ethnographic, life histories, lexical and semantic analyses, then the introduction of many new possibilities, often from neighbouring disciplines.

[19] On the Chicago School, see Bulmer (1984). For details of French life history work, see Heinritz and Rammstedt (1991). They also compare French with German work, in many ways similar and following the same chronology – but used for different topics, emphasizing different modes of data collection; each has related itself to American sociology rather than to the other. They suggest that the form discussion has taken depended on the local alternatives; in France grand theory, in Germany quantification.

and were frequently seen as the only scientific method of data collection (Masson 2008, pp. 47–50, 95), but often analysed in ways alien to America. A mode of data analysis, 'correspondence analysis', invented by the statistician Benzécri, became widespread in the 1970s, especially after it was used in Bourdieu's widely read *La Distinction* (1979). It takes a more inductive approach than that normal in Anglo-Saxon statistics, and is oriented more to description rather than hypothesis-testing, not necessarily aiming to generalize from the sample to the population. It is seen as a way of finding theories, not just testing them (van Meter et al. 1994). Some writers have seen this style of work as typifying a characteristically French approach to sociology more generally.

New methodological possibilities, such as the data archive movement, have been opened up by technical developments in computing. Data archives pool resources by the central deposit of survey data, allowing access to far more material, so that comparative data can be created and increasingly, as time goes by, historical trends can be observed. The data banked are drawn mainly from surveys (often by political scientists, commercial polls, or governmental policy researchers), though moves are now under way to make qualitative data available too. Extensive cross-national collaboration has been built up through a network of institutions such as the International Federation of Data Organisations (IFDO) founded in 1977, the Council of European Social Science Data Archives (CESSDA) formed in 1976, and the Inter-University Consortium for Political and Social Research (ICPSR), established in 1962 at the University of Michigan, which has played a central role. Problems of comparability when independent surveys are compared, and the limits to representativeness when data from only a few countries were deposited, have led to the growth of cooperation in the planning of surveys exemplified in the World Values Survey. This has involved more than eighty countries in surveys planned to permit a wide range of comparison and potential generalizability.[20] The resulting prevalence of secondary analysis has been criticized because researchers are tempted to use what is available rather than collecting data directly addressing their own questions, though early involvement in planning can mitigate the problem. The difficulty of inferring causation when the same units have not been studied at different time points has been met by the creation of an increasing number of cohort studies, whether ad hoc or special samples from census data, and these have become important to work on child development, education, and social mobility.

---

[20] Mochmann (2002) summarizes much information about the movement and its member institutions.

Social constructionism, which sees social 'facts' as socially constructed rather than having a real independent existence, has been especially important (and controversial) in the sociology of science, but has diffused well beyond the application to what natural scientists do. Much unease is expressed at the postmodern relativism of the younger generation, making any version of reality just another version. That is associated with the 'cultural turn', focusing interest on mass media and the internet as the new 'reality'. But while, on the one hand, some may cease to worry about the validity of interview data as representing anything outside the interview situation itself (Holstein and Gubrium 1995, p. 9), on the other hand, formal techniques of increasing sophistication are applied to large-scale, quantitative data. Aspects not previously much considered, such as the logic of comparative study (Ragin 1987) and event history analysis (Allison 1984), have entered the repertoire. We cannot tell what the latest period will look like to historians in 2050, but at present it seems too divided and diverse to summarize.

Conclusion

In the period since 1945 sociology has become fully institutionalized internationally as an academic discipline, but within that outline there have been early and late developers, and different national sociologies have operated under sharply varying intellectual and practical circumstances. The discipline now has a global institutional structure, with many opportunities for movement within it, but one to which members of different groups have varying access and where not all feel at home. Elements of convergence in gender balance, journal style, associations, canon choices, and the repertoire of methods, have been shown, as well as some important differences. Is there a grand historical narrative to which the details can be fitted? Two related candidates are Americanization and globalization.

It is plausible to suggest that from about 1945 to 1965 there was a broad international consensus on what sociology was and how it would do its work, and this demonstrated American hegemony. Parsons and Merton were its lead theorists, while the legacy of Vienna-Circle philosophy of science via America, and the survey methods associated with Lazarsfeld, were dominant. U.S. practical dominance since then seems confirmed by data on publications. The United States led in the number of monographs in sociology produced in 1981–85, with 26.4 per cent of the total; France was next (15.7 per cent), followed by the United Kingdom (8.4 per cent), West Germany (7.6 per cent), the USSR (6.2 per cent), India (6 per cent), and the other eighty-four countries with 29.7 per cent (Kishida and Matsui 1997). (GDP was a major determinant of these differences, though national levels of education also contributed.) The United States has also led in the production of articles: in 1990–92 it had 56.9 per cent of those published in sociology, with the United Kingdom second with 7.6 per cent (Glänzel 1996), and received 76 per cent of the citations to those papers. The general pattern has been for every other country to refer heavily to U.S. work, and secondarily to its own authors more than to others. But this can be seen as simply reflecting the number of U.S. sociologists and their publications. Yitzhaki (1998) found for a 1985–94 sample that, although almost all the U.S. and British citations were to anglophone sources; when this was related to an 'expected' rate based on the proportions of the languages in the sociological literature, it emerged that they had a lower rate of own-language citation than the French or Germans. Similarly, Glänzel found that U.S. citations were somewhat above the world average rate, but the United Kingdom and the USSR did better *relatively* (despite citation shares of only 7.6 per cent and 0.5 per cent, respectively). A numerical lead does not seem quite the same as intellectual dominance. Since the 1960s, many more actors have come on the scene. What shifts may there be with Russia and China entering the international sociological forum?

There has been growing dissatisfaction with United States, anglophone, or Western, dominance, although so far more manifest in programmatic statements than in action. The persistence of the glorious tradition of French resistance to anglophone hegemony was manifest when the president of the Association Française de Sociologie, Dan Ferrand-Bechmann, explained its policy to make links with other countries in southern Europe because it is vital 'faire contrepoids au monde anglo-saxon pour affirmer une culture latine de la sociologie' (Roger 2006) – though she did not indicate what that would consist of. But there are also other sources of resistance now. As former colonies have developed their own sociologies, 'postcolonial theory' and 'subaltern studies' have identified forms of intellectual dominance, seeing what was generally recognized as core sociology as biased to Western issues and concepts, and pressing for 'indigenization' to reclaim and explore the distinctive features of their own societies. Another version of such problems is sketched by Israeli sociologist Azarya (2006), who describes the pressure felt to publish in internationally prestigious places, which must be done by theorizing topics at levels of abstraction that take them away from concrete problems in Israeli society. Others have analysed how Western sociology has presented its empirical results as if they were universal, but those from elsewhere merely local – to the detriment of both (Alatas 2003; Baber 2003; Lee

1994); Alatas applies the concepts of imperialism and dependency to the internal relations of social science.[21] Australian Raewyn Connell extends the argument to a wider 'South' and to general theory; she maintains that so far it has been essentially 'Northern', claiming a universality that is impossible except from the point of view of the metropole, and imposing a grand ethnography of premodern to modern and postmodern which suppresses the particularities of the South. She urges a genuinely global sociology, which must 'at the level of theory as well as of empirical research and practical application, be more like a conversation among many voices', and lists as elements towards that the Islamic debate on modernity, African discussion of indigenous knowledge, Latin American theorization of dependency and globalization, the international feminist critique, and Indian debate on culture, voice, and development (Connell 2006, p. 262).[22]

Other differences have arisen from local intellectual traditions. The system of disciplines has not been the same everywhere – for instance, in India anthropology and sociology are not as clearly distinguished as often elsewhere, while the British separation between 'sociology' and 'social policy' or 'social administration' is not typical (Rodriguez 2007). Abend (2006) found fundamental epistemological differences in the grounds on which claims to truth and scientificity in leading Mexican and U.S. journals were based; for instance U.S. articles, unlike Mexican ones, make assumptions about the regularity of the social world that justify the abstraction of general principles from concrete empirical instances. Seale (2008, p. 12) found, in leading U.S. and British medical sociology journals, greater British concern with 'the production and refinement of social theory … with a relative degree of disdain for empirical work and, in particular, for the use of quantitative methods to document social facts. Instead, there is an abiding preference for what … has now become a social constructionist orthodoxy. …'

In addition, it is natural for local circumstances to affect the issues that are developed, and they have done so. Thus, Canadian concern about U.S. dominance led to an emphasis on methods and data sources which lent themselves to study of the political economy of Canada's relation to the United States. Similarly, the dependency theory of the 1960s related to the felt situation of Latin America, though Davis (1992) analyses the

---

[21] Kennedy and Centeno (2007, pp. 670–2) look at the issue from American sociology, maintaining that in it 'American studies' has had an implicit centrality, with serious attention to other parts of the world only when related to American national interests or intellectual debates.

[22] These arguments have been extended into a book, Connell (2007).

political and institutional reasons, including the ruling party's use of dependency rhetoric for its own purposes, why Mexican sociologists differed from those in Brazil and Chile in being more concerned with social movements and the state. A survey of Australian books seen as shaping the national sociology suggested that 'Australian sociological production ... represents a conscious dialogue with a distinct inheritance of colonial encounters, indigenous presence, migrant arrivals and status in the region ... [which] ... has given rise to a particular brand of critical sociology ...' (Skrbis and Germov 2005, p. 334). Sociology in Korea developed initially under American political control, but it was then found (unsurprisingly!) that what had been learned was not adequate to deal with local experience of national division, neocolonial dependency, military dictatorship, and the suppression of democracy (Park and Chang 1999). The availability of models elsewhere can hinder as well as help. Such local patterns certainly have not excluded foreign influence, but they are among factors that have affected the forms its reception takes – which has sometimes been based on misunderstanding. For instance, several French writers (Simeoni 2000; Wacquant 1993) have criticized what they see as serious misunderstandings of Bourdieu's work in the anglophone world; Matsumoto (2007) shows how cultural differences between Japan and the United States have led to Japanese survey methods differing in several ways; Platt (1995) found that the aspects of Durkheim's *Rules* attended to in the United States changed markedly over time in response to the movement of local discussion. There has been much less discussion of differences unrelated to national identities. However, Edmunds and Turner (2005) suggest that the Internet has been a key factor in creating worldwide 'global generations', cutting across national divisions, and clearly the social movements of the 1960s were also cross-national generational phenomena, while Stehr and Larson (1972, pp. 5–6) found that generational cohort differences tended to persist.

Such factors as those suggest the limitations of Americanization and globalization as grand narratives. A quite different candidate is fragmentation. As sociology has expanded, some who worked on organization theory and industrial sociology have moved to business schools; posts for sociologists in medical settings have increased; women's studies has become a cross-disciplinary field of its own; socio-legal studies and media and/or cultural studies have become separate departments, not just options within sociology. At the same time, some uses of ideas from other established disciplines such as economics and biology have become salient, while the boundaries with politics and social work have never been clear-cut, and commercial social research has its own traditions and associations. Such developments have led to anxiety about the discipline. Is it disintegrating? The BSA initiated a discussion responding to this anxiety, in which Urry (2005) suggested that the period of U.S. hegemony ending in the 1960s, when sociology achieved a homogeneity that rested on ignoring historical change and societal differences, was atypical and not the norm, and Stanley (2005) saw the development of valuably 'hybridic' sociologies in some departments. Such changes can, thus, be seen positively, and even as showing sociology expanding or coming to dominate other fields.[23]

While each of these narratives has clearly corresponded to some social reality, none of them seems adequate to the complexity of events. Several overlapping processes are evident. There has indeed been an international sociology, if not a global one, in the form both of personal contacts and of generally known work. The growth in size has now made room for much more disciplinary diversity than at earlier periods, and has made it impossible to know it all. The history of national sociologies has been influenced by local factors, both longstanding national intellectual traditions and changing historical and political factors as well as simply national size, but also by the state of international sociology at formative stages in their development. Arguably the real unit at intellectual growth points has for researchers become the specialism, which cuts across national boundaries, and this divides those in different fields. But even if that undermines the sense of a shared centre there have been theories, methods, and topics that sociologists everywhere have recognized as part of their field, whether or not they approve them or are expert in them. Those have changed over time, as have the boundaries between sociology and other disciplines or fields of practical work; new sub-disciplines have emerged at the boundaries, and new links in theory and method have been made with other fields. American dominance has owed a lot to its economic and political position in the world system, but also to the size of its educated population, the early development of its sociology, and the happy chance of sharing a language with other former British colonies. As other large countries advance economically and educationally, change is to be expected, but it is likely that the intellectual and social structure of world sociology will remain that of a network of overlapping networks.

---

[23] Mills et al. (2006, p. 68) found that in Britain only half the academic staff with higher degrees in sociology worked in 'sociology' units in 2001, and characterize sociology as an exporting discipline.

REFERENCES

Abbott, Andrew (2001) *Chaos of Disciplines*, Chicago, IL: University of Chicago Press.

Abbott, Andrew& James Sparrow (2007) 'Hot war, Cold War: Structures of sociological action, 1940–1955', pp. 281–313 in ed. Craig Calhoun, *Sociology in America: A History*, Chicago, IL: University of Chicago Press.

Abend, Gabriel (2006) 'Styles of sociological thought: Sociologies, epistemologies, and the Mexican and U.S. quests for truth', *Sociological Theory* 24(1): 1–41.

Alatas, Syed Farid (2003) 'Academic dependency and the global division of labour in the social sciences', *Current Sociology* 51: 599–613.

Alatas, Syed Farid & Vineeta Sinha (2001) 'Teaching classical sociological theory in Singapore: The context of Eurocentrism', *Teaching Sociology* 29: 316–331.

Allison, Paul D. (1984) *Event History Analysis*, Newbury Park, CA: Sage.

Azarya, Victor (2006) '*Academic Excellence and Social Relevance ...*'. Paper given at the XVI ISA World Congress of Sociology, Durban.

Baber, Zaheer (2003) 'Provincial universalism: The landscape of knowledge production in an era of globalisation', *Current Sociology* 51: 615–623.

Baehr, Peter (2002) *Founders, Classics, Canons: Modern Disputes Over the Origins and Appraisal of the Social Sciences*, New Brunswick, NJ: Transaction.

Baert, Patrick (1998) *Social Theory in the Twentieth Century*, Cambridge: Polity Press.

Beilharz, Peter & Trevor Hogan (2005) 'The State of Social Sciences in Australia', pp. 387–417 in ed. J. Germov & T. Renae McGee, *Histories of Australian Sociology*, Melbourne: Melbourne University Press.

Berthelot, Jean-Michel (1991) *La Construction de la sociologie*, Paris: Presses Universitaires de France.

Blackstone, Tessa, K. Gales, R. Hadley & W. Lewis (1970) *Students in Conflict: LSE in 1967*, London: Weidenfeld and Nicolson.

Boudon, Raymond. (1986) 'Mathematical and statistical thinking in the social sciences', pp. 199–217 in ed. Karl W. Deutsch, Andrei S. Markovits & John Platt, *Advances in the Social Sciences, 1900–1980, What Who Where How?* Cambridge, MA: Abt.

Bourdieu, Pierre (1979) *La Distinction: Critique sociale du jugement*, Paris: Minuit.

Brown, Julia S. & Brian B. Gilmartin (1969) 'Sociology today: Lacunae, emphases and surfeits', *The American Sociologist* 4: 283–291.

Bulmer, Martin (1984) *The Chicago School of Sociology*, Chicago, IL: University of Chicago Press.

Burawoy, Michael (2002) 'Candidates announced for ASA officers', *Footnotes* 30.3: 7.

Burt, Ronald S. (1982) *Toward a Structural Theory of Action*, New York: Academic Press.

Camic, Charles (2007) 'On edge: Sociology during the Great Depression and the New Deal', pp. 225–280 in ed. Craig Calhoun, *Sociology in America: A History*, Chicago, IL: University of Chicago Press.

Camic, Charles & Neil Gross (1998) 'Contemporary developments in sociological theory', *Annual Review of Sociology* 24: 453–476.

Cappell, Charles L. & Thomas M. Guterbock (1992) 'Visible colleges: the social and conceptual structure of sociology specialties', *American Sociological Review* 57: 266–273.

Carter, M. P. (1968) 'Report on a survey of sociological research in Britain', *Sociological Review* 16: 5–40.

Cavendish, Ruth (1982) *Women on the Line*, Boston, MA: Routledge and Kegan Paul.

Chapoulie, Jean-Michel (2001) 'Le travail de terrain, l'observation des actions et des interactions, et la sociologie', *Sociétés Contemporaines* 40: 5–27.

Clemens, E. S., W. W. Powell, K. McIlwaine & D. Okamoto (1995) 'Careers in print: Books, journals, and scholarly reputations', *American Journal of Sociology* 101: 433–494.

Chenu, Alain (2002) 'Une institution sans intention. La sociologie en France depuis l'après-guerre', *Actes de la recherche en sciences sociales* 141–142: 46–59.

Claus, Lisbeth M. (1983) 'The development of medical sociology in Europe', *Social Science and Medicine* 17: 1591–1597.

Cole, Stephen (1975) 'The growth of scientific knowledge: Theories of deviance as a case study', pp. 175–220 in ed. Lewis A. Coser, *The Idea of Social Structure: Papers in Honour of Robert K. Merton*, New York: Harcourt Brace Jovanovich.

Coleman, James S. (1986) 'Social theory, social research and a theory of action', *American Journal of Sociology* 91: 1309–1335.

(1990) *Foundations of Social Theory*, Cambridge, MA: Harvard University Press.

Collison, Peter & Susan Webber (1971) 'British sociology 1950–1970: A journal analysis', *Sociological Review* 19: 521–542.

Connell, R. W. (1997) 'Why is classical theory classical?', *American Journal of Sociology* 102: 1511–1557.

Connell, Raewyn (2006) 'Northern theory: The political geography of general social theory', *Theory and Society* 35: 237–264.

(2007) *Southern Theory*, Cambridge: Polity Press.

Converse, Jean M. (1987) *Survey Research in the US: Roots and Emergence 1890–1960*, Berkeley, CA: University of California Press.

Crothers, Charles (2007) '*The changing profile of core publications in the discipline of sociology*', unpublished paper.

(2008) '*New Zealand Sociology Textbooks*', *Current Sociology* monograph 'Introductions to Sociology: History, National Traditions, Paedagogies' 36: 221–234.

Cusset, François (2005) *French Theory*, Paris: La Découverte.

Davis, D. E. (1992) 'The sociology of Mexico: Stalking the path not taken', *Annual Review of Sociology* 18: 395–417.

Delanty, Gerard (ed.) (2006) *Handbook of Contemporary European Social Theory*, London: Routledge.

De Miguel, Jesus, Pau Mari-Klose & Albert F. Arcarons (2007) '*Sociology, from dictatorship to democracy: The case of Spain*', paper presented at the ASA conference, New York.

Devinatz, Victor G. (1999) *High Tech Betrayal: Working and Organizing on the Shop Floor*, East Lansing: Michigan University Press.

Dickens, Peter (2004) *Society and Nature*, Cambridge: Polity Press.

Edmunds, June & Bryan S. Turner (2005) 'Global generations: Social change in the twentieth century', *British Journal of Sociology* 56: 559–577.

Ennis, James G. (1992) 'The social organization of sociological knowledge: Modeling the intersection of specialties', *American Sociological Review* 57: 259–265.

Farrugia, Francis (2000) *La reconstruction de la sociologie française (1945–1965)*, Paris: L'Harmattan.

Ferree, Myra Marx, Shamus Rahman Khan & Shauna A. Morimoto (2007) 'Assessing the feminist revolution…', pp. 438–479 in ed. Craig Calhoun, *Sociology in America: A History*, Chicago, IL: University of Chicago Press.

Finsterbusch, Kurt (1973) 'The 1973 job market for sociologists', *ASA Footnotes* November: 4.

Fisher, Donald (2002) *'Theoretical and methodological shifts within the discipline of sociology in English-speaking Canadian universities, 1950s-1990'*, paper given at the World Congress of Sociology, Brisbane.

Flynn, Pierce J. (1991) *The Ethnomethodological Movement: Sociosemiotic Interpretations*, Berlin: Mouton de Gruyter.

Germov, John & Tara Renae McGee (2005) *Histories of Australian Sociology*, Melbourne: Melbourne University Press.

Giddens, Anthony (1987) *Social Theory and Modern Sociology*, Stanford, CA: Stanford University Press.

Giddens, Anthony & Mitchell Duneier (2000) *Introduction to Sociology*, New York: W. W. Norton.

Glänzel, Wolfgang (1996) 'A bibliometric approach to social sciences: National research performances in 6 selected social science areas, 1990–1992', *Scientometrics* 35: 291–307.

Glaser, Barney G. & Anselm L. Strauss (1967) *The Discovery of Grounded Theory*, Chicago, IL: Aldine.

Goldthorpe, John H. (2000, 2007) *On Sociology*, Oxford: Oxford University Press; Stanford, CA: Stanford University Press.

Grant, Linda, Kathryn B. Ward & Xue Lan Rong (1987) 'Is there an association between gender and methods in sociological research?', *American Sociological Review* 52: 856–862.

Halsey, A. H. (1996) *No Discouragement*, London: Macmillan.

Hammond, Phillip E. (ed.) (1964) *Sociologists at Work*, New York: Basic Books.

Harley, Kirsten (2008) 'Theory use in introductory sociology textbooks', *Current Sociology* monograph 'Introductions to Sociology: History, National Traditions, Paedagogies', 36: 289–306.

Heinritz, Charlotte & Angela Rammstedt (1991) 'L'approche biographique en France', *Cahiers internationaux de Sociologie* 41: 331–370.

Holstein, J. A. & J. F. Gubrium (1995) *The Active Interview*, Thousand Oaks, CA: Sage.

Hout, Michael & Thomas DiPrete (2006) 'What we have learned: RC 28's contributions to knowledge about social stratification', *Research in Social Stratification and Mobility* 24: 1–20.

Kennedy, Michael D. & Miguel A. Centeno (2007) 'Internationalism and global transformations in American sociology', pp. 666–722 in ed. Craig Calhoun, *Sociology in America: A History*, Chicago, IL: University of Chicago Press.

Kilminster, Richard (1998) *The Sociological Revolution*, London: Routledge.

Kishida, Kazuaki & S. Matsui (1997) 'International publication patterns in social sciences', *Scientometrics* 40: 277–298.

Kwasniewicz, Wladyslaw (1994) 'Dialectics of systemic constraint and academic freedom: Polish sociology under socialist regime', pp. 25–38 in ed. M. F. Keen &

J. Mucha, *Eastern Europe in Transformation: The Impact on Sociology*, Westport, CT: Greenwood.

Larsson, Anna (2008) 'Textbooks, Syllabuses and Disciplinary Formation in Sweden', *Current Sociology* 56: 235–51.

Lee, Raymond L. M. (1994) 'Global sociology or "ghettoized" knowledges? The paradox of sociological universalization in the Third World', *The American Sociologist* 25.2: 59–72.

Levine, Donald N., Ellwood B. Carter & Eleanor Miller Gorman (1976) 'Simmel's influence on American sociology', *American Journal of Sociology* 81: 813–844.

Lim, Hyun-Chin (2007) 'Towards a more democratic and just society: An experience of a sociologist from Korea', pp. 145–157 in ed. Mathieu Deflem, *Sociologists in a Global Age: Biographical Perspectives*, Burlington, VT: Ashgate.

Lipset, Seymour M. & Everett C. Ladd (1972) 'The politics of American sociologists', *American Journal of Sociology* 78: 67–104.

Lofland, John (1971) *Analysing Social Settings*, Belmont, CA: Wadsworth.

Marineau, René F. (2007) 'The birth and development of sociometry: The work and legacy of Jacob Moreno (1889–1974)', *Social Psychology Quarterly* 70: 322–325.

Marsden, Peter V. (2005) 'The sociology of James S. Coleman', *Annual Review of Sociology* 31: 1–24.

Masson, Philippe (2008) *Faire de la sociologie: les grandes enquêtes françaises depuis 1945*, Paris: La Découverte.

Matsumoto, Wataru (2007) 'A study on technical and cultural differences in survey methodology between Japan and the US', *International Journal of Japanese Sociology* 16: 23–34.

May, Tim (1995) *Situating Social Theory*, Buckingham: Open University Press.

McFalls, Joseph A., Michael J. Engle & Bernard J. Gallagher (1999) 'The American sociologist: Characteristics in the 1990s', *The American Sociologist* 30: 96–100.

Menzies, Ken (1982) *Sociological Theory in Use*, London: Routledge and Kegan Paul.

Mills, D., A. Jepson, T. Coxon, M. Easterby-Smith, P. Hawkins & J. Spencer (2006) *Demographic Review of the UK Social Sciences*, http://www.esrcsocietytoday.ac.uk/ESRCInfoCentre/PO/releases/2006/february/demographic_review.aspx. Last accessed February 28, 2010.

Mochmann, Ekkehard (2002) *International Social Science Data Service: Scope and Accessibility*, Cologne: GESIS, ZA.

Nakao, Keiko (1998) 'Sociological work in Japan', *Annual Review of Sociology* 24: 499–516.

Oromaner, Mark Jay (1968) 'The most cited sociologists...', *The American Sociologist* 3.2: 124–126.

(1980) 'Influentials in sociological textbooks and journals, 1955 and 1970', *The American Sociologist* 15: 169–174.

Park, Myoung-Kyu & Chang Kyung-Sup (1999) 'Sociology between Western theory and Korean reality', *International Sociology* 14: 139–156.

Peneff, Jean (1990) *La méthode biographique*, Paris: Colin.

(1996) 'Le début de l'observation participante ou les premiers sociologues en usine', *Sociologie du travail* 38: 25–44.

Pfeffer, Richard M. (1979) *Working for Capitalism*, New York: Columbia University Press.

Platt, Jennifer (1995) 'The United States reception of Durkheim's The Rules of Sociological Method', *Sociological Perspectives* 38(1): 77–105.

(1998) *A Brief History of the ISA: 1948–1997*, Madrid: ISA.

(2003) *The British Sociological Association: A Sociological History*, Durham: Sociology Press.

(2004) 'Women's and men's careers in British sociology', *British Journal of Sociology* 55: 187–210.

(2006) 'How distinctive are Canadian research methods?', *Canadian Review of Sociology and Anthropology* 43.2: 205–231.

(2007) 'The women's movement and British journal articles, 1950–2004', *Sociology* 41: 961–975.

(2008a) 'Introduction', *Current Sociology* 56: 147–64.

(2008b) 'British Sociological Textbooks from 1949', *Current Sociology* 56: 165–82.

Pollak, Michael (1993) 'L'efficacité par l'ambiguïté', pp. 300–318 in Pollak, *Une identité blessée*, Paris: Métailié.

Ragin, Charles C. (1987). *The Comparative Method*, Berkeley, CA: University of California Press.

Riley, Matilda W. (1960) 'Membership of the American Sociological Association, 1950–1959', *American Sociological Review* 25: 914–926.

Rodriguez, Jacques (2007) 'Le sociologue, l'expert et le moraliste: à propos de la social administration anglaise', *Socio-logos* 04/12/2007, http://socio-logos.revues.org/document873.html. Last accessed February 28, 2010.

Roger, Christian (2006) '*La sociologie française dans l'Europe*', Soleo 14, http://www.europe-education-formation.fr/docs/Agence/soleo-14.pdf. Last accessed February 28, 2010.

Roth, Guenther (1971) '"Value-neutrality" in Germany and the US' and 'The historical relationship to Marxism', pp. 34–54, 227–252 in eds. Reinhard Bendix & G. Roth *Scholarship and Partisanship: Essays on Max Weber*, Berkeley, CA: University of California Press.

Runciman, W. G. (1998) *The Social Animal*, London: Harper Collins.

Sanderson, Stephen K. & Lee Ellis (1992) 'Theoretical and political perspectives of American sociologists in the 1990s', *The American Sociologist* 23: 23–38.

Savelsberg, Joachim J., Lara L. Cleveland & Ryan D. King (2004) 'Institutional environments and scholarly work: American criminology, 1951–1993', *Social Forces* 82: 1275–1302.

Schrecker, Cherry (2008) 'Textbooks and sociology: A Franco-British comparison', *Current Sociology* monograph 'Introductions to Sociology: History, National Traditions, Paedagogies', 36: 201–219.

Seale, Clive (2008) 'Mapping the field of medical sociology: A comparative analysis of journals', *Sociology of Health and Illness* 30: 655–812.

Shavit, Yossi & Hans-Peter Blossfeld (1993) *Persistent Inequality: Changing Educational Attainment in Thirteen Countries*, Boulder, CO: Westview.

Sica, Alan (1989) 'Social theory's "constituency"', *The American Sociologist* 20: 227–241.

Sica, Alan & Stephen Turner (eds.) (2005) *The Disobedient Generation: Social Theorists in the Sixties*, Chicago: University of Chicago Press.

Simeoni, Daniel (2000) 'Transpositioning social-science capital across borders: The cases of Freud, Weber, Bourdieu', pp. 402–424 in ed. Derek Robbins, *Pierre Bourdieu*, vol. 3, London: Sage.

Sjoberg, Gideon (ed.) (1967) *Ethics, Politics and Social Research*, Cambridge, MA: Schenkman.

Skrbis, Zlatko & John Germov (2005) 'The most influential books in Australian sociology (MIBAS), 1963–2003', pp. 323–342 in ed. John Germov & Tara Renae McGee, *Histories of Australian Sociology*, Melbourne: Melbourne University Press.

Stanley, L. (2005) 'A child of its time: hybridic perspectives on othering in sociology', *Sociological Research Online,* http://www.socresonline.org.uk/10/3/stanley.html. Last accessed March 1, 2010.

Stehr, Nico & L. E. Larson (1972) 'The rise and decline of areas of specialization', *The American Sociologist* 7.7: 1, 5–6.

Sulek, Antoni (2007) '*Polish visitors at American universities in the late 1950s and the development of empirical sociology in Poland*', paper given at 'Voyages transatlantiques' conference, Nancy.

Swedberg, Richard (1991) 'Major traditions of economic sociology', *Annual Review of Sociology* 17: 251–276.

Thompson, John B. (2005) *Books in the Digital Age*, Cambridge: Polity Press.

Turner, Stephen P. & Jonathan H. Turner (1990) *The Impossible Science: An Institutional Analysis of American Sociology*, Newbury Park, CA: Sage.

Ulrich (2004) *Ulrich's International Periodicals Directory*, New York, London: Bowker.

UNESCO (2006) *Global Education Digest*, UNESCO Institute for Statistics Online Database.

Urry, J. (2005) '*Beyond the science of "society"*', *Sociological Research Online*, http://www.socresonline.org.uk/10/2/urry.html. Last accessed February 28, 2010.

van Meter, Karl M., Marie-Ange Schiltz, Philippe Cibois & Lise Mounier (1994) 'Correspondence analysis: A history and French sociological perspective', pp. 128–137 in ed. Michael Greenacre & Jörg Blasius, *Correspondence Analysis in the Social Sciences: recent developments and applications*, London: Academic Press.

Vannier, Patricia (2003) 'Inscription scientifique et mise en norme des savoirs dans le texte sociologique de l'après-guerre', pp. 225–250 in ed. Jean-Michel Berthelot, *Figures du texte scientifique*, Paris: PUF.

Wacquant, Loïc (1993) 'Bourdieu in America', pp. 263–275 in ed. Craig Calhoun, E. LiPuma & M. Postone *Bourdieu: Critical Perspectives*, Chicago, IL: University of Chicago Press.

Warren, Jean-Philippe & Yves Gingras (2007) 'Job market boom and gender tide...', *Scientia Canadensis* 30: 5–21.

Yitzhaki, M. (1998) 'The "language-preference" in sociology: measures of "language self-citation", "relative own-language preference indicator" and "mutual use of languages"', *Scientometrics* 41: 243–254.

Zald, Mayer N. (1995) 'Progress and cumulation in the human sciences after the fall', *Sociological Forum* 10: 455–479.

6

Social Anthropology

Adam Kuper

Origins, Context, Institutions

A history of twentieth century anthropology is impossible. The configuration of the discipline is completely different in the United States and in Britain and France, its main European centres. In North America, anthropology remained, at least until the 1950s, an uneasy coalition of ethnology, archaeology, linguistics, and biological anthropology. 'Cultural anthropology' emerged as a virtually independent discipline in the 1930s, but its overlap with European 'social anthropology' was never complete. While social anthropology in Britain and France – and increasingly in other European centres – identified itself as a social science, 'cultural anthropology' found itself more at home in the humanities. I shall confine myself here to social anthropology, which is essentially a European social science, although with a significant presence in Brazil, India, Japan, Australia, and South Africa, and I shall concentrate on the development of the field in Britain, its major centre, while indicating some parallel developments in France and, more recently, in other European countries. My focus will be less on the internal intellectual history of the discipline than on its institutional contexts, which I believe were decisive for the trajectory taken by the field.

The colonial setting is crucial, though too often represented in polemical terms (as though social anthropologists in the first half of the twentieth century were either collaborators or true scientists). The discipline began to attract funding in the 1930s as the Colonial Office slowly developed policies of social and economic development, and as new administrative structures

The original version of this chapter was delivered as a keynote speech at the European Anthropological Summit held in Lisbon in May 2004, organized by the Instituto de Ciências Sociais da Universidade de Lisboa. It was subsequently published in *Social Anthropology*. The present text is a revised version of the original address.

were put in place in the African and Pacific colonies. During the Second World War, these territories gained a certain strategic importance. After the war, and the traumatic loss of India, the Labour government began to implement strategic planning in the colonies. In the 1950s, African nationalism became a factor, stimulating political adjustments and, in the case of Kenya, military intervention. Missionaries provided a competing social programme, to which colonial governments accommodated. The social anthropologists, however, were the only coherent community of social scientists committed to the study of African and Pacific societies. Their relationship with colonial authorities was often uneasy, even occasionally combative, but from the 1920s to the 1970s, their identity and their research were shaped by the colonial context. In the last third of the twentieth century, the discipline struggled to redefine itself within the social sciences.

Other institutional contexts, often neglected, include relationships with neighbouring disciplines in an increasingly competitive local marketplace and the relationship between 'social anthropology' and the 'cultural anthropology' of the North-American universities. It is also important to consider the restriction of social anthropology in Britain and France to a handful of high-status institutions. Social anthropology has the same elite profile as archaeology and classical studies. Because of this largely deliberate isolation from the mass universities, the discipline remained small throughout the century.

In some ways it makes sense to think of social anthropology not so much as a discipline equivalent to psychology or sociology, but rather as a school of thought within the social sciences. It is defined by its object of study (once the primitive, then the colonial, subject; now, effectively, and with some exceptions, the ex-colonial subject), and its method, called 'ethnography', reliant on participant observation, at once individualist and subjective, and contrasted always with the survey methods of the other social sciences.

If social anthropology is treated as a school of thought, perhaps even a movement, there are obvious parallels – as well as interactions – between its inception and the more or less contemporary development of the Vienna circle of psychoanalysis, the launch of Durkheim's *Année Sociologique*, or the formation of the *Annales* school of social historians led by Lucien Febvre and Marc Bloch. In each case, a small network of marginal intellectuals, attracted by charismatic leaders, created new and enduring research programmes that introduced novel objects of study, methods of research, and applications.

Internalist histories of British social anthropology, written by practitioners or, more commonly, regurgitated in lecture courses, conventionally begin with a contrast between Malinowski and the old-style ethnographers, and emphasize the radically innovative way in which he went about his fieldwork in the Trobriand Islands between 1915 and 1918. The great symbolic image, inevitably flashed on the screen, is of Malinowski pitching his tent in the village. His slogan is quoted: 'The anthropologist must relinquish his comfortable position on the verandah, where he has been accustomed to collect statements from informants' (1926, p.147). From that point on, ethnographers had to go out into the village, cultivate a garden, join in the dances, exchange gifts and generally muck in. 'The main principle of my work in the field', Malinowski wrote in a note to himself in the Trobriand Islands, '[is to] avoid artificial simplifications. To this end, collect as concrete materials as possible: note every informant; work with children, *outsiders, and specialists. Take side lights and opinions*' (Young 2004, p. 560; cf. Roldán 1995, p. 138). Above all, customs and institutions now had to be studied as they really are rather than as they might once have been.

There is, of course, more than an element of myth-making here. Certainly the Trobriand study became the touchstone for Malinowski's students, but some of them remarked that their teacher did not always follow his own rules in the field. Michael Young has worked out that 'his tent was folded for almost half his time in Kiriwina' (Young 2004, p. 502). And it could be argued that Malinowski's methodological originality lay elsewhere, in his insistence that ethnographers must provide what he called concrete documentation, such as maps, measurements, multicoloured synoptic charts, gardening diaries, and texts in the vernacular. There can be no question but that he broke with the established, questionnaire-led form of inquiry. An off-the-shelf ethnographer's aid was available, the Royal Anthropological Institutes' checklist for fieldworkers, *Notes and Queries in Anthropology*. Malinowski had made use of it while writing up the results of a short, apprentice field-study in Mailu, organizing his material to fit its rigid categories. The format facilitated cross-cultural comparisons, but a mechanical inventory of customs and beliefs could not bring out the connections between different activities and institutions. Malinowski's aim in his Trobriand fieldwork was to tease out the various strands – magic, economics, kinship, politics – that were woven together in even the most essential work, like house building, sailing, or gardening.

Malinowski's fieldwork in Kiriwina is often seen as marking the decisive breach between the generation of Haddon, Rivers, and Marett and the new social anthropology, even if the precise nature of his ethnographic innovations might be called into question. However, conventional histories also remark on a more or less contemporary theoretical shift. Malinowski himself insisted on introducing theory into the very process of what he called the construction of facts. After all, like his American counterpart Franz Boas, he had written a doctoral thesis that addressed issues in the philosophy of science. This was an account of Mach's positivism, though Malinowski ended up with a more permissive empiricist doctrine, 'nothing without experience'. Working in the Trobriands, he sometimes felt himself 'almost swamped by detail', but his philosophy of science indicated that experience had to be shaped, and that theory must come before description (Young 2004, pp. 79–90). The description of facts required precise concepts that only theory could provide. The ethnographer should build up synthetic facts, informed by theoretical considerations, and tackle strategic issues ('problems, not peoples').

The theory that came to define social anthropology in its heyday – the half-century between the early 1920s and 1970s – was called 'functionalism', and the main inspiration was the school of Durkheim. Since the 1860s, ethnographic data had been collected in order to address historical and geographical questions. The new research questions had to do with the workings of social institutions in the here and now, not with historical reconstructions. But Malinowski and Radcliffe-Brown, the other leading figure in the movement, famously did not agree on sociological theory. Malinowski was always an individualist. Radcliffe-Brown was an orthodox Durkheimian, and like his French opposite number, Durkheim's nephew Marcel Mauss, he was a collectivist. In his *Essay on the gift*, in 1925, Mauss rewrote the *kula* ethnography in terms of Durkheimian collective sentiments. Malinowski in turn recast reciprocity as a matter of enlightened self-interest in his *Crime and Custom in Savage Society* in 1926.

Durkheimian sociology defined itself in opposition to psychology, but both Malinowski and Radcliffe-Brown flirted with the possibility that the new anthropology would be allied with specific research programmes in psychology. Rivers had argued in his paper 'Sociology and Psychology' in 1916 that anthropologists could operate either as sociologists or as psychologists. 'Those who follow one path will devote themselves to the study of the body of customs and institutions which make up social behaviour, while those who follow the other path will inquire into the instincts, sentiments, emotions, ideas, and beliefs of mankind' (reprinted in Rivers 1926, p. 6). In a letter to Rivers, Radcliffe-Brown responded that 'the only difference between us is at what stage in the progress of sociology we should take up the fundamental psychological problems. I wish to take them up at once, whereas you wish to postpone them' (Kuper 1989, p. 79). Rivers was a cognitive psychologist who later became a Freudian, but both Radcliffe-Brown and Malinowski were more inclined to seek inspiration from the movement that became social psychology. Both were particularly drawn to the theory of sentiments of the now forgotten English psychologist A. F. Shand, whom Malinowski described as 'one of the greatest psychologists of our time' (Malinowski 1927, p. 240; see Kuper 1990).

The in-house histories then move on to the professionalization of the discipline, a process that was accompanied by the commitment to 'functionalist' theory – that is, to a variety of sociology that imagined societies to be bounded, equilibrium systems. The students of Malinowski and Radcliffe-Brown established new departments, debated variants of functionalist theory, and wrote the classic monographs of the 1930s and 1940s. Was there a relationship between the type of people who went into the subject and the theoretical orthodoxy? Discussing the classical phase of British functionalism, George Stocking writes that 'there are many today (especially, perhaps, in the United States) for whom the real problem for historical understanding would seem now to be: how could so many intelligent anthropologists have been so long infected by such a sterile and/or derivative viewpoint'. While fastidiously distancing himself from these crude characterizations, Stocking suggests that the theoretical trajectory of social anthropology is to be explained with reference to the British national character (Stocking 1984, pp. 181–2). This is unpersuasive, if only because so many of the leading figures in the story, from Westermarck and Malinowski to Fortes, Nadel, Gluckman, and Schapera were foreigners.

A paper by Edmund Leach, provocatively entitled 'Glimpses of the Unmentionable in the History of British Social Anthropology', pays special attention to the preponderance of foreigners, Jews, and women in the functionalist generation. Leach claimed that 'differences of social class played a critical role in what happened in British anthropology during the first forty years of the this [the twentieth] century' (Leach 1984, p. 2). He observed that the early-twentieth-century pioneers of British social anthropology – Rivers and Haddon – were not really gentlemen. For that simple reason they had failed to establish the discipline in Cambridge, then the headquarters of British science. When Malinowski came on the scene, it was obvious that he was not an English gentleman, and so not a candidate for Oxbridge. He found a niche in the socialist and marginal London School of Economics (LSE), which Leach described as being 'a very low status institution' in the 1920s and 1930s (Leach 1984, p. 11). And his students were largely foreigners or women, which, somewhat paradoxically, Leach believed led to a conservative faith in equilibrium theories of societies and a touching attachment to British institutions, and in particular to the ancient universities.

A Colonial Science?

An alternative perspective became popular in the 1970s, taking a lead from Franz Fanon and Edward Said. Social anthropology was represented as a colonial science, a form of Orientalism, 'a kind of western projection onto and will to govern over the Orient' (Said 1978, p. 95). This proposition is now taken for granted by many students (and quite a few American anthropologists), but a number of authors have pointed to the anticolonialism of certain leading anthropologists, and the contemptuous rejection of anthropological expertise by some colonial governors and high officials. Several of the South African anthropologists who entered British anthropology brought with them a thorough-going critique of colonialism (Kuper 1999b). A more persuasive objection is that British anthropologists often endorsed the mandarin preference for pure science, uncontaminated by policy concerns, a view expressed in particular by Evans-Pritchard and Leach but preached in the 1950s even by Fortes and Gluckman, who had been among the partisans of applied research in the 1930s and 1940s.

By and large, recent historians have resisted the designation of social anthropology as a colonial science (see, for example, Goody 1995). George Stocking's very lengthy history of modern British social anthropology, *After Tylor* (1995), devotes only part of one chapter to the colonial context, amounting to only some twenty pages in a work running to 570 pages in all. Few reviewers of Stocking's book seem to have found this at all odd. But clearly this refusal to engage with the colonial context will not do either. As Benoît de L'Estoile writes,

> What needs to be addressed … is precisely what is meant by anthropological knowledge being a 'colonial science'. We need to understand the specific historical configuration in which some discourses and practices could be held as 'scientific', while at the same time unambiguously belonging to the colonial world. (de l'Estoile 2004a, p. 343)

In his thesis, 'L'Afrique comme Laboratoire. Expériences Réformatrices et Révolution Anthropologique dans l'Empire Colonial Britannique (1920–1950)' (de L'Estoile 2004b), de l'Estoile protests against the juxtaposition of an independent science of anthropology with another, supposedly distinct entity termed colonialism. He also criticizes the conventional opposition between pure science and the compromised and compromising applied studies. Rather, he argues that, beginning in the late 1920s, British social anthropology was effectively reconstituted. This happened by way of social and intellectual exchanges between academic anthropologists, other intellectuals, missionaries, and colonial policymakers. And de L'Estoile describes a second and more fundamental Malinowskian revolution that occurred in the 1930s, as Malinowski drew his students into a dialogue with the leading policymakers who were concerned with Britain's African empire.

This story begins with the formation of the International Institute of African Languages and Cultures (IIALC) in 1926. Initially dominated by missionary societies, the IIALC concerned itself at first with linguistics particularly, which was crucial to bible translation and to education. However, its moving spirits recast its programme as they appealed for funds. The key actor here was J. H. Oldham, secretary of the International Missionary Council, who became administrative director of the IIALC in 1931 and worked closely with Malinowski. Oldham's plan was to establish the Institute as a privileged interlocutor of the colonial office, whose main preoccupation was the government of Britain's African colonies. Policymakers were casting about for social scientists who might help them to put flesh on the bones of Lugard's proposals for a system of indirect rule in Africa. The IIALC and Malinowski seized this opportunity.

Drawing on letters, minutes of meetings, and often unpublished internal reports, de L'Estoile traces the social networks that drew anthropologists, missionaries, and policymakers together – the weekend parties at Lugard's country house, the committees and meetings of the IIALC, and Malinowski's LSE seminars. Malinowski's strategy was to forge a new space for a science of African social policy centred upon the anthropology department of the LSE. In the process, he refashioned the functionalist anthropology that he had propagated in the 1920s. He now conceded that his own work on the Trobriand Islands represented an inadequate model for the kind of ethnography that the circumstances of the African empire required. *Argonauts of the Western Pacific*, published in 1922, opened with a lament for the 'cruel irony that just as the importance of the facts and conclusions of ethnological research is … becoming recognised, … the material of our science is vanishing'. In a paper published in 1929 in *Africa* entitled 'Practical Anthropology', Malinowski demanded an 'anthropology of the changing native' (Malinowski 1929).

He had his reward. With Oldham's crucial support, Malinowski was able to tap the funds of the Laura Spelman Rockefeller Memorial. An immediate consequence was a shift in ethnographic focus. The pioneering field expedition of British anthropology had been to the Torres Straits in 1898. Rivers, Haddon, Radcliffe-Brown, and Malinowski himself had conducted field research largely in the Pacific. The Rockefeller fellows were now funded to undertake sociological studies in British African colonies. Malinowski and Oldham ruthlessly shut out the old guard. The Cambridge students of Haddon and Rivers, who had worked on kinship problems in the Pacific, were passed over. At Oxford, Marrett was starved of funds. Within the LSE, Seligman was sidelined, despite the fact that he was the sole African specialist at the School and had worked closely with the government of the Anglo-Egyptian Sudan. Even after Malinowski left England in 1938, his most loyal followers were able to control the Colonial Social Science Research Council, which was founded in 1944. Firth became the secretary, seconded by Audrey Richards, who had served as a temporary principal at the Colonial Office and worked with Hailey on postwar African policy before being appointed special lecturer in Colonial Studies at the LSE in 1944 (Mills 2002).

This reorientation of British social anthropology to focus on colonial policy was part of a general trend in the 1920s, as governments began to develop more comprehensive social programmes, creating a market for scientific advice. The social sciences redefined themselves as policy sciences (even if they might serve at times as sources of critical commentary). A historian of social science, Dorothy Ross, points to 'a movement toward modernist historical consciousness, the growing power of professional specialisation, and the sharpening conception of scientific method', which together produced a 'slow paradigm shift in the social sciences … away from historico-evolutionary models … to specialised sciences focused on short-term processes' (Ross 1991, p. 388).

Leach represented Malinowski's situation at the LSE as a handicap. After all, Oxbridge was the base of the establishment. However, the LSE was one of the very few substantial centres for social science research in Europe in this period. Moreover, it had developed its own ideology of public service and social reform. Malinowski's inner circle – Firth, Richards, and Mair – were working with Lord Hailey on proposals for colonial research, at the same moment that the welfare state in Britain was being planned by Beveridge, the director of the LSE.

By the early 1930s, Malinowski had effectively reinvented British social anthropology as the social science that addressed colonial policy. In practice, the Colonial Office was concerned above all with the government of African societies. (The India Office was a separate and much more prestigious institution.) It was the African colonial context that shaped the topics that were studied by the new generation of social anthropologists. But this did not dictate the stance taken by individual scholars, who could, and did, adopt a variety of intellectual and even political positions. In their public statements, Malinowski and Radcliffe-Brown tended to insist that there should be a division of labour. The anthropologist presented the facts, and the colonial official decided what was to done. But both men broke this rule at times and wrote critical, occasionally intemperate, commentaries on aspects of colonial government in the 1920s and 1930s.

There was another option, however. This was to insist on the purity of scientific research. Evans-Pritchard and Radcliffe-Brown reacted to Malinowski's initiative by demanding that social anthropology should be a strictly academic pursuit. Evans-Pritchard started referring to the LSE in his correspondence as the '£.S.D,' and in 1934 he wrote from Cairo to Meyer Fortes:

> The racket here is very amusing. It would be more so if it were not disastrous to anthropology. Everyone is advising government – Raymond [Firth], Forde, Audrey [Richards], Schapera. No one is doing any real anthropological work – all are clinging to the Colonial Office coach. This deplorable state of affairs is likely to go on, because it shows something deeper than making use of opportunities for helping anthropology. It shows an attitude of mind and is I think fundamentally a moral deterioration. These people will not see that there is an unbridgeable chasm between serious anthropology and Administration Welfare work. (quoted in Goody 1995, p. 73)

De L'Estoile persuasively suggests that this purist discourse was later mobilized to promote the new institute of social anthropology at Oxford, which had been established in 1937 under Radcliffe-Brown. He and his younger associates, Evans-Pritchard and Fortes, set out to challenge the LSE. And in 1940, they published the classic statement of British Africanist anthropology in this period, *African Political Systems*. Edited by Fortes and Evans-Pritchard, and with a preface by Radcliffe-Brown, the book was presented at the time as a pathfinding contribution to a new political science: political anthropology. This was not a mere smoke screen. *African Political Systems* was, among other things, a transformation of the classical debates inaugurated by Henry Maine and Lewis Henry Morgan, and perpetuated the Victorian two-stage model of kin-based societies and states (Kuper 2005, chap. 8). The editors also touched on classical issues in British political theory (see, e.g., Kuklick 1984 and de Zengotita 1984). But de L'Estoile argues persuasively that the book issued more immediately from the debates on indirect rule in the 1930s, which framed the issues and determined the way in which it was read in Britain at the time. *African Political Systems* addressed precisely the issues that arose within the context of indirect rule. Who were the leaders? What were the structures of administration?

Even more telling was that the contributors accepted that the 'tribes' on which they reported were genuinely distinct societies, although, as African historians were soon to demonstrate, these so-called tribes were in very large part the product of indirect rule. But recent colonial history was written out of even the most innovative 'theoretical' ethnographies. Leach's *Political Systems of Highland Burma* (1954) challenged key features of the model that had been presented in *African Political Systems*. Leach argued that lineage systems and states were stages in one, often cyclical, process, and he represented the tribal units as unstable and intricately interconnected social fields, shaped by ambitious individuals. But like all the contributors to *African Political Systems*, with the notable exception of the South African, Max Gluckman, Leach neglected the impact of colonial overrule. Somewhat paradoxically, this was the price of abjuring 'applied' research.

While critics on the left condemned British social anthropologists for serving the Empire, functionalist anthropology was criticized more commonly in the 1930s and 1940s for ignoring social change and failing to analyse the colonial context. Its defenders pointed out that, on the contrary, functionalists produced a number of studies of local government, migrant labour, land tenure, the work of the courts, and so on, and that there were several attempts at developing a theory of social change. However, such studies came to be considered as constituting a special category, termed 'applied' work. After the Second World War the academic purists stigmatized this sort of research as less scientific and prestigious than what came to be termed 'theoretical' studies. An ostentatious refusal to analyse the colonial context became the hallmark of theoretical contributions in social anthropology, because any acknowledgement of colonial realities would mean engaging directly, rather than implicitly, in debates on colonial policy. Yet *African Political Systems* unwittingly proved that the colonial context did in fact determine the units of study, the tribes. Colonial preoccupations also made certain topics seem naturally more important than others.

The study of tribal political or legal systems was effectively mandated by colonial governments. Policies on religion, education, and the family were generally delegated to missionary societies. In response, anthropologists made applied studies of Christian influences, the economics of bride price, or the impact of migrant labour on family life. They also undertook 'theoretical studies' on the same institutional complexes, but these were ostentatiously pure in thought, dealing with initiation ceremonies, traditional religion, witchcraft, kinship taboos, and lineage systems. No missionaries appeared in these 'theoretical' texts, except as straw men who took a moralizing view of African practices.

After Empire: Sociology and Development Studies

In the 1940s and 1950s, the Rhodes-Livingstone Institute, under Godfrey Wilson and later Max Gluckman, and the East African Institute of Social Research, under Audrey Richards, were mature embodiments of applied anthropology in Africa. They represented the apotheosis of Malinowski's project. But Africa was changing. As colonial policymakers looked forward to the independence of African states, the anthropologists were sidelined. At the LSE, Lucy Mair tried to turn applied anthropology into development studies, but applied studies were effectively excluded from departments of social anthropology in British universities after the African empire came to an end in the mid-1960s. Within the university departments, the purists won out.

At this critical juncture, the social anthropologists began to lose ground within British universities. Britain's system of higher education entered a phase of rapid expansion in the 1960s, but social anthropology stagnated institutionally. Given the requisite political will on the part of the leading anthropologists, it might have been possible to establish a number of new departments of social anthropology as the universities expanded and new ones were founded. A particular growth area was social science. Sociology became a popular subject and established itself in all the new universities. Social anthropology, however, remained a small elitist discipline, positioned most securely at Oxford, Cambridge, and the LSE. Given Leach's thesis about the nature of British science, this might be regarded as a plus point, but it froze the institutional development of the discipline. (Leach himself was one of those responsible for this defensive, conservative strategy.) By the 1970s, when Malinowski's students retired, there were about 150 academic social anthropologists in Britain, and the figure remained stable for another decade. Today, after a generation in which the universities have expanded enormously, there are 230 full-time academic positions in social anthropology in British universities. There are also a number of fixed-term appointments, many of them post-doctoral positions, and a few appointments in museums, which might bring the total to 300 (Mills 2003a, p. 22).

As the institutional basis of the discipline within the universities stagnated, and even began to shrink in the 1980s, the decade of the 'cuts,' the collective institutions of British social anthropology became bastions of conservatism, not to say reaction (Mills 2003b). The anthropology subcommittee of the Social Science Research Council, the Royal Anthropological Institute, the Association of Social Anthropologists, the anthropological section of the British Academy, all remained under the control of a few increasingly elderly professors. Raymond Firth was calling the shots in most of these institutions when he was well into his eighties, and his close ally Edmund Leach remained a key player until his death, although he had insisted in his Reith lectures that in our 'runaway world … no one should be allowed to hold any kind of responsible administrative office once he has passed the age of 55' (Leach 1968).

Having lost an empire, the social anthropologists found themselves struggling in this dismal institutional environment to find a role. And just at this moment they were challenged on their own turf, within the universities. Hamstrung by the sclerotic institutional structure of the profession, they were confronted by the rise of development studies and sociology. The anthropologists naturally refused to be drawn into development studies, which moved into the space that had been vacated by the old colonial science. Third-world development projects provided the infrastructure and ideological impetus for a fresh surge of social anthropology in Scandinavia and in the German-speaking countries, while in the Netherlands, new departments of 'non-western sociology' split off from the old departments of ethnology in order to tap the generous funds being made available by the Dutch government for overseas 'development projects'. In Britain, however, any anthropologist who specialized in development studies would be unlikely to find encouragement, or employment, in departments of social anthropology (Grillo 1985).

The rise of sociology presented a more alarming challenge. At Oxford and Cambridge the professors were frankly terrified that their students would desert en masse to this more radical and more relevant social science. When, at last, the university established a chair of sociology at Cambridge, Meyer Fortes used his political skills to secure the appointment of a social anthropologist, John Barnes. Elsewhere, a few social anthropologists were placed as professors of sociology in the new departments. In Manchester, Peter Worsely split acrimoniously from Max Gluckman to found a separate sociology department, while Victor Turner, equally acrimoniously, turned away from the sociology of the Manchester school and took up the hermetic analysis of systems of ritual symbolism.

The problem presented by sociology went beyond competition for jobs and for students, or even for funds in the Social Science Research Council. The social anthropologists were obliged to think again about what kind of social science their discipline could claim to be. The general impulse was to redefine social anthropology in opposition to sociology. Sociology was about modern, industrial, Western societies. Therefore, social anthropology was defined as the science of the rest, the 'other cultures', even if these were now less often distinguished as 'primitive.' (There was a search for euphemisms, 'pre-literate' being popular for a time.)

The implication was that social anthropologists had no business doing research in Britain, unless it was among migrants from a formerly colonial country. This view was deeply entrenched in the profession until the 1980s, and it remains the implicit doctrine in some circles. In contrast to other European countries, there was no alternative tradition of *Völkskunde*. The folklore movements of the nineteenth century had never established an academic base in English universities. Malinowski's Trobriand research inspired ethnographic experiments at home, but not by professional anthropologists. George Orwell's *Down and Out in Paris and London* and *The Road to Wigan Pier* followed in the Victorian footsteps of Christopher Mayhew, but equally they were Malinowskian experiments in participant observation. Mass observation, launched in 1937, aimed to stimulate a popular ethnography of everyday life, carried out by amateur observers. In the 1950s came the Bethnall Green studies of Peter Wilmott and Michael Young. All of these men were social reformers, attuned to the issues facing politicians. Young had been secretary of the Labour Party's research department in the run-up to the general election of 1945, the election that opened the way for the implementation of Beveridge's welfare plans. But they also operated outside academia. As sociology consolidated its base within the universities, the leading sociologists pronounced that community studies were unreliable. Scientific research required large surveys and statistical evidence.

But this tradition of urban, British ethnography did not attract anthropologists. Evans-Pritchard denounced Malinowski as 'a bloody gas-bag' because he looked kindly on 'the mass-observation bilge' (Goody 1995, p. 74). Firth and Richards organized studies of British kinship in the 1950s and early 1960s, but had little immediate impact on their colleagues. Few young anthropologists undertook field research in Britain in the 1960s and 1970s; they did, however, begin to move into new areas. With the end of the African empire, India and Indonesia increasingly attracted ethnographers, and the Australian government encouraged research in New Guinea. Anthropologists might even venture into Europe, but only to the periphery, looking for lineages in a Greek island, or dowry systems in Andalucia, or perhaps describing an isolated community in a windswept and very uncomfortable collection of rocks somewhere between Scotland, Norway, and Iceland. But anyone who insisted on doing fieldwork in Britain was liable to find themselves exiled to departments of sociology.

The leading anthropologists also stuck with the traditional subjects of 'pure' research: kinship and ritual. The advent of structuralism gave a fresh impetus to these fields of study, but anthropologists paid little attention to new intellectual movements in the other social sciences. And the methods of field research continued to be those associated with Malinowski, at least in the mythology.

And so, by and large, the British anthropologists beat a retreat in the face of sociology. They distanced themselves from issues of public interest. And increasingly they tended to redefine their project as the study of cultural variation. They chose to study isolated, traditional, if perhaps no longer 'primitive' societies, and even anthropologists working in societies under-going revolutionary changes in India, China, Indonesia, or Latin America typically concerned themselves exclusively with rituals or with kinship ter-minologies and rules of marriage.

Some influential figures began to argue that it had been a mistake to define social anthropology as a form of sociology in the first place. Evans-Pritchard asserted in a public lecture in 1950 that social anthropology was not a science in search of laws but 'a kind of historiography, and therefore ultimately of philosophy or art', and represented it as a complement to ori-ental studies (Evans-Pritchard [1950] 1962, p. 26). He and Schapera now preferred to describe themselves as ethnographers. According to Godfrey Lienhardt, Evans-Pritchard's shift was an accommodation to the intellec-tual climate of Oxbridge, which was inhospitable to social science at the time (Lienhardt 1974), but the problem was even more acute in less conser-vative universities, where sociology and the other social sciences flourished in the 1960s and 1970s.

Nor was this a problem only for British anthropology. Social anthro-pologists had to face up to the challenge of sociology in most European universities, and they either asserted their own social science creden-tials or drew in their skirts. In France, for instance, Georges Balandier advocated a colonial sociology in the mould of the Rhodes-Livingstone school. He was opposed by Claude Lévi-Strauss, whose project was purist and idealist (Gaillard 1990). Some of Balandier's leading students experi-mented with a Marxist anthropology in the 1960s, but like the American Marxists associated with Julian Steward and Leslie White, the younger members of the school also turned in the 1970s to a culturalist anthropol-ogy, associated in France with Lévi-Strauss and Louis Dumont, who had taught at Oxford in the 1950s, had been influenced by Evans-Pritchard, and had become somewhat Parsonian. Like the American Parsonians Clifford Geertz and David Schneider, Dumont came to the conclusion that anthropologists should treat cultural systems, and systems of values in particular, as independent realities, without taking social processes into account.

The American Challenge and Cultural Studies

As British social anthropologists fought their desperate rear-guard action, they began to pay attention to developments in the United States. They had felt remote from the central scientific project of Boasian anthropology, which had spent two generations patiently assembling microhistories of the North American Indians. They had scorned the culture and personality school of the 1930s. The four-field conception of anthropology – including biological anthropology, archaeology, and linguistics alongside social or cultural anthropology – had few prominent advocates in Europe after the Second World War. But by the 1960s, American anthropology was in the throes of radical change.

American anthropologists had been drawn into policy studies and intelligence work during the Second World War (Price 2008). This was not altogether a new development. The Boasians had addressed racism in the United States in important theoretical papers and in popular books, although they were strangely reticent about conditions on the Indian reservations. But now, anthropologists were given desks in Washington and talked directly to administrators and politicians. Mead, Bateson, and their associates drew on psychoanalysis and developmental psychology to produce profiles of enemies and allies for the benefit of government policymakers and planners. George Peter Murdock served during the war as an officer in the U.S. Navy and masterminded the production of ethnographic guides to strategic Pacific islands, guides that were later to form the model for his World Ethnographic Survey. This generation of American anthropologists were not, however, interested in sociology, economics, or political science. It was only when, in the aftermath of victory, the United States was drawn into nation building in Japan and, as the Cold War began, in the Philippines and Indonesia, that anthropologists started to collaborate with other social scientists. And now, for the first time, significant numbers began to specialize in societies beyond North America.

This entailed a redefinition of the project of cultural anthropology. At Harvard, Talcott Parsons and Clyde Kluckhohn envisaged the discipline changing its image and becoming a partner in a global social science project. Collaborating with sociologists and psychologists, anthropologists would become specialists in culture. But the culture in which they were to be the experts was not Tylor's culture. For Parsons, culture meant the ideological dimension of social life: the realm of ideas and values expressed in symbols. Anthropologists were to take culture, in this sense, as their specialism, not 'primitive peoples', and then they were to report back to the sociologists, who would synthesize an explanation of social action (Kuper 1999a).

Clifford Geertz was in many ways the exemplary figure in this new generation. He was one of the early products of Parsons's new School of Social Relations at Harvard, and his work in Java was conceived as part of a team effort in which anthropologists collaborated with economists and political scientists. On his return to the United States, he worked with development economists at MIT (writing reports that were later elaborated and published as monographs, such as *Agricultural Involution* and *Peddlers and Princes*, both of which appeared in 1963). He spent the 1960s, together with Lloyd Fallers, as a member of the Committee for the Comparative Study of New Nations at the University of Chicago, which was directed by a conservative ally of Parsons, Edward Shils. Other anthropologists were engaged in comparable projects in Latin America, some of which, it turned out, were bankrolled and perhaps directed by the Central Intelligence Agency.

However, the moment of neo-imperial anthropology passed quickly. There was a scandal over the use of anthropologists and other social scientists by American intelligence in Operation Camelot in Chile in the early 1960s, but the great divide was, of course, the Vietnam War. One of the casualties of the radicalization of the campus in the 1960s was the Parsonian project. At the end of the decade, Geertz moved from Chicago's troubled campus to the mandarin calm of the Institute of Advanced Study at Princeton. Here he began to redefine anthropology as an autonomous discipline. Its subject matter was still culture, in Parsons's sense – the realm of ideas, values and symbols – but its future lay not with sociology but with the humanities. Cultural anthropology was to be a study of texts in action, its aim not explanation but the explication of meaning. In 1973, Geertz welcomed 'an enormous increase in interest, not only in anthropology, but in social studies generally, in the role of symbolic forms inhuman life. Meaning … has now come back into the heart of our discipline' (Geertz 1973, p. 29). His essays placed anthropology within a new configuration of disciplines, linking up particularly with literary theory and linguistic philosophy.

The established alternative tradition in American anthropology, a form of evolutionism often linked with Marxism, had attracted some young radicals, and produced its new stars, Marshall Sahlins, Roy Rappaport, and Eric

Wolf. But Sahlins was also converted at the end of the 1960s to a culturalist position. Even Rappaport began to recast his ecological determinism
to give it a culturalist edge. The new generation of American anthropologists that graduated in the 1960s and 1970s was effectively formed in an
anthropology that defined its object as the realm of values, ideas, and symbols. Its members had been caught up in the campus radicalism of the time,
and they remained politically engaged, but from now on radical politics on
campus increasingly meant identity politics. Cultural relativism became the
common orthodoxy.

American influence came to predominate in all the sciences and social
sciences after the war, and anthropology was no exception. The disarray of
European social anthropology in the 1970s and 1980s made Americanization
more palatable, even attractive. Although American anthropologists liked
to cite French philosophers, all the innovations in anthropology from the
late 1960s crossed the Atlantic from west to east: the study of gender, the
body, medical anthropology, the revamped field of material culture studies,
the anthropology of film. And more generally, Western European anthropologists absorbed the American discourse on culture. In the 1990s the
postmodernist version of interpretive anthropology – which Marcus and
Fischer defined as 'nothing other than relativism, rearmed and strengthened
for an era of intellectual ferment' (Marcus and Fischer 1986, p. 33) – seemed
set for a while to sweep the board on both sides of the Atlantic. For a time it
appeared that even in its heartlands, social anthropology was barely resist-
ing translation into cultural studies.

In the event, the social science tradition in European social anthropology
survived the cargo cults of the 1980s. In the 1990s social anthropology
became an established and popular discipline in a number of European
countries, displacing older traditions of descriptive ethnology. A new
generation is committed to Malinowskian fieldwork – often in their own
societies – and draws upon a range of contemporary sociological discourses. Younger scholars also engage with characteristically European
concerns about immigration, ethnicity, and the interplay of local, national,
and European institutions. In many ways marginal to the established social
sciences, their role is nevertheless important. My back-of-the-envelope
calculation suggests that only 2–3 per cent of social science funding in
Europe goes on studies carried out in non-Western societies, but clearly
there is a need for a broader perspective, for a discipline that can ask
whether the theories of the other social sciences apply to human behaviour or only to the circumstances of life in modern, industrialized,
Western societies.

REFERENCES

de L' Estoile, Benoît. 2004a. 'From the Colonial Exhibition to the Museum of Man. An alternative genealogy of French anthropology', *Social Anthropology* 11: 341–61.

2004b. '*L'Afrique comme laboratoire. Expériences réformatrices et révolution anthropologique dans l'empire colonial britannique (1920-1950)*' (PhD dissertation, EHESS, Paris).

de L' Estoile, Benoît, and Michel Naepels (eds.) 2004. *Frontières de l'anthropologie*. Special issue of *Critique*, Jan–Feb, 680–1.

de Zengotita, Thomas. 1984. 'The functional reduction of kinship in the social thought of John Locke', in G. Stocking (ed.), *Functionalism historicised. Essays in British social anthropology* [History of Anthropology, vol. 2]. Madison, WI: University of Wisconsin Press.

Evans-Pritchard, E. E. 1962. *Essays in social anthropology*. London: Faber and Faber.

Fortes, Meyer, and E. E. Evans-Pritchard (eds.) 1940. *African political systems*. London: Oxford University Press for the International African Institute.

Gaillard, Gerald. 1990. *Répertoire de l'ethnologie française, 1950–1970*. Paris: CNRS.

Geertz, Clifford. 1973. *The Interpretation of Cultures*. New York: Basic Books.

1988. *Works and lives. The anthropologist as author*. Stanford, CA: Stanford University Press.

1995. *After the fact*. Cambridge, MA: Harvard University Press.

Gingrich, Andre, and Richard G. Fox (eds.) 2002. *Anthropology, by comparison*. London: Routledge.

Goody, Jack. 1995. *The expansive moment. Anthropology in Britain and Africa, 1918–1970*. Cambridge: Cambridge University Press.

Grillo, Ralph. 1985. 'Applied anthropology in the 1980s. Retrospect and prospect', in R. Grillo and A. Rew (eds.), *Social anthropology and development policy*. New York: Tavistock.

Kuklick, Henrika. 1984. 'Tribal exemplars. Images of political authority in British anthropology, 1885-1945', in G. Stocking (ed.), *Functionalism historicised. Essays in British social anthropology* [History of Anthropology, vol. 2] pp. 59–82. Madison: University of Wisconsin Press.

1991. *The savage within. The social history of British social anthropology, 1885-1945*. Cambridge: Cambridge University Press.

Kuper, Adam. 1989. 'Radcliffe-Brown and Rivers. A correspondence', *Canberra Anthropology* 11: 49–81.

1990. 'Psychology and anthropology. The British experience', *History of the Human Sciences* 3: 397–413.

1999a. *Culture. The anthropologists' account*. Cambridge, MA: Harvard University Press.

1999b. 'South African anthropology. An inside job', in Adam Kuper, (ed.), *Among the anthropologists. History and context in anthropology*, pp. 145–170. London: Athlone Press.

2005. *The Reinvention of Primitive Society*. London: Routledge.

Leach, E. R. 1954. *Political systems of highland Burma*. London: Athlone Press.

1968. *A runaway world?* [Reith Lectures]. London: BBC.

1984. 'Glimpses of the unmentionable in the history of British social anthropology', *Annual Review of Anthropology* 13: 1–23.

Lienhardt, Godfrey. 1974. 'E-P. A personal view', *Man* 74: 299–304.

Malinowski, Bronislaw. 1926. *Crime and custom in savage society*. London: Routledge and Kegan Paul.

1927. *Sex and repression in savage society*. London: Kegan Paul.

1929. 'Practical anthropology', *Africa* 2: 22–38.

Marcus, George E., and Michael M. J. Fischer. 1986. *Anthropology as cultural critique. An experimental moment in the human sciences*. Chicago, IL: University of Chicago Press.

Mills, David. 2002. 'British anthropology at the end of empire: The rise and fall of the Colonial Social Science Research Council, 1944–1962', *Revue d'Histoire des Sciences Humaines* 6: 161–88.

2003a. 'Quantifying the discipline. Some anthropology statistics from the UK', *Anthropology Today* 19 (3): 19–22.

2003b. 'Professionalising or popularising anthropology? A brief history of anthropology's scholarly associations in the UK', *Anthropology Today* 19 (5): 8–13.

Price, David H. 2008. *Anthropological intelligence: The deployment and neglect of American anthropology in the Second World War*. Durham, NC: Duke University Press.

Rivers, W. H. R. 1926. *Psychology and ethnology*, ed. G. E. Smith. London: Kegan Paul.

Roldán, Arturo Alvarez. 1995. 'Malinowski and the origins of the ethnographic method', in Hans F. Vermeulen and Arturo Alvarez Roldán (eds.), *Fieldwork and footnotes. Studies in the history of European anthropology*. London: Routledge, pp. 143–58.

Ross, Dorothy. 1991. *The origins of American social science*. Cambridge: Cambridge University Press.

Said, Edward. 1978. *Orientalism*. New York: Pantheon.

Stocking, George W. 1984. 'Radcliffe-Brown and British social anthropology', in G. Stocking (ed.), *Functionalism historicised. Essays in British social anthropology* [History of Anthropology, vol. 2]. Madison, WI: University of Wisconsin Press.

1995. *After Tylor. British social anthropology, 1888–1951*. Madison, WI: University of Wisconsin Press.

Young, Michael. 2004. *Malinowski. Odyssey of an anthropologist, 1884–1920*. New Haven, CT: Yale University Press.

7

Human Geography

Ron Johnston

Introduction

Although some aspects of the study of geography are common across a large number of countries, nevertheless a marked 'geography of geographies' has emerged since the Second World War. Until then, there was considerable common ground that geography was the study of areal differentiation or chorology; it described and provided accounts for inter-regional differences in environments, human activities, and the interactions between the two. The widely adopted foundations for such an approach were laid down by German and French geographers – with a major American defence of that approach published in 1939 (Hartshorne 1939; see also Entrikin and Brunn 1990; Hartshorne 1959).

Those foundations were rapidly eroded in the anglophone world during the immediate post-war decades. Human geography in the United Kingdom, the United States, and most of the former British Empire took a new set of paths and contacts with practices in other language realms declined, although Scandinavia and the Netherlands were exceptions – much of the research done there is published in English and contacts with English-speaking geographers were strengthened post-1950, with the anglophone 'new geographies' adapted to local circumstances (Öhman and Simonsen 2003). Some national traditions were sustained in other language realms, such as the dominance of the regional monograph in French practice (Clout 2009; see also Clout 2003), but many aspects of the 'new paths' taken within anglophone geography were later adopted there in some form, fostered by two-way contacts (not least attendance at the annual meetings of the Association of American Geographers, which took on a pronounced

My thanks to Les Hepple and Alec Murphy for valuable comments on a draft of this chapter.

international complexion from the 1990s on). 'Indigenous' developments elsewhere have had very little influence in the English-speaking world, however.[1] Several decades of relative isolation – exacerbated by declining linguistic competence among English-speaking geographers and lessening interest in the geography of 'other parts of the world' – stimulated considerable concerns from geographers in non-English-speaking countries regarding a perceived Anglo-American hegemony over disciplinary changes (see Harris 2001).[2] Those concerns and the related debates lie outside the scope of this chapter, however; I focus on changing practices within human geography in the English-speaking, predominantly Anglo-American world, which, for much of the second half of the twentieth century, had relatively little sustained contact with geography as practiced in other language realms (Dunbar 2002; Johnston and Claval 1984).

Contemporary Anglo-American human geography is almost unrecognisable from the discipline's composition sixty years ago. In the first two post–Second World War decades, few human geographers identified themselves as social scientists. Their somewhat small and introverted discipline's strongest external links were with geology, history, and, in a few places, anthropology. Similarly, few members of other disciplines considered geography to fall within the social scientific orbit. Although there are still some lingering doubts as to whether their discipline is a social science (exemplified by the lack of any coverage of links between geography and sociology in Halsey and Runciman 2006), however, there is now general acceptance among human geographers that the great majority of its practitioners are correctly situated in the social sciences. That was resisted in the 1960s by some U.K. geographers – who identified firmly with the pre-war humanities tradition – when their discipline belatedly obtained recognition by and entry to the U.K.'s Social Science Research Council (Chisholm 2001; Johnston 2004b). Similar cases had to be made in the United States (Taaffe 1970) alongside arguments stressing the discipline's credentials to the scientific community more generally, recognising the more centralised structure of the academy there (NAS/NRC 1965, 1997); in most U.S. universities with

---

[1]   This is in considerable contrast to the impact of 'continental' social theorists – such as Derrida, Deleuze, and Foucault – on British human geographers.

[2]   Interestingly, since the Prix Vautrin Lud (claimed to be the highest honour awarded within geography and modelled on the Nobel prizes) was established in 1991 by the Festival International de Géographie, held at Saint-Dié-des-Vosges annually, the eighteen recipients have included ten from either the United Kingdom or the United States. Anglo-American geography has clearly had a major impact on the successive juries, predominantly drawn from western European, non-English-speaking countries, who nominate the lauréats.

academic structures separating out the sciences, humanities, and social sciences, geography is now located within last of those three divisions.

The Institutional Context

Understanding human geography's growing pluralism, especially since the 1970s, requires appreciating not just the wider post-war intellectual milieu but also particular institutional settings. As an academic discipline, geography is a late-nineteenth- and early-twentieth-century creation, preceding the institutionalisation of several other social sciences. Geography as a subject is very much older than that, however, and geographical material was being taught at the United Kingdom's ancient universities for much of the modern period, albeit not necessarily identified as geography per se (Livingstone 2003a; Withers and Mayhew 2002). The Royal Geographical Society (RGS) was founded in the 1830s to promote geography in the widest sense, and comparable societies were established in several provincial cities – mainly to sustain commercial interests – during the subsequent fifty years, alongside similar societies in the United States and elsewhere. [The American Geographical Society (AGS) was established in 1851 with similar goals.]

Many contemporary disciplines have been created by individuals/groups promoting a new research agenda, usually by 'breaking away' from a 'parent discipline'. In the United Kingdom, however, geography was largely created to meet a perceived teaching need. In the mid-nineteenth century, RGS officers became concerned with the quality of geography teaching in secondary (mainly public, i.e., private) schools, and commissioned a report that would draw international comparisons. This provided material that was used to press for more – and more rigorous – geographical teaching throughout the school curriculum, focused on the emerging grammar schools. Geography lacked status and credibility within educational circles because it was not taught at the 'ancient' English universities of Cambridge and Oxford, however, so the RGS campaigned to get it taught there, providing funds that sustained the staffing for several decades (Scargill 1976; Stoddart 1986). A diploma course for intending school teachers was provided, alongside – at Oxford – very large and successful summer schools for those already teaching geography who wanted a formal qualification in the subject.

Full degree schemes were not established at Oxford and Cambridge until the 1930s, by which time small geography departments offering honours degrees were available at several other universities (Slater 1988). Many originated in a demand for 'service teaching', providing geographical material for degrees in, for example, economics, history, and geology. Most soon found a rationale in the preparation of grammar (i.e., state, selective high) school teachers, for whom there was a continuing demand because of successful campaigns winning a substantial place for geography in school curricula and the relevant public examination systems. The Geographical Association, established in 1893 to promote geography teaching (Balchin 1993), remains a potent disciplinary lobbyist – not least in the post-1988 debates over a national curriculum (Rawling 2001; Walford 2001). The interaction between schools and universities sustained the subject in both milieux, ensuring a continual flow of students to the small university departments.

By 1950 there was a small geography department, headed by a professor, in almost all U.K. universities and university colleges. These prospered in the first post-war decades with the increased flow of students wanting to study a subject they enjoyed at school and that offered clear career opportunities – not only in school teaching but also the burgeoning profession of town and country planning. But geography's status was not high in some institutions as research became more important in universities' missions and individual academics' career trajectories (Johnston 2003a). Geography struggled for several decades to establish a viable, recognised research-based foundation. For most practitioners (and many others outside the discipline), its rationale remained the study of regions, synthesising material on the natural environment (some drawn from other disciplines and some from specialist studies by physical geographers) with that on human occupance (Wooldridge and East 1958). The goal was to depict different assemblages of physical and human features – at a range of spatial scales – comprising a mosaic of milieux with their own genres de vie. To many outside the discipline – and increasingly some within (see David 1958) – this was not a rigorous scientific practice. Geography was tolerated in the universities because it could attract students and 'pay its way' (something that still characterises the discipline), but it was not seen as a major research discipline. A learned society – the Institute of British Geographers (IBG) – was founded in 1933 to promote the academic practitioners' interests (many of whom – especially human geographers – felt that the RGS largely ignored their work; Steel 1983). It launched a serial (*Transactions*) at the outset, which only published occasional monographs and did not become a regular journal carrying papers until the 1950s. Research was not a high priority among the country's human geographers – perhaps one reason why none were elected to the

British Academy until 1967 (a historical geographer, Clifford Darby, was the first).

The situation was very different in the United States, where geography has never established a secure foundation in high school curricula and – in part because of the lack of political activity by leading geographers – was outflanked by the development of social studies in the early twentieth century (Schulten 2001). At the same time, the National Geographic Society, through its highly successful monthly *National Geographic*, presented a widely adopted view of geography that stressed the representation of exotic places (Johnston 2009). There was some demand for universities and normal schools to train geographers to become school teachers, but the lack of a separate geography stream in most states' high school systems meant that this was relatively slight. Generalist social studies teachers were expected to cover the needed geographical material, and geography was not considered a discipline requiring specialist teachers with university-level qualifications. Some small university geography departments were established to provide service teaching to undergraduates in other disciplines and a number – as at Berkeley, Clark, and Chicago – instituted graduate schools; the discipline only established a narrow foothold in the Ivy League institutions, however, and just one – at Dartmouth – survived into the 1990s.[3] The graduate schools were sustained by the provision of large, introductory undergraduate classes to students almost all of whom lacked any background in the subject, and there were very few geography majors; most American academic geographers thus have a wide range of undergraduate backgrounds, whereas most of those educated in the United Kingdom had specialised in the subject (along with two or three others only) from the age of sixteen.

The presence of a small number of graduate programmes stimulated the creation of a professional learned society – the Association of American Geographers (AAG) – founded to promote geographical research, not least through its *Annals*. (The AGS was significantly restructured at about the same time, with its journal – *The Geographical Review* – also adopting a research focus.) One of the discipline's most active promoters then, and

---

[3] Harvard did have a Laboratory for Computer Graphics and Spatial Analysis headed in the late 1970s by a geographer (Brian Berry, who had been appointed a professor of city and regional planning). A Center for Geographic Analysis was opened there in 2006, providing a 'technology program in the Institute for Quantitative Social Science'; its director is also a Professor of East Asian Languages and Civilizations and none of its permanent staff, who offer a range of expertise in Geographical Information Science, has a Ph.D. in geography.

first AAG President, William Morris Davis, was initially trained as a scientist and engineer at Harvard, and later as a geologist; he was appointed a full professor of physical geography there in 1890.[4] Alongside his massive geomorphological research contributions, he did much to promote geography as the study of environment–society interactions (Chorley, Beckinsale, and Dunn 1973), although in other hands this became translated into a naïve determinism and geography – as in the United Kingdom – failed to gain equal status with other research-based disciplines; geographical research as practised by AAG members became marginalised by the National Geographical Society and other influential organisations (Poole 2004; Schulten 2001).

The emphasis on interaction between humans and their physical environments in the British conception of geography points to a crucial feature of the intellectual context there. All U.K. university geography departments, to a greater or lesser extent, include both physical and human geographers, the former practising as natural/earth scientists. In the early twentieth century, most physical geographers were also 'regional specialists', teaching about areal differentiation in one part of the world. From the 1950s on, their specialist interests – notably in geomorphology (the study of landforms and landforming processes), but also in biogeography and climatology – came to predominate. As a result, and as human geographers too deserted the regional focus, the two 'halves' of geography have become more separate activities, with distinct sets of research practices. Nevertheless, for political reasons at least, the two have remained together institutionally, offering students courses in both social and natural science approaches to the discipline (with most degree schemes allowing specialisation in one or the other during the later years of their degree). The consequences of this togetherness for the development of each are difficult to unravel (given the absence of a substantial counterfactual case), but there can be little doubt that it was crucial in the 1960s to 1970s in the development of quantitative methodologies for spatial analysis and has sustained work on society–nature interactions.

This physical–human symbiosis was less apparent in U.S. universities, especially during the period when areal differentiation held sway as the discipline's *raison d'être*; many adopted the stance advanced by Hartshorne (1939) that, while this called for descriptive accounts of the physical environment, research into, for example, landform creation was not needed [see also some of the essays in James and Jones (1954)]. As a result, geography departments rarely encouraged research in physical geography and

---

[4]   He was also president of the American Geological Society.

some excluded it (the University of Washington still does); a commemorative volume for the AAG's seventy-fifth anniversary had no specific physical geography contributions (Marcus 1979). From the 1980s on, this rift was healed, in part responding to increasing concern over human–nature inter-actions, and most U.S. university departments now include physical geog-raphy, but it generally lacks the status sustained and enhanced in the United Kingdom over the last sixty years.[5]

Until the 1960s–1970s, geographers had few contacts with the burgeoning social sciences – the relatively 'new' disciplines of politics and sociology as well as the longer-established fields of economics and anthropology. (Exceptions include the links with anthropology at Berkeley in the United States, led by Carl Sauer; the foundation chair at Aberystwyth in the United Kingdom, first held by H. J. Fleure, is in geography and anthropol-ogy.) Geography was, for example, largely ignored by the 'new universities' established in the United Kingdom in the late 1950s, where the social sciences flourished (Johnston 2004a). The discipline continued to expand very substantially where it was already well-established in U.K. universi-ties, however, and suffered less than some other natural and social science disciplines that experienced downturns in popularity during subsequent decades. Similarly in the United States, geography was not perceived as a key discipline in either form of science. Indeed, it is absent from a signifi-cant number of U.S. universities and relatively small in other institutions when compared with the three core social sciences, but it is large in absolute terms and had big graduate schools before comparators were established in the United Kingdom. In the 1960s to 1970s, many British students went to North America to do a doctorate. Some stayed; others returned and had a substantial impact on the British departments that had appointed them. Increasingly U.K. geographers made regular trips to the United States: a contingent of several hundred can usually be found at the AAG's annual conference, for example. The discipline has become very much an Anglo-American construct though with important differences (Johnston and Sidaway 2004b, 2007; Murphy 2007).

Five Tumultuous Decades

Until the early 1960s, change in geographical practices was slow and slight, linked, for example, to developments in cartography and the discipline's

---

[5] In Canada, as in Australia and New Zealand, the U.K. model prevailed with university departments containing both human and physical geographers – at least until the 1990s.

core tool – the map. Geography and cartography had been linked for many centuries – exploration, the production of maps, and description of their contents being at the heart of geographical practices long before its institutionalisation as an academic discipline. Indeed, map-making was a major activity into which that new academic discipline was integrated (Kain and Delano-Smith 2003), with geography incorporating that particular visual medium as a major differentiating factor from other disciplines – what Balchin (1972) termed 'graphicacy'. Maps remain at the core of geography for many outside the discipline, but changes in the technology of their production has seen a decline of geographers' interest in cartography – at the same time as there has been a massive expansion in the generation, display, and analysis of geographic information, increasing amounts of which are geo-coded and so amenable to cartographic treatment (Rhind 2003). Geographers remain map generators (especially of thematic maps), analysers, and interpreters – although maps are much less a feature of their publications now than in the past – but the technology of their production now lies elsewhere.

This shift away from the visual was one of the foundations being laid for a major 'revolution' in geographical practices during the 1950s. The regional focus predominated in most departments' teaching portfolios then, although physical geographers were beginning to develop specialist research agenda linked to work in geology and other natural sciences. There was less movement in human geography, however, although with some marked exceptions. Historical geography, emphasising landscape change illustrating the discipline's visual perspective (Cosgrove 2001, 2007; Rose 2003, 2007), and led by scholars such as Clifford Darby in the United Kingdom (Darby 2002; Prince 2000), was one of the largest 'specialist' interests; some places developed particular niches based on links to anthropology – notably at Aberystwyth (see Buchanan 2006) and in the 'Berkeley School' developed by the highly influential Carl Sauer (Leighly 1963). The interests of scholars such as Darby and Sauer in various aspects of landscape change were brought together in a major Wenner-Gren symposium on 'man's role in changing the face of the earth' (Thomas 1956).[6] There was little economic geography beyond descriptive studies of, for example, resource availability and manufacturing activities, however, and virtually no study of towns or of social geography; political geography was somewhat discouraged because of perceived links to the Nazi practice of *geopolitik* (Agnew 2002).[7]

---

[6] That symposium was updated – and its contents illustrate geographers' continued interest in landscape change – in Turner et al. (1990).

[7] I was an undergraduate at the University of Manchester from 1959 to 1962 – a large department with eleven staff and an intake to the honours school of forty-eight. There

As what one leading geographer referred to as 'the highest form of the geographer's art' (Hart 1982), regional geography predominated until the 1960s – especially among human geographers. For some critics, their works were little more than gazetteers or catalogues, involving mapping areas on major thematic variables (such as climate and soils), dividing them into regions with similar characteristics – usually based on their physical environments – and then providing descriptive accounts of each region's particular features [what Gould (1979, p. 139) called 'banal, factual boxes']. Little attention was paid to the local cultural milieux, what Vidal de la Blache (1911) termed their *genres de vie* in his classic work on French rural *pays*. But others, by 'adopting a foreign land' and immersing themselves in it, were able to deploy the regional approach to illuminate life and lives in a selected area (on which see Mead 2007).

The First 'New Geography'

A so-called 'theoretical and quantitative revolution' was launched in the late 1950s, although as with so many revolutions earlier indicators can be found (Harris and Ullman 1945; Ullman 1941). It had three salient characteristics. The first was the need for *rigour in description*, particularly quantitative description – empirical statements should be replicable and unambiguous (Cole 1969). A pioneering text on statistical methods was written by a British climatologist (Gregory 1963) and a specialist study group on quantitative methods was established within the IBG in the mid-1960s, but by then the use of statistical procedures had been widely promoted for a decade among U.S. geographers.

The second key characteristic was the *search for spatial order*, for underlying principles not only in the operation of the physical processes studied by geographers interested in landscapes and the natural environment, but also in the spatial patterning of human occupance of the earth's surface (Johnston 2003b). In the United States, the dominant centre for this re-orientation was the University of Washington, Seattle, based around two key individuals. Edward Ullman was one of a large number of geographers

were specialist courses in geomorphology, biogeography, and climatology in the second year (all compulsory) but only in historical geography within human geography. There were compulsory regional courses in both second and third years (Great Britain and Ireland in the former; Western Europe in the latter), plus a range of regional options and something of a rag-bag of other 'specialist courses' (e.g., history of geography; applied geography). Although a 'revolution' was already being fomented across the Atlantic and could be accessed through some journals, it had no impact on the Manchester department then – or many others.

recruited by the OSS in Washington, D.C. during the war, where they worked in multidisciplinary teams (Barnes 2006; Barnes and Farish 2007). He and a few others realised that their discipline lacked core principles and an adherence to scientific procedures that could produce generalised, applicable knowledge rather than detailed information about unique places. He wrote about models of the distribution of urban settlements and their internal structures, developing an approach to human geography around principles of spatial interaction, based on the key variable of transport and communication costs (Ullman 1941, 1956). A group of graduate students – quickly known as the 'space cadets' – went to work with him at Seattle, but found greater inspiration from another faculty member, William Garrison, who taught pioneering courses on location theory and statistical analysis (gaining stimuli from parallel developments in the earth sciences that were being adopted by some physical geographers). The group Garrison mentored rapidly spread the new ideas into other graduate schools, and from there – via visiting students – to the United Kingdom and elsewhere in the English-speaking world (Haggett 2008a; King 2007).

A separate node for similar developments – lagging those in the United States by a few years – emerged at the University of Cambridge with two young academics at its heart. One was a physical geographer, Dick Chorley, who was strongly influenced by those bringing the hypothetico-deductive method associated with systems thinking to geomorphology when doing graduate work in geology in New York (Barnes 2008; Haggett 2008b); the other was a human geographer, Peter Haggett, who, although he specialised in geomorphology as an undergraduate and some of his early research was in biogeography, spent several years developing a course of lectures that became an influential text on *Locational Analysis in Human Geography* (Haggett 1965). Chorley and Haggett and a growing range of contributors also promoted this 'new geography' to schoolteachers through a series of summer schools, leading to major edited volumes that became important university texts (Chorley and Haggett 1965, 1967). Haggett moved to Bristol in 1966, establishing another 'pole of development' there, and graduates from the two universities, as well as from a number of other centres (Johnston et al. 2008), rapidly colonised the discipline as more departments embraced the need to teach and research in this 'new geography' – albeit somewhat grudgingly in the case of some senior staff. Adherents to the 'new' were welcomed but few members of the 'older generation' were fully converted to the cause (Johnston 1978, 2003b; Taylor 1976).

Much impetus to work on spatial order came from outside the discipline, and the bibliography to Haggett's 1965 book illustrates how much he drew on work by economic theorists such as von Thünen, Hoover, Lösch, and Weber, and sociologists such as Zipf and Stouffer. Papers by the Seattle 'space cadets' and others illustrated the technical inspiration gained from cognate disciplines, adopting methods from psychometrics, biometrics, sociometrics, and econometrics, for example, as well as from the earth sciences. There were two exceptional endogenous developments, however. *Central place theory* is an idealisation of settlement patterns produced by a German geographer – Christaller (1933) – that assumes rational economic behaviour by both service providers and their customers, deducing that this results in hierarchical arrangements of settlements of various sizes serving hexagonal market areas; it had little impact until taken up at Seattle in the mid-1950s. The spatial *diffusion of innovations* was the subject of pioneer studies by Swedish geographer Torsten Hägerstrand (1953). His detailed studies of migration identified a 'distance-decay' pattern in that and other interactions – as indeed contemporaneously did sociologists and 'social physicists' – but his work was largely ignored by Anglo-American human geographers until he visited Seattle in the later 1950s (Duncan 1974; Morrill 2005). The space cadets who took up these and other ideas and techniques stressed their applied value, exemplified by a wide range of studies pioneered by one of them – Brian Berry – at the University of Chicago in the 1960s and 1970s (Yeates 2001).[8]

The impact of these ideas launched on a largely unsuspecting geographical community in the mid-1960s was massive and rapid – and also traumatic. Some established figures in the discipline were reluctant to embrace the rejection of the regional approach. Pressures to accommodate new ways of thinking were strong, however, and in a period of expansion it was not long before most departments contained at least one practitioner of the 'new human geography'. Teaching practices were very substantially altered: compulsory courses in statistics became *de rigueur*, accompanied in some by parallel courses in computer use and programming (Lavalle, McConnell, and Brown 1967; Whitehand 1970).

This rapidly named 'new geography' had a third key characteristic, introducing students not just to procedures associated with the hypothetico-deductive 'scientific method', but also to aspects of the *philosophy of science*. The key book was Harvey's (1969) *Explanation in Geography*, which

---

[8]   There is a strong tradition of work in 'applied geography', although its nature has changed very substantially since the early books by Stevens (1921) and Stamp – one of the discipline's pioneers in the United Kingdom who served on a number of important government committees in the 1940s through 1950s – were published (Stamp 1960). [On Stamp see Embleton and Coppock (1968).]

emphasised rigorous methodology exemplified by mathematical reasoning and statistical analysis. Human geography was to become a spatial science, as earlier propounded by Bunge (1966).

The foundations laid down by these pioneers have endured, although contemporary practices differ substantially from the originals. In statistical analysis, for example, by the end of the 1960s researchers – particularly Haggett and his Bristol colleagues – had identified major problems when applying standard techniques from the general linear model to spatial data, because of biases in coefficients and their error terms introduced by spatial autocorrelation (an extension to two dimensions of the one-dimensional temporal autocorrelation of such importance in econometrics). Development of valid spatial analytical tools was initiated and continues in the rapidly expanding field of spatial econometrics and 'local statistics', with a growing number of researchers across the social sciences appreciating the need for such an approach (Anselin et al. 2004). In this, as in so much else, change has not only been facilitated but in some cases made possible by developments in computing technology. Spatial statistical analysis is now an extremely sophisticated activity.

One aspect of computing technology fundamental to much of this development is the creation of geographical information systems (GIS), which combined computer hardware and software for the capture, storage, checking, integration, manipulation, display, and analysis of spatially referenced data (Longley et al. 1999, 2001). Geographical information systems integrate data that can be 'mapped' (in the widest sense of that term), providing a technology that is at the core of developments in spatial analysis across many disciplines, as well as an enabling technology for a wide range of service industries – and the potential for commercial contract work (Longley and Clarke 1995). This has stimulated the growth of geographical information science (GISc) with geography at the fore (Goodchild 1992, 2008) – and providing, in the United States more than the United Kingdom, a key rationale for the academic discipline's financial survival (Murphy 2007).

The nature of the theory driving spatial analysis has also changed. Much of the original inspiration came from reading the small volume of work by economists on locational issues, such as von Thünen on agricultural land use patterns around market centres (Chisholm 1962; Hall 1966), Alfred Weber (1929) and Hoover (1948) on industrial location, and Lösch (1954) on settlement patterns; Garrison (1959–1960) overviews these stimuli. The 'space cadets' also developed close links with the attempts by economist Walter Isard to develop a new discipline of regional science, which stimulated cross-disciplinary contacts through national and international conferences of the Regional Science Association (Barnes 2004b; Berry 1993, 1995; Isard 1956, p. 200).[9] It was soon realised that most models of economically rational behaviour were, however, too unrealistic to be applied to contemporary behavioural patterns – especially in spatial studies, because they incorporated strong assumptions that distance (reflecting the time and cost involved in crossing it) was a major constraint to spatial behaviour. [Pred (1967–1969) is a full critique.] An alternative *behavioural geography* was formulated, which sought regularities in rigorous but more inductive ways – teasing out patterns within the context of general theories of how people make decisions in and about space (Golledge and Stimson 1997).

In the early years of this 'new geography', many research papers tested theoretically derived hypotheses. A large number investigated aspects of spatial form – analysing point and line patterns and various surfaces [as synthesised in Berry and Marble (1968)], whereas others studied spatial patterns of human behaviour in the context of, for example, 'gravity models' applied to migration patterns and the diffusion of diseases. As the location theories that provided the original stimuli declined in popularity, increasing attention was given to other forms of behaviour – looking, for example, at the characteristics of different types of social area within a city and how these provided contexts for behavioural variations in such aspects as health and voting, and using techniques from the developing field of spatial econometrics (in many cases within GIS frameworks) to evaluate the mapped spatial patterns. Place rather than space became the leitmotif; rather than focus on ordered patterns that could be mapped (or maps that could be deconstructed as representations of spatial order), human geographers moved to study spatially varying contexts and their influence on behaviour patterns. Economic theories never entirely disappeared, but were more sophisticated in their treatment of behavioural patterns, as, for example, recent work on 'evolutionary economic geography' (Boschma and Martin 2007). Geographers, on the other hand,

---

[9]   Few of the 'space cadets' had any formal training in economics – one of the exceptions was Brian Berry, who did a joint degree in economics and geography at University College London and was taught economic geography – including Hoover and Lösch – by Brian Law: Hoover and other (non-technical) approaches to economic location decisions were also taught at the London School of Economics in the early 1950s [see also Rawstron (2002)]. Leslie Curry (2002) reports that he read many of those 'continental' classics when he was a graduate student at Johns Hopkins University in 1951, a few years before they became major stimuli to the Seattle graduate school.

distanced themselves from the 'new economic geography' launched by Paul Krugman and others in the 1990s (e.g., Krugman 1993), claiming that this bore too close a resemblance in its assumptions regarding economic behaviour to the discredited theories that characterised the early years of geography's 'quantitative and theoretical revolution' (Martin 1999).

The 'Radicals' Arrive

No sooner had human geographers accommodated changes in research and teaching practices induced by the 'quantitative revolution', than a new 'would-be revolution' arrived. This was partly a product of social unrest focused on American concerns about the Vietnam War but also covered issues such as social and economic inequality, poverty, and civil rights. It stimulated negative reactions to spatial science, arguing that its quantitative descriptions and attempted 'explanations' of spatial patterns and behaviour were largely irrelevant to those major concerns, having little to offer scholars who wished to tackle – rather than just ameliorate – such problems and create a more just and equal society. The alternative offered was Marxism.

A pioneer of this approach was David Harvey, who had been at the forefront of the previous revolution and was now in the vanguard of the next. His essays in *Social Justice and the City* (1973) galvanised postgraduates and young academics, not only with excoriating views on approaches he supported a few years earlier but also through his promotion of a Marxist (or historical-materialist) approach. While Harvey supported and was personally involved in local political campaigns, he stressed the importance of a deep grounding in Marx's thinking and dialectic methods to provide a basis within which understanding of the particular circumstances could be set. Capitalism had to be understood theoretically, and he extended Marxian thinking by incorporating a spatial element – most notably in *The Limits to Capital* (1982) and several works on urbanisation (e.g., Harvey 1985a).

This 'radical revolution' stimulated some to abandon human geography as a spatial science but its influence on the discipline differed from its predecessor's. Some 'radicals' were appointed to geography departments and introduced courses/research that broadened institutional portfolios, but this was not widespread – certainly nothing like the rapid and deep spread of 'quantification'. In part this reflected the context. British universities in particular were contracting and losing staff in the 1970s and 1980s, and many lacked space for individuals promoting the new approach – especially as they were also being pressed to become more commercially minded rather than critical of the apparatus of capitalism and the contemporary state. There was no take over.

There was, however, a broad acceptance of the radicals' case that studying capitalism's superstructure – the spatial patterns of settlements and individual behaviour within them, for example – offered neither a full appreciation of its underpinnings (the so-called infrastructure) nor tools to do other than manipulate that superstructure. Fundamental problems of inequality could not be addressed within geographers' largely descriptive paradigm, however quantitatively rigorous. Few established academics embraced Marxism fully (in part, perhaps more so in the United States, because of rhetorical links between Marxism and the 'cold war'), let alone associated reform agenda, but recognised the argument that 'real explanation' required more than a distance-decay regression equation.

Further impetus towards this appreciation came from two directions. The first was Derek Gregory's (1978) classic, *Ideology, Science and Human Geography*, which introduced the discipline to a wide literature in the philosophy of science, social science, and the humanities, focusing attention on the role of human agency in the continuous re-creation of structures (including spatial structures) – what later became known through Giddens' (1984) work as structuration. Andrew Sayer's (1984) *Method in Social Science: A Realist Approach* broadened the agenda by setting the base-infrastructure-superstructure model in a wider, not-necessarily Marxist, context. Such books and subsequent debates resulted in a more philosophically aware human geography, which distanced itself from the geometrical determinism of some aspects of spatial science and the economic determinism of some forms of Marxism by stimulating awareness of spatially varying structure-agency interactions as people made their own histories and geographies but not in circumstances of their own choosing. Place was again replacing space as geographers' leitmotif through this re-orientation of human geographical work: Harvey, for example, built space into Marx's basic arguments regarding capitalist dynamics – not only through his major theoretical essays on movements of capital and their geopolitical consequences (Harvey 1982, 1985b), but also his interpretations of late capitalism and neo-liberalism (Harvey 2003, 2007); Massey's (1984; Massey and Meegan 1982) empirical studies set the changing geography of British manufacturing employment during the recession of the 1970s and 1980s into a clear realist framework, showing how a decline in profitability both constrained locational choices and yet, at the same time, offered restructuring organisations a range of spatial opportunities.

A further 'radical' agenda reflected an inequality within geography itself, as well as society more widely. Feminism's arrival within human geography focused initially on the small number of women geographers and the discipline's institutionalised patriarchy (Maddrell 2009; Rose 1993), as well as the invisibility of women in so much geographical scholarship. The agenda – led by a Women and Geography Study Group established within the IBG in the early 1980s, which produced a collective text on *Geography and Gender: An Introduction to Feminist Geography* (1984) – soon broadened, however, drawing on a wide range of inter-disciplinary sources concerned with difference and positionality, and the politics thereof [a switch reviewed in McDowell (1993a, 1993b); Women and Geography Study Group (1997)]. This informed not only a growing volume of work in feminist geography – and a significant change in the composition of the academic discipline – but also wider concerns with the politics of difference applied to other marginalised groups. The feminist impulse also introduced human geographers to a wider range of cultural theory than heretofore encountered.

Followed by the 'Cultural Turn'

From the late 1980s on, growing appreciation, and participation in the development, of cultural theory added a further major strand to human geography's portfolio. It was not the first attempt to promote the role of individual agency. Alongside the 'radical revolution', a small number of dissenting voices criticised both spatial science for denying individual free will in a form of spatial (or geometrical) determinism and Marxism for privileging economic imperatives. A range of philosophies – such as phenomenology, idealism, and existentialism – was explored. None achieved more than a token following, but the basic point was appreciated even if largely unrealised until the 'cultural turn' a decade or so later. Increasingly, geographers acknowledged the importance of constrained free-will within structural imperatives, which were themselves changing markedly as capitalism was being restructured through globalisation and neo-liberalism.

The change was initiated in the late 1980s in a small number of departments (especially in the United Kingdom at first, where there was greater freedom for academics and their students to experiment relatively unconstrained by financial imperatives). It came to the fore in the early 1990s as the 'cultural turn', drawing much inspiration from the burgeoning multi-disciplinary enterprise of cultural studies. It emphasised hybridity, seeking to break down barriers between different 'types' of geography – economic, social, political, urban, etc. – through an awareness that common human traits and behaviour patterns ('culture') underpin most (if not all areas) of life and are inscribed in spatial structures that constrain and yet facilitate further action.[10]

One particular impetus for a substantial number of human geographers was post-modernism and its stresses on heterogeneity, particularity, and uniqueness. This was expressed in work that (at least implicitly) respected arguments derived from Marxist, realist, and structurationist scholars but distanced itself – often aggressively so – from spatial science. The latter was seen as failing to 'to take seriously the complexity of human beings as creative individuals' (Cloke et al. 1991, p. 17), with behavioural geographers restricting themselves to 'a fairly narrow conception of how human beings think and act' (Cloke et al. 1991, p. 67). Instead, geographers were offered a range of approaches that, according to a major introductory textbook promoting the genre:

avoids the easy and ultimately dull options of retreating into worlds of compiled fact or modelled fantasy. It engages with real life and real lives, embracing their wonderful complexity. It seeks to do more than record or model; it tries to explain, understand, question, interpret and maybe even improve these human geographies (Cloke et al. 1999, p. ix)

focused, according to a parallel book, on describing and explicating the 'meaningful nature of life' (Cloke et al. 2004, p. 283).

Such arguments challenged much that continued to be done within human geography, especially within spatial science and geographical information science, creating deep breaches that facilitated some portraits of the discipline as irrevocably split. Others have been at least partly reconciled with the 'cultural turn', as in Harvey's (1989) interpretation of societal and economic change since the 1970s within his firmly held Marxist approach, in the major thrust within economic geography involved with understanding new forms of capitalism associated with globalised neo-liberalism and economic regulation, and in the appearance of a structurally based

---

[10] One attempt, using citations, to explore the interactions among the discipline's various branches – which suggests relatively little success at breaking down the barriers – is Sluyter et al. (2006).

critical human geography emphasising the 'ought' as much as the 'is', concerned with ethics and justice (Harvey 1996; Smith 1994). But the challenge has gone much further, with geographers addressing material way beyond previous agenda – as in feminist-inspired studies of the body, of sexuality, and of children's geographies – and much rethinking about the relationships between humans and not only nature – as illustrated by the burgeoning field of political ecology (Robbins 2004) – but also a wide range of other 'things', such as texts. Indeed, the substantive content of human geography has become extremely wide ranging, generating very considerable intra-disciplinary fragmentation as separate communities of workers pursue their own agenda – not least through the various specialist groups within the main learned societies [those within the AAG having been used to structure discussions about progress within the discipline (Gaile and Willmott 2004)].

Geographers' focus on subjectivity and the social construction of knowledge is grounded by stressing the crucial role of place (at a range of spatial scales, a concept of much contemporary concern) as where identities are created and re-created, and political strategies are enacted. There is talk of this stimulating a wider 'spatial turn' within the humanities and some social sciences, reflecting appreciation of the key concept of place in the constitution of society. Space and place have been introduced to subjects and narratives that, according to geographical protagonists, have been for too long dominated by time. Geography and history should run in parallel (if not interweave), rather than the latter being privileged.

Inspiration has also been drawn from post-structuralism, emphasising language, texts, discourse, and power. Drawing on stimuli such as French philosophers and social scientists Foucault, Derrida, Deleuze, and Latour, this emphasises problematics involved in representing empirical worlds (not only worlds of 'things' but also non-representational worlds of, e.g., emotion and affect). Writing and other textual forms – including geographers' traditional medium, the map (Olsson 2007) – as well non-textual representations (such as landscapes) reflect their authors' positionality, and their interpretation reflects the readers'. The transmission of 'facts' and meanings is thus unstable, as texts are constructed and deconstructed hermeneutically in spatial contexts (Livingstone 2003b, 2005).

This approach is illustrated by work on geopolitics, notably Gregory's (2004) *The Colonial Present*, which deals with the contemporary conflicts in Afghanistan, Iraq, and Israel–Palestine, much influenced by Edward

Said's work on the (re)presentation of 'others'. Its stress on the role of political power in creating, maintaining, and challenging such representations characterises critical geopolitics' emphasis on the role of asymmetric cultural creations in international relations. The book also provides an intriguing counterpoint to a Marxist-inspired interpretation of much of the same subject matter in Harvey's discussion of *The New Imperialism* (2003).

The difference between approaches influenced by the 'cultural turn' and earlier work characteristic of the 'quantitative revolution' has been sharply drawn in Barnes's (2004a) comparison of studies in economic geography – what he terms 'the 1960s science of space versus the millennial culture of place'. This involved a shift, he suggests, 'from abstract spaces to concrete places', whereas a characteristic paper in the 1960s used regression analysis to test hypotheses regarding central place patterns in part of Iowa (Berry and Barnum 1962), one from the 1990s on workers in the City of London's financial markets stressed the cultural performances in their working practices – what they wore, how they spoke, how they held their bodies (McDowell 1997). In spatial science, he argues,

the intent is to deploy formal transformations that render all places comparable, to turn them into one continuous homogeneous space that is mathematically tractable, and hence explainable by abstract logic

whereas

the cultural turn is about keeping places intact, not transforming them into a theoretical calculus, but working away at their contingent concreteness, materiality and singularity ... (Barnes 2004a, p. 58)

The 'cultural turn' has altered human geography at least as much in the last twenty years as quantification did between 1960 and 1980. Much of this reflects the power of the ideas and their attractiveness to new generations of scholars, but the rate and extent of change has been facilitated by the altered academic environment. Universities have expanded rapidly in the United Kingdom since 1988, and more recently in the United States, with (many) geography departments enjoying the fruits of this growth (albeit constrained by financial circumstances, which have not expanded to the same extent); they have attracted students, many of whom in the United Kingdom then discover that they have enrolled into a very different discipline from that studied in school. Operation of intra-disciplinary politics has enabled geographers associated with the 'cultural turn' to capture a significant proportion of the discipline's available resources – such as new/replacement staff positions – and rewrite undergraduate curricula to emphasise their practices (Johnston 2006). This has not gone unchallenged in some departments, or in the discipline more widely; spatial science and/or GIS remain strong contenders for disciplinary resources (Jackson et al. 2006). But just as the discipline in 1975 bore little resemblance to that of 1945 or 1955, so the discipline in 2005 is different again.

Putting It All Together?

This review of changes in human geography over six decades has stressed issues of geographical practice – what geographers do – rather than changes in geographical knowledge – what geographers study and how their knowledge is used. Not surprisingly, changing practices have been linked to changing subject matter – although, as often claimed, the key geographical concepts of space, place, scale, and environment have remained at the discipline's core.

Changes in geographical knowledge have involved both a broadening and a deepening of disciplinary content. Clearly defined sub-disciplines were few in the first ten to twenty years of the period; most practitioners identified themselves simply as human geographers, usually with a regional specialism. By the late 1970s, although there were still some geographers teaching in a regional context, few identified an areal specialism as the main focus of their research. Instead, there were economic geographers and social geographers, urban geographers, industrial geographers and transport geographers, resource geographers – even quantitative geographers. In the United Kingdom few were called cultural geographers until the 1990s, however, the term being generally associated with the school of human-environment studies founded by Carl Sauer at the University of California, Berkeley, in the 1920s through 1930s. From then on, many more identified themselves as cultural geographers, but the intra-disciplinary boundaries became less rigid (Cosgrove and Jackson 1987).

Human geographers are sometimes placed in just two main groups – spatial analysts and social theorists (Sheppard 1995). Although an over-simplistic binary split, this emphasises the main difference in their dominant practices – quantitative versus qualitative. Although some individuals practice on both sides of the divide – either in different substantive areas of study or by successfully deploying elements of both sets – nevertheless this clear distinction can be found throughout the contemporary discipline, including the practices emphasised in some departments and their teaching programmes.

The presence of two sets of distinctive portfolios of geographical practices in the contemporary discipline indicates that – as in other social sciences – the changes that have occurred in human geography do not conform to Kuhn's (1970) model of normal science interrupted by occasional revolutions (Johnston and Sidaway 2004a). None of the attempted 'revolutions' has been totally successful in eliminating previous practices (although some, like 'traditional' regional geography, slowly disappeared as their adherents retired from the scene). Instead, they have increased the range of work and fostered a wide portfolio of (sometimes ill-defined) sub-disciplines. Geography, at least since the early 1960s, has been multi-paradigmatic, at every scale of that concept.

The two major changes in human geography since 1945, in terms of volumetric contribution to the discipline's portfolio, occurred during periods of university growth; new practices could be more readily incorporated when more students were being recruited and more staff appointed. This may have been a necessary condition for change, but certainly not a sufficient one. Those wishing to alter the disciplinary agenda had to convince others of the desirability of adding the new to the old – as a precursor, for some proponents at least, to replacing it and engineering a complete revolution (Johnston 2006). This political task involving competition for resources provides a further exemplar of structuration processes, of human agency operating within structural and contextual constraints to change those structures. Some agents have been more successful than others; the results stand out in human geography's recent history and contemporary situation – and in the variety of practices emphasised within and between institutions.

Geography, therefore, has a number of traditions that characterise practitioners' approaches to their discipline (Livingstone 1992). Rarely has there been a wide consensus about their relative value, however, and as their breadth has increased in recent years, the discipline has become an even more contested enterprise. In this, human geography differs little, if at all, from other social sciences where similar contests are being played out as various academic social movements seek to dominate disciplinary spaces (Frickel and Gross 2005; Johnston 2006). That alone does not make human geography a social science, and it is still not recognised as such by all social scientists. Nevertheless, as this essay has shown, English-speaking human geographers on both sides of the Atlantic have adopted and adapted the social sciences' main precepts over the last six decades. There can be no doubt that they practice as social scientists and that their practices are increasingly recognised, and adopted, by other social scientists.

In embracing the social sciences, however, geographers have very largely foresaken their traditional role of developing citizen awareness, through education at all levels, of the world's great diversity. The emphasis on space in the first of the post-1950s portfolios, with its focus on the search for universals in spatial patterns and behaviour, largely ignored the areal differentiation of physical environments, cultures, histories, and political economies on which those templates were being laid, and the subsequent replacement of space by place as the discipline's post-1970s leitmotif involved only a partial return to the long-established concern with areal differentiation; what one internal critic claimed was 'the highest form of the geographer's art' (Hart 1982) enjoyed no major revival. Thus, perhaps surprisingly to an outsider, geographers play at best only a minor role in inter- and multi-disciplinary area studies teaching and research programmes, where the core disciplines are more likely to be history, literature, and political studies. Geographers' embrace of science and social science in their various paradigmatic forms over the last six decades or so has meant that 'what (academic) geographers do' has little in common with what they are popularly believed to do (Johnston 2009).[11]

---

[11] An interesting reflection of this occurred in early 2009. In 1995 the Royal Geographical Society (RGS) merged with the Institute of British Geographers, established in 1933 as a learned society for academic geographers. The RGS had a long tradition of supporting explorations – for the discovery of 'new worlds' in the nineteenth century and for filling in our knowledge of relative unknown parts of the world in the twentieth. The newly merged society decided not to mount any more major international expeditions but to support research on a wider range of subjects as being more cost-effective and relevant. In 2009 a group of (non-academic) Fellows challenged this policy arguing that the Society should continue to mount such expeditions. The proposal was lost at a Special General Meeting (see http://www.rgs.org/AboutUs/Governance/SGM/SGM. htm), but its protagonists have said they will continue to fight that decision (http:// thebeaglecampaign.com. Last accessed 2 March 2010.). Meanwhile, a number of press articles and commentaries poured considerable scorn on contemporary academic geography (e.g., http://www.telegraph.co.uk/news/5301118/Stanley-Johnson-has-the-Royal-Geographical-Society-lost-its-sense-of-adventure.html. Last accessed 2 March 2010.).

REFERENCES

Agnew, J. 2002. *Making political geography.* London: Arnold.

Anselin, L., Florax, R. J. G. M. and Rey, S. J. (eds). 2004. *Advances in spatial econometrics: methodology, tools and applications.* Berlin: Springer.

Balchin, W. G. V. 1972. Graphicacy. *Geography* 57: 185–195.

1993. *The Geographical Association: the first hundred years, 1893–1993.* Sheffield: The Geographical Association.

Barnes, T. J. 2004a. 'L'évolution des styles: de l'analyse spatiale des années 1960 à la culture du lieu des années 2000 dans la géographie économique anglo-américaine. *Géographie et Culture* 49: 43–58. (An English translation is at http://www.geog.ubc.ca/~tbarnes/ pdf/PAPER_Styles_of_the_times.pdf. Last accessed 22 February 2010.)

2004b. The rise (and decline) of American regional science: lessons for the new economic geography? *Journal of Economic Geography* 4: 107–129.

2006. Geographical intelligence: American geographers and research and analysis in the Office of Strategic Services 1941–1945. *Journal of Historical Geography* 32: 149–168.

2008. Geography's underworld: the military-industrial complex, mathematical modelling and the quantitative revolution. *Geoforum* 39: 3–16.

Barnes, T. J. and Farish, M. 2007. Between regions: science, militarism and American geography from world war to cold war. *Annals of the Association of American Geographers* 97: 807–826.

Berry, B. J. L. 1993. Geography's quantitative revolution: initial conditions 1954–1960, a personal memoir. *Urban Geography* 14: 434–441.

1995. Whither regional science? *International Regional Science Review* 17: 297–306.

Berry, B. J. L. and Barnum, H. G. 1962. Aggregate relations and elemental components of central place systems. *Journal of Regional Science* 4: 35–68.

Berry, B. J. L. and Marble, D. F. (eds). 1968. *Spatial analysis.* Englewood Cliffs NJ: Prentice-Hall.

Boschma, R. and Martin, R. L. 2007. Constructing an evolutionary economic geography. *Journal of Economic Geography* 7: 537–548.

Buchanan, R. H. 2006. Emyr Estyn Evans (1905–1989). In P. H. Armstrong and G. J. Martin, (eds), *Geographers: biobibliographical studies,* Volume 25. London: Continuum, 13–33.

Bunge, W. 1966. *Theoretical geography* (second edition). Lund: C. W. K. Gleerup.

Chisholm, M. 1962. *Rural settlement and land use.* London: Hutchison.

2001. Human geography joins the Social Science Research Council: personal recollections. *Area* 33: 428–430.

Chorley, R. J., Beckinsale, R. P. and Dunn, A. J. 1973. *The history of the study of landforms, volume 2: the life and work of William Morris Davis.* London: Methuen.

Chorley, R. J., and Haggett, P. (eds). 1965. *Frontiers in geographical teaching.* London: Methuen.

(eds). 1967. *Models in geography.* London: Methuen.

Christaller, W. 1933. *Die zentralen Orte in Süddeutschland.* Jena: G Fischer. (Translated by C. W. Baskin as *Central places in southern Germany.* Englewood Cliffs NJ: Prentice-Hall, 1966.)

Cloke, P., Crang, P. and Goodwin, M. (eds). 1999. *Introducing human geographies.* London: Arnold.

2004. *Envisioning human geographies.* London: Arnold.

Cloke, P. J., Philo, C. and Sadler, D. 1991. *Approaching human geography: an introduction to contemporary theoretical debates.* London: Paul Chapman.

Clout, H. D. 2003. Place description, regional geography and area studies: the chorographic inheritance. In R. J. Johnston and M. Williams (eds), *A century of British geography.* Oxford: Oxford University Press for the British Academy, 247–274.

2009. *Patronage and the production of geographical knowledge in France: the testimony of the first hundred regional monographs, 1905–1966.* London: Royal Geographical Society (with the Institute of British Geographers), Historical Geography Research Group.

Cole, J. P. 1969. Mathematics and geography. *Geography* 54: 162–173.

Cosgrove, D. 2001. *Apollo's Eye: a cartographic genealogy of the Earth in the western imagination.* Baltimore MD: Johns Hopkins University Press.

2007. *Geography and vision: seeing, imagining and representing the world.* London: I. B. Tauris.

Cosgrove, D. and Jackson, P. 1987. New directions in cultural geography. *Area* 19: 95–101.

Curry, L. 2002. A random walk in terra incognita. In F. R. Pitts and P. R. Gould (eds), *Geographical voices: fourteen autobiographical essays.* Syracuse: Syracuse University Press, 81–98.

Darby, H. C. 2002. *The relations of geography and history.* Exeter: University of Exeter Press.

David, T. 1958. Against geography. *Universities Quarterly* 12: 261–273.

Dunbar, G. S. (ed.). 2002. *Geography: discipline, profession and subject since 1870: an international survey.* Amsterdam: Kluwer.

Duncan, S. S. 1974. The isolation of scientific discovery: indifference and resistance to a new idea. *Science Studies* 4: 109–134.

Embleton, C. and Coppock, J. T. (eds). 1968. *Land use and resources: studies in applied geography – a memorial volume to Sir Dudley Stamp.* London: Institute of British Geographers, Special Publication 1.

Entrikin, J. N. and Brunn, S. D. (eds). 1990. *Reflections on Richard Hartshorne's 'The nature of geography'.* Washington DC: Association of American Geographers.

Frickel, S. and Gross, N. 2005. A general theory of scientific/intellectual movements. *American Sociological Review* 70: 204–222.

Gaile, G. L. and Willmott, C. J. (eds). 2004. *Geography in America at the dawn of the 21st century.* Indianapolis: Bobbs Merrill.

Garrison, W. L. 1959–1960. Spatial structure of the economy: I, II and III. *Annals of the Association of American Geographers* 49: 238–249 and 471–482, and 590, 357–373.

Giddens, A. 1984. *The constitution of society.* Cambridge: Polity Press.

Golledge, R. G. and Stimson, R. J. 1997. *Spatial behaviour: a geographic perspective.* London: Guilford.

Goodchild, M. F. 1992. Geographical information science. *International Journal of Geographical Information Systems* 6: 31–45.

2008. Statistical perspectives on geographic information science. *Geographical Analysis* 40: 310–325.

Gould, P. R. 1979. Geography 1957–1977: the Augean period. *Annals of the Association of American Geographers* 69: 139–151.

Gregory, D. 1978. *Ideology, science and human geography*. London: Hutchinson.

2004. *The colonial present: Afghanistan, Palestine, Iraq*. Oxford: Blackwell Publishers.

Gregory, S. 1963. *Statistical methods and the geographer*. London: Longman.

Hägerstrand, T. 1953. *Innovationsförloppet ur korologisk synpunkt*. Lund: C W K Gleerup. (Translated by A. Pred as *Innovation diffusion as a spatial process*. Chicago, IL: University of Chicago Press, 1967.)

Haggett, P. 1965. *Locational analysis in human geography*. London: Edward Arnold.

2008a. The spirit of quantitative geography. *Geographical Analysis* 40: 226–228.

2008b. The local shape of revolution: reflections on quantitative geography at Cambridge in the 1950s and 1960s. *Geographical Analysis* 40: 336–352.

Hall, P. 1966. *The isolated state* (a translation, by Carla Wartenberg, of J. H. von Thünen's *Die isolieert Staat*, originally published in 1826). Oxford: Pergamon Press.

Halsey, A. H. and Runciman, W. G. (eds). 2006. *British sociology: seen from without and within*. Oxford: Oxford University Press for the British Academy.

Harris, C. D. 2001. English as international language in geography: development and limitations. *The Geographical Review* 91: 675–689.

Harris, C. D. and Ullman, E. L. 1945. The nature of cities. *Annals of the American Academy of Political and Social Science* 242: 7–17.

Hart, J. F. 1982. The highest form of the geographer's art. *Annals of the Association of American Geographers* 72: 1–29.

Hartshorne, R. 1939. *The nature of geography*. Lancaster PA: Association of American Geographers.

1959. *Perspective on the nature of geography*. Chicago, IL: Rand McNally for Association of American Geographers.

Harvey, D. W. 1969. *Explanation in geography*. London: Edward Arnold.

1973. *Social justice and the city*. London: Edward Arnold.

1982. *The limits to capital*. Oxford: Blackwell Publishers.

1985a. *The urbanization of capital*. Oxford: Blackwell Publishers.

1985b. The geopolitics of capitalism. In D. Gregory and J. Urry, (eds), *Social relations and spatial structures*. London: Macmillan, 128–163.

1989. *The condition of postmodernity*. Oxford: Blackwell Publishers.

1996. *Justice, nature and the geography of difference*. Oxford: Blackwell Publishers.

2003. *The new imperialism*. Oxford: Oxford University Press.

2007. *A brief history of neo-liberalism*. Oxford: Oxford University Press.

Hoover, E. M. 1948. *The location of economic activity*. New York: McGraw Hill.

Isard, W. 1956. *Location and space economy*. New York: John Wiley.

2003. *History of regional science and the Regional Science Association International: the beginnings and early history*. Berlin: Springer.

Jackson, A., Harris, R., Hepple, L. W., Hoare, A. G., Johnston, R. J., Jones, K. and Plummer, P. 2006. Geography's changing lexicon: measuring disciplinary change through content analysis. *Geoforum* 37: 447–454.

James, P. E. and Jones, C. F. (eds). 1954. *American geography: inventory and prospect*. Syracuse: Syracuse University Press.

Johnston, R. J. 1978. Paradigms and revolution: observations on human geography since the Second World War. *Progress in Human Geography* 2: 189–206.

2003a. The institutionalisation of geography as an academic discipline. In R. J. Johnston and M. Williams (eds), *A century of British geography*. Oxford: Oxford University Press for the British Academy, 45–97.

2003b. Order in space: geography as a discipline in distance. In R. J. Johnston and M. Williams (eds), *A century of British geography*. Oxford: Oxford University Press for the British Academy, 303–346.

2004a. Institutions and disciplinary fortunes: two moments in the history of UK geography in the 1960s – I: geography in the 'plateglass universities'. *Progress in Human Geography* 28: 57–78.

2004b. Institutions and disciplinary fortunes: two moments in the history of UK geography in the 1960s – II: human geography and the Social Science Research Council. *Progress in Human Geography* 28: 204–226.

2004c. Communications technology and the production of geographical knowledge. In S. D. Brunn , S. L. Cutter and J. W. Harrington Jr. (eds), *Geography and technology*. Boston: Kluwer, 17–36.

2006. The politics of changing human geography's agenda: textbooks and the representation of increasing diversity. *Transactions of the Institute of British Geographers* NS31: 286–303

2009. Popular geographies and geographical imaginations: contemporary English-language geographical magazines. *GeoJournal* 74: 347–362.

Johnston, R. J. and Claval, P., (eds). 1984. *Geography since the Second World War: an international survey*. London: Croom Helm.

Johnston, R. J., Fairbrother, M., Hayes, D., Hoare, T. and Jones, J. 2008. The Cold War and geography's quantitative revolution: some messy reflections on Barnes' geographical underworld. *Geoforum* 39: 1802–1806.

Johnston, R. J. and Sidaway, J. D. 2004a. *Geography and geographers: Anglo-American human geography since 1945* (sixth edition). London: Arnold.

2004b. The trans-Atlantic connection: 'Anglo-American' geography reconsidered. *GeoJournal* 59: 15–22.

2007. Geography in higher education in the UK. *Journal of Geography in Higher Education* 31: 57–80.

Kain, R. and Delano-Smith, C. 2003. Geography displayed: maps and mapping. In R. J. Johnston and M. Williams, (eds), *A century of British geography*. Oxford: Oxford University Press for the British Academy, 371–427.

King, L. J. (ed.). 2007. *North American explorations: ten memoirs of geographers from down under*. Victoria BC: Trafford Publications.

Krugman, P. 1993. *Geography and trade*. Cambridge MA: The MIT Press.

Kuhn, T. S. 1970. *The structure of scientific revolutions*. Chicago, IL: University of Chicago Press.

Latour, B. 1999. *Pandora's hope: essays on the reality of science studies*. Cambridge MA: Harvard University Press.

Lavalle, P., McConnell, H. and Brown, R. G. 1967. Certain aspects of the expansion of quantitative methodology in American geography. *Annals of the Association of American Geographers* 57: 423–436.

Leighly, J. (ed.). 1963. *Land and life: a selection from the writings of Carl Ortwin Sauer*. Berkeley, CA: University of California Press.

Livingstone, D. N. 1992. *The geographical tradition: episodes in the history of a contested enterprise.* Oxford: Basil Blackwell.

2003a. British geography 1500–1900: an imprecise review. In R. J. Johnston and M. Williams (eds), *A century of British geography.* Oxford: Oxford University Press for the British Academy, 11–44.

2003b. *Putting science in its place: geographies of scientific knowledge.* Chicago: University of Chicago Press.

2005. Science, text and space: thoughts on the geography of reading. *Transactions of the Institute of British Geographers* NS30: 391–401.

Longley, P. and Clarke, G. P. (eds). 1995. *GIS for business and service planning.* Cambridge: GeoInformation International.

Longley, P., Goodchild, M., Maguire, D. and Rhind, D. W. (eds). 1999. *Geographical information systems: principles, techniques, applications and management (second edition).* New York: John Wiley.

Longley, P., Goodchild, M., Maguire, D. and Rhind, D. W. 2001. *Geographic information systems and science.* New York: John Wiley.

Lösch, A. 1954. *The economics of location.* New Haven CT: Yale University Press.

McDowell, L. 1993a. Space, place and gender relations: part I. Feminist empiricism and the geography of social relations. *Progress in Human Geography* 17: 157–179.

1993b. Space, place and gender relations: Part II. Identity, difference, feminist geometries and feminist geographies. *Progress in Human Geography* 17: 305–318.

1997. *Capital culture: gender at work in the city.* Oxford: Blackwell.

Maddrell, A. 2009. *Complex locations: women's geographical work in the UK 1850–1970.* Chichester: Wiley-Blackwell.

Marcus, M. G. 1979. Coming full circle: physical geography in the twentieth century. *Annals of the Association of American Geographers* 69: 521–532.

Martin, R. L. 1999. The 'new geographical turn' in economics: some critical reflections. *Cambridge Journal of Economics* 23: 65–92.

Massey, D. 1984. *Spatial divisions of labour: social structures and the geography of production.* London: Macmillan (second edition, 1995).

Massey, D. and Meegan, P. A. 1982. *The anatomy of job loss.* London: Methuen.

Mead, W. R. 2007. *Adopting Finland.* Helsinki: Niilo Helander Foundation.

Morrill, R. L. 2005. Hägerstrand and the 'quantitative revolution': a personal appreciation. *Progress in Human Geography* 6: 333–336.

Murphy, A. B. 2007. Geography's place in higher education in the USA. *Journal of Geography in Higher Education* 31: 121–141.

NAS/NRC 1965. *The science of geography.* Washington DC: National Academy of Sciences/National Research Council.

1997. *Rediscovering geography: new relevance for science and society.* Washington DC: National Academy of Sciences/National Research Council.

Öhman, J. and Simonsen, K. (eds). 2003. *Voices from the North: new trends in Nordic human geography.* Aldershot: Ashgate.

Olsson, G. 2007. *Abysmal: a critique of cartographic reason.* Chicago, IL: University of Chicago Press.

Poole, R. M. 2004. *Explorer's house: 'National Geographic' and the world it made.* New York: Penguin Books.

Pred, A. 1967–1969. *Behavior and location: foundations for a geographic and dynamic location theory. Parts I and II.* Lund: C. W. K. Gleerup.

Prince, H. C. 2000. *Geographers engaged in historical geography in British higher education, 1931–1991.* London: Historical Geography Research Group, Publication 36.

Rawling, E. 2001. *Changing the subject: the impact of national policy on school geography 1980–2000.* Sheffield: The Geographical Association.

Rawstron, E. M. 2002. Textbooks that moved generations. *Progress in Human Geography* 26: 831–836.

Rhind, D. 2003. The geographical underpinning of society and its radical transition. In R. J. Johnston and M. Williams, (eds), *A century of British geography.* Oxford: Oxford University Press for the British Academy, 428–461.

Robbins, P. 2004. *Political ecology: a critical introduction.* Oxford: Blackwell.

Rose, G. 1993. *Feminism and geography.* Cambridge: Polity Press.

    2003. Just how, exactly, is geography visual? *Antipode* 35: 212–221.

    2007. *Visual methodologies: an introduction to interpreting visual materials.* London: Sage.

Sayer, A. 1984. *Method in social science: a realist approach.* London: Hutchinson.

Scargill, D. I. 1976: The RGS and the foundations of geography at Oxford. *The Geographical Journal* 142: 438–461.

Schulten, S. 2001. *The geographical imagination in America, 1880–1950.* Chicago, IL: University of Chicago Press.

Sheppard, E. 1995. Dissenting from spatial analysis. *Urban Geography* 16: 283–303.

Slater, T. R. 1988. Redbrick academic geography. *The Geographical Journal* 154: 169–180.

Smith, D. M. 1994. *Geography and social justice.* Oxford: Blackwell Publishers.

Stamp, L. D. 1960. *Applied geography.* London: Penguin.

Steel, R. W. 1983. *The Institute of British Geographers: the first fifty years.* London: The Institute of British Geographers.

Stevens, A. 1921. *Applied geography.* Glasgow: Blackie.

Stoddart, D. R. 1986. *On geography and its history.* Oxford: Blackwell Publishers.

Sluyter, A., Augustine, A. D., Bitton, M. C., Sullivan, T. J. and Wang, F. 2006. The recent intellectual structure of geography. *The Geographical Review* 96: 594–608.

Taaffe, E. J. 1970. *Geography.* Englewood Cliffs NJ: Prentice-Hall.

Taylor, P. J. 1976. An interpretation of the quantification debate in British geography. *Transactions, Institute of British Geographers* NS1: 129–142.

Thomas, W. L. Jr. (ed.). 1956. *Man's role in changing the face of the earth.* Chicago, IL: University of Chicago Press.

Turner, B. L., Clark, W. C., Kates, R. W., Richards, J. F., Matthews, J. T. and Meyer, W. B. (eds). 1990. *The earth as transformed by human action: global and regional changes in the biosphere over the past 300 years.* Cambridge: Cambridge University Press.

Ullman, E. L. 1941. A theory of location for cities. *American Journal of Sociology* 46: 853–864.

    1956. The role of transportation and the bases for interaction. In W. L. Thomas, (ed.), *Man's role in changing the face of the earth.* Chicago, IL: University of Chicago Press, 862–880.

Vidal de la Blache, P. 1911. Les genres de vie dans la géographie humaine. *Annales de Géographie* 20: 193–212.

Walford, R. 2001. *Geography in British schools 1850–2000* London: Woburn Press.

Weber, A. 1929. *Alfred Weber's theory of the location of industries* (translated by C. J. Freidrich of the German version published in 1909). Chicago: University of Chicago Press.

Whitehand, J. W. R. 1970. Innovation diffusion in an academic discipline: the case of the 'new' geography. *Area* 17: 277–283.

Withers, C. W. J. and Mayhew, R. J. 2002. Rethinking disciplinary history: geography in British universities, c. 1580–1887. *Progress in Human Geography* 27: 11–29.

Women and Geography Study Group, 1984. *Geography and gender: an introduction to feminist geography*. London: Hutchinson.

1997. *Feminist geographers: explorations in diversity and difference*. Harlow: Longman.

Wooldridge, S. W. and East, W. G. 1958. *The spirit and purpose of geography*. London: Hutchinson.

Yeates, M. H. 2001. Yesterday as tomorrow's song: the contribution of the 1960s 'Chicago School' to urban geography. *Urban Geography* 22: 514–529.

8

Toward a History of the Social Sciences

Roger E. Backhouse and Philippe Fontaine

We need to characterize American society of the mid-twentieth century in more psychological terms ... for now the problems that concern us most border on the psychiatric.

C. Wright Mills (1951, p. 160).[1]

The Second World War and Its Aftermath

It is hard to overestimate the significance of the Second World War for the social sciences as a whole, even though its importance varied from one social science to another. The war and its aftermath brought about profound changes in Western societies, creating new problems that provided opportunities for social scientists to demonstrate their expertise. In the postwar decades, notably the 1960s, as a result of their efforts to tackle urgent social problems, the traditional domains of the social sciences were redefined. Of course many of the conceptual frameworks or paradigms within which social scientists operated had roots that went much further back, but the changed context brought about profound transformations. The most obvious change concerned the political position of the United States in relation to Europe: to quote British historian Tony Judt (2007, p. 13), "Europe in the aftermath of the Second World War offered a prospect of utter misery and desolation. ... Europeans *felt* hopeless, they *were* exhausted – and for good reason." The physical destruction had been immense, the death toll, especially among civilians, vastly higher than that in the First World War, and at the end of the war tens of millions of people were displaced, in part as a result of "an unprecedented exercise in ethnic cleansing and population

For acknowledgments relevant to this chapter, see the Preface to the volume.

[1] Quoted in Herman (1995, p. 7; 1998).

transfer" (p. 24): Europe was in chaos and the split between East and West was accentuated.[2]

An important effect of this turmoil was that many Germans and other East Europeans had been forced to migrate westward, most of them ending up in the United States. Though the process had started in the early 1930s, its effects were more visible after the war. Germany, a key pole in the social sciences until the 1920s, had clearly lost this position by 1945.[3] The émigrés included large numbers of social scientists. The academic credentials of those who obtained academic posts by virtue of their Nazi- party connections were often weak. The leading German economists were either forced to migrate or, like Walter Eucken in Freiburg, severely constrained in their activities (Hagemann 2000). Postwar economic policy in West Germany was set by the Freiburg School, dominated by Eucken, whose members were among the minority who had resisted the Nazis. Economics in East Germany was reduced to a Marxist–Leninist orthodoxy. In psychology, a high proportion of full professors remained in their post until the 1950s when they were replaced by a younger generation. But aside from this weakening of German academia, the dire economic position of Germany in the postwar years meant that it was both very difficult and unattractive for American social scientists to visit, unless the visits were linked to the occupying forces.[4] After the war, American occupation officials and foundations helped reconstruct parts of German sociology, a relationship that would have been inconceivable earlier in the century.[5] Human and material resources had become overwhelmingly concentrated in the United States. As with European culture more generally, the combination of profound change and American dominance fed, in

---

[2] To put this in perspective, Judt (2007, pp. 22–32) notes that the U.N. Relief and Rehabilitation Administration (UNRRA) and other Allied agencies were responsible for looking after almost 7 million people, with a similar number placed under Soviet authority.

[3] Manicas (1991, p. 48) recalls "that the majority of the 9,000 Americans who studied in Germany between 1820 and 1920 did their studies in the 'social sciences' in the last decades of the nineteenth century."

[4] An interesting example is provided by Talcott Parsons who visited Germany and other countries in the summer of 1948. Parsons was sent by the Russian Research Center with a view to exploring the possibilities of an interview program with Soviet escapees. On that occasion, Parsons met with military government personnel and a number of émigrés themselves (Diamond 1992, p. 89; Gerhardt 2002, p. 179). Other examples include the economist John Kenneth Galbraith and political scientist Gabriel A. Almond, who both worked in Germany for the U.S. Strategic Bombing Survey (Almond and Krauss 1999; Parker 2005, pp. 177–88)

[5] For examples, see Weyer (1984) and Gerhardt (2007). We are indebted to Jennifer Platt for these references.

the ensuing decades, into discussions of whether the social sciences had become Americanized.[6]

Many social scientists had been recruited to the war effort on both sides. In the United States, social scientists from many disciplines had become involved in intelligence work, often through the Office of Strategic Services.[7] Working alongside natural scientists and engineers, economists tackled problems related to military strategy and tactics as well as more traditional economic topics.[8] Objectives were much more clearly defined than in peacetime, with the result that the emphasis was generally on efficient resource allocation. Economists, therefore, came increasingly to see their subject in terms of social engineering in order to achieve goals that were externally given (Morgan 2003). This led many economists to part company with sociology and political science (except in relation to the parts of those disciplines that took up the rational choice model). Until the 1950s, there were several departments of "economics and sociology" in the United States and several departments of "economics and political science" in Canada, but the trend, except in very small institutions, was for these disciplines to separate.[9]

Psychologists were likewise involved in the war effort and their attention to practical problems took up a more collective dimension, going from the natural inclination to address personal difficulties to the handling of group problems and, more generally, social forces (Capshew 1999; Geuter 1992). Psychologists became more aware of the demands for social management, and decision makers in government and business realized that the experts

---

[6] Needless to say, the academic success of many of these German (and other) émigré social scientists depended on the degree of coherence between their methods and objectives on the one hand and the practices of the relevant social sciences in the United States on the other. That is especially true of political science where Gerhard Loewenberg (2006, pp. 597–8) has underscored the impact of Leo Strauss and Hannah Arendt on political theory, Hans Morgenthau on international relations, Theodor W. Adorno on social theory, and Henry Ehrmann, John Herz, Otto Kirchheimer, Franz Neumann, and Sigmund Neumann on comparative politics.

[7] James G. Miller (1996) provided a lively and instructive account of his work as a psychologist at the OSS selection program during the Second World War. On the OSS's Research and Analysis Branch (R&A), the so-called Chairborne Division, see Katz's *Foreign Intelligence* (1989).

[8] Economists were especially active at OSS, the Enemy Objectives Unit, and the Statistical Research Group (see Guglielmo 2008). One example is Walt Rostow whose "job was to identify which German military targets were most vulnerable to Anglo-American bombing" (Milne 2008, p. 32; see also Lodewijks 1991).

[9] It is worth noting that these changes, when combined with the massive expansion of the higher education system in the United States, served to bring about a very marked, and comparatively rapid, generational shift in many disciplines.

charged with handling postwar problems could benefit from results of psychological research (Hermann 1995).

Sociology witnessed a parallel movement: "The career experience of sociologists in the war comprised two types of service – in war-related research and in the military" (Abbott and Sparrow 2007, p. 286). Sociologists were especially present in the Department of Agriculture. In the process, empirical research, already widespread before the war, was consolidated alongside attempts at generalization as an essential part of the discipline. By the mid-1940s, in a context where sociologists may have felt that their subject enjoyed greater academic acceptance, several voices were rising to show the compatibility between the two approaches. In an issue commemorating the fiftieth anniversary of the *American Journal of Sociology*, Robert Merton (1945, p. 462), for instance, was confident that "[g]eneralizations can be tempered, if not with mercy, at least with disciplined observation; close, detailed observations need not be rendered trivial by avoidance of their theoretical pertinence and implications." However, in the late 1950s, some sociologists (e.g., Mills 1959) still regarded these two orientations as distinct if not opposed, and by the time Alvin Gouldner's critique of scientism was articulated in *The Coming Crisis of Western Sociology* (1970), the debate had shifted away from Merton's emphasis on the possibility of mutual coexistence.[10]

In social anthropology, there had been a reorientation of the discipline toward policy issues before the war. Whereas they had previously focused on Southeast Asia, anthropologists became involved, in the 1920s and 1930s, in the search for a system of indirect rule in Britain's African empire (see Kuper, Chapter 6, pp. 142, 144–5). Anthropologists could participate in the war effort, for they knew about many of the Asian societies in which fighting took place. Following the death of Franz Boas in 1942, anthropology gained momentum in the United States, bringing about a shift to cultural anthropology. This shift reflected Boas's particularism – "his stress on the uniqueness of each culture and its historical particularity" (Applebaum 1987, p. 2).[11] Though serving to establish cultural anthropology, during and after the war, the value of such work lay in its military relevance. Thanks to their linguistic and cultural skills, anthropologists became indispensable to

---

[10] Abbott and Sparrow (2007, p. 285) note that by 1955, "the discipline was dominated ... by the odd marriage of survey analysis and Parsonian theory, symbolized by the pairings of Stouffer and Parsons at Harvard and Lazarsfeld and Merton at Columbia."

[11] Following Franz Boas's denunciation, in a letter to *The Nation* in 1919 (reprinted in Simpson 1998, pp. 1–2) of the use of anthropologists as spies in the First World War, there had been considerable discussion of ethical issues in the discipline.

the military and intelligence agencies, and they were employed in a number of activities from espionage and training guerilla fighters, to producing manuals for the use of military personnel (Price 2008).

Geography did not exist as a social science before the Second World War and geographers had few contacts with social scientists (see Johnston Chapter 7, p. 156). This changed with the war. Susan Schulten (2001, p. 204) reminded us that "[o]n Friday, February 20, 1942, President Roosevelt asked Americans to buy a map of the world. In his noontime radio address Roosevelt announced that he would explain the nation's wartime strategy over the airwaves the following Monday and that a clear sense of geography would greatly facilitate this task." The war brought to the front new realities that geography could help understand better if only because of its familiarity with maps and their power to create knowledge. In a sense the war, because of its demands for practical knowledge, fostered the dialogue between the traditional social sciences and geography, and in the process helped the latter gained a better understanding of the techniques, concepts, and theories of the former.[12] As Schulten observed, the "power of geography to shape history is difficult to apprehend" (2001, p. 241). However, as Neil Smith (2003) showed in his detailed study of the career of Isaiah Bowman, "Roosevelt's geographer," geographers played a far from negligible part in the U.S. advance toward world hegemony.

The war brought about changes the nature of which was still unclear to many in the mid-1940s. Sociologist George A. Lundberg, in "The Social Sciences in the Post-War Era" (1945, p. 138), betrayed some of these uncertainties when he wrote: "That attitude [toward social research] has been, to a large extent, that social research was a kind of luxury to which surplus funds might be devoted as a sort of advertising stunt reflecting the benevolence of the donors, or in any event as a side issue not vitally concerned

---

[12] Barnes (2006) provides a telling account of the contributions of a number of American geographers, including Richard Hartshorne, to the Research and Analysis Branch of OSS. Barnes notes that in early 1943, "the former discipline-based grid of organization at R&A [including the Geography Division] was abandoned. After that date, research and analysis was organized geographically by theatre area" (p. 154), which increased geographers' exposure to other social sciences. In particular, geographers had "to translate their vocabularies and skills into the new form of military intelligence" (p. 158), which eventually helped geography's quantitative revolution from the mid-1950s. On the latter's origins in Cold War military imperatives, see Barnes (2008). Drawing on the U.K. case, Johnston et alii (2008) suggest that the origins of the quantitative revolution in geography were more diverse and messy. Robic (2003, p. 379) also notes increasing interactions between geography and other social sciences in the postwar era though she emphasizes its integration into the human sciences as opposed to the earth sciences.

with the serious business of managing society. If social research is really to flourish, this view must change. Sooner or later it will change." It did.[13]

Nevertheless, despite this uncertainty, the social sciences emerged from the Second World War greatly strengthened and less divided. Wartime projects encouraged cross-disciplinary endeavors among social sciences themselves and between social sciences and other disciplines as well. Economics had demonstrated its value both to the government and the armed forces through assisting in the solution of highly technical problems; it was needed after the war to ensure that the events of the 1930s were not repeated. Psychology also achieved a reputation for having been essential to the war effort – paradoxically, because the psychological screening of recruits had failed to achieve its intended objective. After the war, psychologists were needed to deal with the mental health problems of ex-servicemen; most psychologists were engaged in clinical and personnel work (Britt and Morgan 1946). At the same time, anthropologists began increasingly to engage with other social sciences, with the case of Clyde Kluckhohn at the Harvard Department of Social Relations being exemplary in that respect. Human geographers, who were beginning to see themselves as social scientists, began to develop relations with traditional social sciences. Finally, political science, institutionally a purely American discipline before the war, established an independent existence in many European universities.[14]

Social Science, Politics, and Society

The postwar period was one in which social scientists were often led to emphasize their scientific credentials. Labels such as "positive economics," "positivism," "behaviorism," and the techniques for empirical analysis developed under them sought to aim at objective inquiry, not tainted by opinion or ideology. "Opinion" and "ideology" were to be the subjects of scientific analysis, not its drivers. This was perhaps clearest in political science in which, while political philosophy involving the study of classic texts on the normative theory of politics might still serve as a unifying factor in the curriculum, the focus shifted to the analysis of how political processes worked: public opinion became something measurable to be used alongside

[13] Solovey (2004) has provided a telling illustration of the uncertain future of the social sciences in the context of the immediate postwar national science debate.

[14] Vout (1991), for instance, describes the emergence of political science in postwar England between 1945 and 1960, with special emphasis on Oxford.

the analysis of how political parties worked. Though the theory of pluralism, developed by Robert Dahl and others, which dominated American political science in the 1960s (Merelman 2003), could be seen as offering a political philosophy to justify American democratic institutions, it was, at least ostensibly, rooted in analysis of how democracies worked. As such, it was connected with some of the attempts to develop a pluralist theory of democracy in the 1920s (Gunnell 2004). This perspective of the social role of the social scientist lay behind the focus on elites in work as different as the Yale school's pluralism (see Gilman 2003, pp. 50–2) and sociologist Wright Mills's Marxian analysis of *The Power Elite* (1956).[15] However, politics did not concern social science only as an object of research, for the social sciences were themselves subject to political pressures.[16]

The Second World War was soon followed by the Cold War, which was in large part a cultural war in which the battle zones were first the newly liberated countries of Europe and later the people of Africa, Latin America, and Asia. Social scientists were involved in this cultural war, as well as becoming

---

[15] Mills was arguably not a Marxist in that his concept of the power elite differentiates his approach from Marx's analysis in terms of a ruling class, but it was clearly inspired by Marx. This shared attitude reflects the closeness between political science and sociology in this period. Paul Lazarsfeld (1901–76), an Austrian forced by political developments to migrate to the United States, provides a clear illustration. He was "one of the pioneers in using the survey method for social science purposes" (Barton 1979, p. 6), seeking to make the study of public opinion more quantitative. After studying economics, political theory, and mathematics (where he got his doctorate), he began to use surveys in the analysis of social phenomena in the late 1920s and early 1930 at the Psychological Institute in Vienna (Lazarsfeld 1969). While in the United States on a Rockefeller fellowship to visit universities and research centers, in 1933–34, civil war and the banning of the socialist party in Austria made the prospects of going back unappealing. As a result, Lazarsfeld stayed in the United States. In the fall of 1937, he was associated with a project, proposed by Princeton social psychologist Hadley Cantril and funded by the Rockefeller Foundation, to study the social effects of radio on American society. The project resulted in the setting up of an Office of Radio Research (ORR) at Princeton though Lazarsfeld continued to work in Newark. Thanks to his appointment at Columbia, however, the ORR was moved there in 1940 and later renamed the Bureau of Applied Social Research. With the help of sociologists, including Merton (from 1941) and to a lesser extent Wright Mills (from 1945), Lazarsfeld used survey research to examine a variety of human behavior, with the classic study of the American Presidential election of 1940 and its final report, *The People's Choice* (1944), standing as a major contribution to the analysis of voting behavior (Converse 2006, p. 605).

[16] Cantril also wrote *Invasion from Mars*, a 1940 study of the events associated with the Orson Welles's "War of the Worlds" radio broadcast of October 1938. Regarding the relatively limited multidisciplinarity of the Bureau in comparison with similar postwar ventures, it should be noted that it took a surprisingly long time for the Columbia administration to recognize the significance of the Bureau's work and to provide adequate support for its activities.

caught up in a regime, stemming from the Second World War, in which a significant part of their funding came from private foundations, such as Carnegie, Ford, and Rockefeller; from the Social Science Research Council (SSRC); and from military research agencies. By the late 1950s, a second patronage system began to take form, in which civilian, federal agencies, such as the National Science Foundation and the National Institutes of Health, were especially influential (Crowther-Heyck 2006a).[17] In the United States, there was also the spectre of McCarthyism – the rooting out of communists, former communists, or suspected communists within the United States. When, in the 1960s, the Cold War evolved into full-scale American military involvement in Vietnam, the political context changed.[18] Radical ideas from the left challenged the social sciences in all countries. However, such movements were overtaken by the economic crisis of the mid-1970s and the rise of radical conservatism, which set the agenda for the rest of the twentieth century and the opening years of the twenty-first.

American culture came to Europe during the war, symbolized by the contrast between the young, confident, and affluent GIs and the defeated German soldiers. This American culture appealed to the young who wanted to rebel against their parents' generation, reinforced in occupied countries by their desire to distance themselves from Nazi and Fascist ideologies. The devastation of Europe meant that there was no effective local competition. But on top of this was a concerted attempt, starting from the activities of the Office of War Information, to create a favorable image of the United States. American expenditure on cultural foreign policy grew substantially until, by 1953, over 13,000 people were employed in foreign cultural programs (Wagnleitner 1994, p. 57). These extended to popular culture, in which radio was particularly important (Wagnleitner 1994), to longer-established cultural activities (such as educational exchanges and libraries) and attempts to draw intellectuals away from communism (Berghann 2001; Saunders 1999).[19]

---

[17] Among organizations committed to social and behavioral sciences, the Russel Sage Foundation should also be mentioned (Wheeler 1994).

[18] Robin Winks's *The Cold War: From Yalta to Cuba* (1964) provides an informative and telling account of world uncertainties right before the Vietnam War. Solovey (2001) analyses the military-sponsored Project Camelot, which was canceled in 1965 while controversy was raging over the connections between military patronage and American social science.

[19] Mention should be made as well of the project to bring unity to diversity, which was organized within the Social Sciences Department of Unesco in the late 1940s and early 1950s. Influenced by the SSRC model, that project encouraged cross-disciplinary orientations (Selcer 2009).

Clearly, social scientists will not have been immune to these developments, and some were caught up with activities such as the Central Intelligence Agency (CIA)-funded Congress for Cultural Freedom. However, their implications ran deeper, for social scientists were caught up in this cultural cold war through the project of making the "cold war enemy" (Robin 2001). The analysis of communist societies and the planning of anticommunist propaganda required a wide range of social scientists. This financial support was part of a much broader Cold War funding of science that included the social sciences. Social science clearly received much less funding, in absolute terms, than the natural sciences, but government funding of social science was nonetheless very substantial and helped underwrite the massive expansion that took place between the Second World War and the 1970s (Crowther-Heyck 2005). In the United States, this came through a variety of channels but the political justification was the need to strengthen American science in the context of the Cold War. The National Science Foundation (NSF) , established in 1950, initiated a Social Science Research Program in 1957. Despite the failure to establish a separate National Social Science Foundation, in 1968 social science was eventually granted "the formal status it initially lacked as part of the NSF mandate" (Herman 1998, p. 114; see also Solovey 2009). There was also significant funding of science through the CIA and the armed forces. Not only did it become far more common for individual social scientists to acknowledge financial support for their research, a substantial part of such funding came from defense-related sources, such as the Office of Naval Research. There was also very substantial support for research centers across the social sciences. Close links developed between providers of government funding and private foundations, such as Ford and Rockefeller. It is impossible to avoid the conclusion that such funding must, through selection bias if nothing else, have influenced the course of social science research. Yet, though some academics may have avoided contentious research in order to obtain funding, it remains true that much highly controversial social science research was undertaken (Crowther-Heyck 2005, p. 427).[20]

---

[20] Another issue is that some characteristics of academic research from the late 1940s and early 1950s were already in place during the Second World War or even predated it. David Engerman (2003) criticizes the Cold War overdeterminism of those narratives that tend to use the image of pure universities to emphasize emerging political interference in the Cold War era. Instead, he strives to "put the Cold War back into American history and into the international history of the twentieth century" (Engerman 2007, p. 621; see also Engerman 2009). In her study on Stanford, Rebecca Lowen (1997) similarly argues that in order to understand the way universities responded to the Cold War, consideration of prewar conflicts and concerns is necessary.

CIA involvement in social sciences is clearly illustrated by the emergence of area studies, which was driven by the need for intelligence. McGeorge Bundy, Dean of Arts and Sciences at Harvard for much of the 1950s, and National Security Adviser to Presidents Kennedy and Johnson, observed that,

> It is a curious fact of academic history that the first great center of area studies [was] in the Office of Strategic Services. It is still true today [1964], and I hope it always will be, that there is a high measure of interpenetration between universities with area programs and the information-gathering agencies of the government. (quoted in Cumings 1998, p. 163)

In 1943, the Office of Strategic Services (OSS) established a USSR division, comprising sixty social scientists under the direction of a historian, Geriod T. Robinson, Professor of Russian History at Columbia. After the war, Robinson obtained support from the Rockefeller Foundation, effectively to continue this work in the Russian Institute at Columbia, established in 1946. Complemented in 1949 by institutes of Asian and European studies, this formed part of the School of International and Public Affairs (Cumings 1998, p. 163). Controversially, for some academics argued that such methods would produce dilettantes rather than serious scholars, it aimed to provide multidisciplinary training for those who had roots in a single discipline. Russian studies centers were established at Harvard and Berkeley in 1948, and by 1960 were to be found in thirteen universities. This paralleled a broader investment in area studies and language programs, into which the Ford Foundation alone put $270 million, spread over thirty-four universities, between 1953 and 1966 (p. 163). Ford's activity initially focused on Asia and the Middle East, followed first by Africa and eventually the Soviet Union and Eastern Europe, the region that eventually became the largest recipient of funds from its Foreign Area Fellowship Program. Such investment also took place outside the United States. The British journal *Soviet Studies*, for example, came from the University of Glasgow's Department for the Study of the Social and Economic Institutions of the USSR, with the aim of broadening the study of the Soviet Union beyond what was being undertaken in departments of Russian, in which the study of the Russian language was linked to literature rather than to Soviet society (Miller and Schlesinger 1949).[21]

---

[21] The journal had enough leftist sympathies for the Americans to contemplate the creation of an alternative scholarly outlet, *Soviet Survey*, with less colorful acquaintances. We are grateful to David Engerman for drawing our attention to this.

These developments started in the Second World War, but were continued as part of the Cold War. For example, as one of many actions taken in response to the launching of Sputnik, the National Defense Education Act (NDEA) of 1958 made significant funds available for area studies. In the early Cold War years, the main focus in area studies was the Soviet Union, but as the political climate changed, the emphasis shifted to other regions – China, Latin America, and Asia (Cumings 1998, pp. 160–2).[22] In Britain, a government report in 1961 by a committee chaired by a former diplomat, Sir William Hayter, led to the creation of ten centers for area studies, covering Asia (four), the Middle East, Africa, and Eastern Europe (two each). Attaching importance to the permeation of area studies into existing disciplines, 150 academic posts were earmarked for universities that wanted to appoint area specialists within nonlanguage departments (Hayter 1975).[23]

Another of the political pressures confronting postwar American academics was McCarthyism, a point made forcefully by Ellen Schrecker's *No Ivory Tower* (1986).[24] Before the publication of her book, it was common knowledge that government employees and artists had been the main targets of McCarthyism, but it was less appreciated that many in academe had suffered a similar ordeal. One thing that comes out of Schrecker's detailed investigation is that the notion of academic freedom was not only threatened during that period, but also more importantly, that no consensual definition could easily be identified at the height of the McCarthy era (p. 13).[25]

---

[22] As regards relations between disciplines, three points are relevant. (1) Though drawing on established disciplines, by virtue of being located in specialist centers, with their own specialist journals, and being involved in work that their disciplinary colleagues might not be able to follow because of language barriers, area studies had many of the features associated with academic disciplines. (2) Whereas early work brought together sociologists, anthropologists, historians, economists, and psychologists, the balance shifted firmly toward political science. Bonnell and Breslauer (2003, p. 12) point out that the number doctoral students supported by the Ford Foundation, a major source of such support, covered large numbers of political scientists, and hardly any sociologists or anthropologists. (3) Centers funded by State Department under the NDEA focused more on the humanities and history, as did United States-Soviet academic exchange programs.

[23] It is worth noting that the Committee visited U.S. universities and was supported by the Rockefeller Foundation.

[24] The situation was, of course, different elsewhere. At this time, Marxism flourished in many Western European countries. In the Soviet Union, the political pressures were even stronger and more direct.

[25] In the wake of the Senate's censure of McCarthy, Samuel Stouffer's *Communist, Conformity, and Civil Liberties* (1955) and Lazarsfeld and Wagner Thielens's *The Academic Mind* (1958) had already offered important insights into the subject.

The argument has been made that the fear of McCarthyism led to caution in tackling controversial issues and to the adoption of clearly "scientific" language. Economist Paul Samuelson (in Colander and Landreth 1996, p. 172), for example, has argued that his best-selling textbook prospered, where an earlier text with substantially the same content had fallen victim to anticommunist agitation, because his was written "carefully and lawyer-like."[26] However, it remains unclear whether the need to avoid antagonizing McCarthy and his acolytes directly influenced the way social scientists constructed their theories. That would have implied having a clear-cut idea of what the latter expected from academe, whereas it seems that McCarthy and his associates were less interested in controlling what was being written than in getting rid of real, past, and suspected Communists. At university, the red scare often meant that being, having been, or being suspected of being a Communist was simply incompatible with the normal duties of an academic teacher.

The social sciences were close to politics in a different way with the rise of radicalism at the time of the Vietnam War. This came at the end of a decade that saw a second massive increase in higher education, an expansion in which social science was, again, very significant. In Britain, for example, expansion involved the establishment of new universities, many of which (e.g., Sussex, Essex, Warwick) chose to specialize in social science. Aside from satisfying rising student demand for social science education, this strategy aimed to establish concentrations of social scientists that were large enough to challenge the dominance of established institutions. In France, there were similar developments, with the establishment of universities with strong humanities divisions such as Paris 8 – Vincennes (1969) and Paris 10 – Nanterre (1970). The creation of these universities played a significant part in absorbing the increasing flow of students from the mid-1960s, but it also reflected the political and social changes affecting French society. More open to the outside world, these universities were especially permeable to the social agitation of the late 1960s, and were also more inclined to pedagogical experimentation and innovation. By the mid-1970, social science education had become more firmly established, this being exemplified by the transformation of the Sixth Section of the École pratique des hautes études into the École des hautes études en sciences sociales.[27] In the United States, with its much less centralized university system, new universities were not

---

[26] For a fuller account of the episode in question, see Colander and Landreth 1998.
[27] The Sixth Section of the École pratique des hautes études was created in 1947 thanks to the financial assistance of the Rockefeller Foundation (Mazon 1988).

established in the same way, but between 1960 and 1970, the number of social science degrees almost tripled, rising from 13 percent to 19 percent of the total.[28] The closest parallel with European experience is probably the rise in the prestige of social science departments in some of the Midwestern universities that took advantage of the reluctance of established centers such as Harvard and Princeton to become involved in quantitative work. For example, the University of Iowa established its "stock market" in political candidates, and Ohio State and Michigan State established reputations relating to Congress and the Supreme Court.[29]

These changes were compounded with the social, political, economic, and intellectual challenges of the 1960s and 1970s, which were sufficiently powerful to alter the balance of power within many social science disciplines. However, permeability to social change varied according to every discipline. In economics and political science, radicalism hardly took hold. The strong disciplinary identity of economics meant that it could be comparatively immune to outside intellectual influences. Radical economics could develop, as it did in the Union for Radical Political Economy (URPE), established in 1968, but after a brief flurry of interest, it was marginalized (Mata 2009). Similarly, whereas at least three other social science associations responded to police treatment of demonstrators at the 1968 Democratic Convention by removing their annual meetings from Chicago, the American Economic Association, even though it was under the presidency of Quaker pacifist Kenneth Boulding, did not, despite radical pressure to do so (Coats 2002). The discipline's distance from political concerns may even have been constitutive of its reputation of objectivity and neutrality in the eyes of policy makers.

In political science, the situation was different though the end result was not. Though it was highly fragmented, mainstream political science succeeded (at least for a certain time) in keeping the changes of the 1960s at a reasonable distance from theory. The accommodating power of pluralism and its capacity to assume multiple forms (Merelman 2003) may have delayed the absorption of the events of the 1960s. Radicalism surrounding the Vietnam War did, however, contribute to the rejection of political theory as the center of the discipline. In sociology, permeability to outside events was greater than in economics and political science. It

---

[28] .Number of degrees awarded, taken from various issues of the *Statistical Abstract of the United States* are: 1960, 479,215 (total), 59,037 (social science); 1970, 1,072,581 (total), 182,593 (social science).

[29] We are grateful to Bradley Bateman for pointing us to these examples. On American research university in the postwar era, see Geiger (1993).

is not surprising that following a decade of agitation, Gouldner (1970) contemplated *The Coming Crisis of Western Sociology*. Likewise, it is hard not to connect the resurgence of radicalism throughout the decade with the diminishing influence of Parsons's structural functionalism and the greater recognition of Mills's *Sociological Imagination* at the end of the 1960s.[30]

The legacy of the 1970s, during which the world experienced economic turbulence not seen since the 1930s, was not the society for which student radicals of the 1960s had struggled. By 1980, the conservative neoliberalism of Margaret Thatcher and Ronald Reagan was in the ascendant (Cockett 1995 [1994]; Kelley 1997; Harvey 2005; Mirowski 2009; Tribe 2009). Not only had academia suffered in many countries due to economic crisis and cuts in government spending – this was the decade when academic social science stopped expanding – but it entered an environment in which many decision makers were hostile to social science, seen as tainted by association with the left. Friedrich Hayek, an influence on both Thatcher and Reagan, may have been a social scientist (an economist who had later turned to psychology and political theory), but he was an outsider to the trends that had dominated postwar social science, hardly taken seriously until his award of the Nobel Memorial Prize in 1974.

This change was accentuated by the fall of the Berlin Wall in 1989 and the dissolution of the Soviet Union two years later, both encouraging a form of

---

[30] This is not to suggest that there were no internal factors behind the difficulties encountered by the Parsonian project. Nichols (1998, pp. 84–5) and Johnston (1998, pp. 30–1) have explained that the story of the Department cannot be dissociated from the unhappy departmental situations of its four founding members. Psychologists Allport and Murray did not necessarily recognize themselves in a scientific psychology based on the experimental method which some of their colleagues endorsed. Kluckhohn, who was already a peculiar social anthropologist, felt remote from the archaeology and physical anthropology dear to most of his colleagues. Finally, Parsons, as is well known, did not get along with Sorokin. In all three departments, there existed divisions concerning disciplinary identity and some of these survived the creation of the Department of Social Relations. Parsons's colleague at Harvard, George C. Homans (1964), took the opportunity of his Presidency of the American Sociological Association, to launch an attack on "structural-functionalism" in his presidential address "Bringing Men Back In" (see Moss and Savchenko 2006, p. xiv). And by the late 1960s, the attempts at integrating the social sciences through the Department of Social relations had failed resulting in the reestablishment of an independent Department of Sociology, with Homans as its chair (Johnston 1998, p. 37). As of the early 1960, Lipset and Smelser (1961, pp. 45–6) noted significant tensions around functionalism in American sociology and mentioned three main oppositions regarding the place of history in the analysis of social systems, the role of conflict in society and the place of politics in the discipline. On the reasons for *The Sociological Imagination*'s popularity, Brewer's (2004) provides an instructive account centered on the biographical context.

Cold War triumphalism (Schrecker 2004). Supporters of free markets used this to argue that the very idea of socialism should be abandoned; market economies had triumphed. This was translated into politics through Francis Fukuyama's *The End of History and the Last Man* (1992) in which it was claimed that liberal democracy might represent the "end point of mankind's ideological evolution" and the "final form of human government." Though neoliberal political philosophy was challenged by U.S. foreign policy failures in the 2000s, and free-market economics by the banking crisis of 2008, such views were clearly still being taken very seriously at the turn of the century.

The Intellectual Context

Perhaps the most frequently recurring theme in the methodology of postwar social science has been "positivism." Regardless of whether the term has become too elastic to have identifiable content, it has served as "an important folk category among social scientists": it has been both the butt of criticism and, under varying labels, defended in other branches of the social sciences (Steinmetz 2005, p. 30). The origins of postwar positivism are commonly traced to the logical positivism of the interwar Vienna Circle, which formed the basis of what came to be known as the received view in the philosophy of science, albeit under labels that reflected modifications of some of the early doctrines (Suppe 1977). However, logical positivist ideas overlapped with ideas developed independently in the United States, such as operationalism, of which the physicist Percy Bridgman was the most notable exponent. Tracing the significance of positivist ideas is, moreover, difficult because claiming a link with Vienna Circle positivism or Bridgman's operationalism was sometimes used to establish the authority of social scientific arguments, even if the author had never seriously engaged with the ideas of the authors being cited. Much work went under the label of positivism, even though it might not stand up well to being judged against the criteria proposed by the Vienna Circle or Bridgman (Platt 1996, chap. 3; Platt and Hoch 1995).[31] At the core of positivism, as the term was generally used in social science, lay the separation of statements about the world from ethical judgments, enabling the ruthless application to science of logical analysis. It suggested that there could be a generic science, represented by Merton's (1942) norms of

---

[31] It could be argued that such failings made "positivism" an all too easy target for the plethora of critics that emerged in the 1960s.

universalism, communism, disinterestedness, and organized skepticism (Hollinger 1996, pp. 80–96).[32]

This conceptualization of science fitted the science-funding model established in the Second World War in which research would be commissioned by the U.S. armed forces, but carried out in universities, and controlled only indirectly. In the Cold War, this model continued, augmented by the development of think-tanks, of which RAND was the archetype. When the postwar science-funding model was being discussed, the inclusion of the social sciences was controversial, critics being skeptical of disciplines that included scholars committed to political engagement, normativity, and ethical judgment. Solovey (2004, p. 416) has argued that the U.S. Social Science Research Council's "deliberations and actions were of critical importance in defining the enterprise of American social science in a nonthreatening fashion, with an emphasis on technical, nonpartisan, and value-neutral professional expertise."[33] In both economics and political science there was a decisive move away from Deweyian pragmatism toward positivism. This marked an important transition for the social sciences, involving a break with the social engagement of scholars ranging from John Dewey to Karl Mannheim and Gunnar Myrdal, whose voices, though still heard, became marginal to the mainstream of postwar social science.

This positivism emerged in many forms. The emphasis was on testability and quantification as methods whereby social science could escape subjectivity and dependence on metaphysical notions that had no "scientific" content. The most obvious example is perhaps behaviorism in psychology, represented by B. F. Skinner. Laboratory techniques were developed to explore relationships between measurable observed behavior of human or animal subjects and the environment. Speculation on unobservable mental processes was redundant. In economics, Milton Friedman's "Methodology of Positive Economics" (1953), though denying

---

[32] There may be a link between the emergence of this view of science and the emerging tendency to view rationality as a technical notion, shorn of any ethical connotations; Mirowski (2005) has argued for a historical link between philosophy of science (reflecting the Mertonian view of science) and operations research (in which rationality was a purely technical concept).

[33] The American Social Science Research Council (SSRC) should be clearly distinguished from the British institution with the same name (until it was renamed the Economic and Social Research Council in 1983). Both were established at the initiative of social scientists, and though both played a role in the distribution of research funding, the British SSRC, founded in 1965, was a government institution whereas the American, founded in 1923–4, was not. The latter was influenced by Merriam's vision of the prospects for cross-disciplinary social science research. For "official" histories of the two institutions, see Worcester, 2001, and Economic and Social Research Council, undated). For reasons of

that economics could be a laboratory science, argued that it should be concerned with observable behavior, not with motives for action. This might be translated into an emphasis on measurement and testing, as advocated in the "positive economics" that Richard Lipsey (1963) endorsed in his best-selling textbook, or it might be used to justify the pursuit of mathematical theorizing even though theories could not in practice be tested. This resembled what in political science came to be known as "behavioralism" (not to be confused with behaviorism in psychology), associated primarily with Charles Merriam and members of the next generation who were trained at Chicago, including Harold Lasswell, Gabriel Almond, and Herbert Simon (Dahl 1961). In a presidential address to the American Political Science Association in 1925, Merriam had argued that "Some day we may take another angle of approach than the formal, as other sciences do, and begin to look at political behavior as one of the essential objects of inquiry" (Merriam 1926, p. 7).[34]

Positivism, especially in its logical positivist variant, was a profoundly empirical doctrine. However, it could mesh closely with other approaches to social science that shared its commitment to objectivity – to being "scientific" and rigorous. Individualism and rationality were arguably metaphysical notions, commitment to which might be thought inconsistent with positivism, yet in practice models of individual maximizing behavior and rational choice were seen by many economists as providing a basis for rigorous, scientific theorizing that also served to provide an ideology to counter Soviet collectivism (Amadae 2003). Sociologists and anthropologists in the 1950s and 1960s turned not to rational choice but to functionalism: explaining social phenomena in terms of the contribution they make to social and cultural life.

In the 1960s, however, things began to change. As noted by Quentin Skinner (1985, p. 6), the "empiricist and positivistic citadels of English-speaking social philosophy have been threatened and undermined by successive waves of hermeneutics, structuralists, post-empiricists, deconstructionists and other invading hordes." In the immediate postwar era, social scientists often found

space, aside from this point, the role of research councils and national academies in shaping social science is an issue not discussed here.

[34] It is worth noting that Merriam cited with approval, and as echoing his own approach, Wesley Mitchell's Presidential Address to the American Economic Association a year earlier. It is perhaps worth noting that Friedman had spent many years in the National Bureau of Economic Research, which institutionalized Mitchell's vision of economic research. Friedman, of course, studied in Chicago in 1932–3 and was a researcher there in 1934–5, though in economics, not political science.

it opportune to point out similarities between the natural sciences and social sciences so as to make the latter more appealing to various decision makers. At a time when the future of the social sciences was uncertain and perhaps threatened, the idea that they could conform to a naturalistic methodology had more supporters than detractors. Yet, the consolidation of the social sciences after the Second World War and throughout the 1950s paved the way for the reaction of the 1960s.[35]

One of the most obvious criteria used to assert the specificity of the social sciences has often been to underscore that they should take into account the representations individuals form about social phenomena because the understanding of the social world is directly connected with the meanings invested into it. With the publication of the widely read *The Idea of a Social Science* (1958), the British philosopher Peter Winch crystallized opposition to emulating the natural sciences in the social sciences. With the model of the natural sciences being increasingly challenged in the 1960s, social scientists turned once again to *Verstehen*. As a method for understanding social phenomena, it allows for a number of variations among which the hermeneutic approach stands as a convenient illustration. In emphasizing the meaning individuals confer on their actions, that approach echoed the participatory mood associated with the politically loaded environment of the 1960s. It suggested the possibility for social scientists to understand the world by putting themselves in the shoes of the social actors they studied. German philosopher Hans-Georg Gadamer played no minor role in the re-emergence of empathetic understanding as a method for understanding the social world; though, like many social scientists, he was aware of its inherent difficulties.[36]

Equally important for the development of the hermeneutic approach was the French philosopher and theologian Paul Ricoeur. Kurzweil (1980,

---

[35] Scott Gordon (1991, pp. 51–4) notes six major points of difference between the social and natural sciences. As far as writing history is concerned, Gordon insists on the significance of Carl G. Hempel's "The Function of General Laws in History" (1942) in triggering the debates between those who think that narrative accounts of the past should be cast "in a form that is fundamentally the same as that employed by the natural sciences" (Gordon 1991, p. 392) and those who place more weight on the social sciences. Another important opposition concerned the sciences and the humanities, and was revived in the 1960s thanks to C. P. Snow's emphasis of "a gulf of mutual incomprehension" in his famous *The Two Cultures and the Scientific Revolution* (1959, p. 4).

[36] As with all such attributions of significance to philosophical developments, it is important to remember that, especially in relation to the United States, care should be taken in assessing the influence of explicit philosophical discussions in relation to empirical studies that were widely taken as paradigmatic.

pp. 92–3) explains that "at first he tried to limit the definition of hermeneutics to the interpretation of symbolic language, whereas more recently
[in the 1970s], he links hermeneutics to the written texts and looks at the
problem of language as such rather than, as previously, at the structures
of will or at the symbolism of myth." When *La Pensée Sauvage* was published in 1963, Ricoeur criticized Claude Lévi-Strauss for limiting himself
to a "structural explanation," in which an outside observer accounts for an
unconscious system. By neglecting the hermeneutic approach, in which an
observer interprets myths from within, the observer produces a synchronic,
as opposed to a historicized, reading. Whereas hermeneutics encouraged
the immersion of the subject into the social world, structuralism, it was
argued, tended to avoid it.

One can hardly speak of structuralism without at the same time pointing
to those French intellectuals who personified it. Among them, Lévi-Strauss
has often been regarded as a father figure, with a progeny of no less talented
scholars, such as Louis Althusser, Roland Barthes, Jacques Derrida, Michel
Foucault, and Jacques Lacan (Sturrock 1979; Kurzweil 1980). Some of these
intellectuals – and the term here warrants a better grasp of this eminently
cultural enterprise – would perhaps not qualify as professional social scientists, especially if one looks at the French postwar intellectual landscape
from an American perspective. However, unlike in the United States, postwar social sciences and human sciences in France overlapped.[37] That being
said, there is no question that the "structuralists" played a significant role
in some of the debates of postwar social science in Europe and to a lesser
extent in the United States.

Interestingly, the "father of structuralism" had some direct experience of
American social science at a time when it went through dramatic changes.
Yet, his six-year stay at the highly unusual New School for Social Research
in New York,[38] should not be taken to imply that Lévi-Strauss simply
adapted the American model to France's postwar underdeveloped social
science.[39] Had this been the case, his work and, more generally, structuralism would probably have been better understood in the United States when

---

[37] Perrin Selcer (2009, p. 314) argued that "in the late 1940s, [f]or many European
intellectuals, the 'social sciences' belonged with the humanities."

[38] The New School was notable for the University in Exile, established in 1933 as a base for
social scientists fleeing Nazi persecution. See Krohn (1993).

[39] In a report to the French Government, dated June 1957, Henri Longchambon (1958,
p. 94), President of the Conseil supérieur de la recherche et du progrès technique, noted
that unlike the *sciences humaines*, the "new social sciences," including political economy,
sociology, ethnography, social psychology, biometrics and demography, were no reason
for pride.

it became fashionable there.[40] Still, his American experience, especially his contact with cross-disciplinary ventures, changed Lévi-Strauss to the point that upon returning to France in December of 1947, he could reconnect with his intellectual origins without feeling hampered by them. If anything, structuralism *à la* Lévi-Strauss went against what Kurzweil (1986, p. 115) has called "the fragmentation of knowledge into academic disciplines." In other words, Lévi-Strauss found the greater institutionalization of American social science disciplines especially helpful in comparison with the more intellectually ambitious, but less professionalized, French *sciences humaines*. The American model showed that disciplinary boundaries could sustain cross-disciplinary research ventures.[41] At the same time, structuralist ideas could made themselves felt beyond anthropology because of the deep philosophical roots and hence generalist orientations of social scientific discourse in France.[42]

By the early 1960s, following the publication of Lévi-Strauss's *Tristes Tropiques* (1955) and *Anthropologie Structurale* (1958), the idea that there were universal mental structures that the social scientist could elucidate through studying a variety of systems, became increasingly appealing to a number of French intellectuals.[43] Though they were written in France, these two works bore the mark of the New York experience especially as Lévi-Strauss had befriended Roman Jakobson there and in the process got interested in structural linguistics, which he subsequently strove to apply to the study of kinship structures and more generally social phenomena. One aspect of that approach that perhaps deserves to be emphasized because of the distinct orientations of American social science is that empirical observation was considered inadequate to account for social phenomena, unless the latter were at the same time recognized as sets of symbolic relationships (Kurzweil 1980, p. 17). This, in turn, can be partly explained by the significance of psychoanalysis for structuralists whose effort at unveiling unconscious structures resembles "a kind of cultural psychoanalysis"

---

[40] Edith Kurzweil (1980) argued that structuralism is a good example of an intellectual movement being fashionable and yet misunderstood.

[41] Annie Cohen-Solal (2000, p. 254) rightfully observed that "Another American novelty Lévi-Strauss discovered [during his stay in the U.S] was that the borders between disciplines seemed more distinctive and yet less rigid than in France."

[42] It may be useful to remember that most structuralists were trained as philosophers.

[43] Lévi-Strauss realized the importance of the notion of system thanks to Jakobson's structural linguistics in the 1940s. A decade later, however, the main influence behind the recognition of that notion in the United States was Ludwig von Bertalanffy and his General Systems Theory. Interestingly, natural scientists were then more receptive than social scientists.

(p. 19).[44] Finally, very much like Parsons's structural functionalism in the United States, Lévi-Strauss's structuralism declined in France in the late 1960s. Associated with political conservatism, its emphasis on universal mental structures made it difficult to accommodate the concrete political demands of the age. It is not surprising then that by the late 1960s French sociologist Raymond Boudon, who is not especially known for his structuralist sympathies, asked "A quoi sert la notion de structure?" in his eponymous book of 1968. And it is no less so that, on the other side of the Channel, the British sociologist W. G. Runciman (1968, pp. 263–4) asked "What Is Structuralism" and concluded that it "should not be claimed to constitute a novel, coherent and comprehensive paradigm for sociological and anthropological theory."[45]

A more radical challenge to positivism came in the 1970s. David Hollinger (1997, p. 339) has argued that, in the 1970s, four movements came together to create a radically new context for social science: "'Kuhn,' antiracism, feminism and 'Foucault.'" Knowledge came to be seen not simply as local but also as historicized. Though these movements were rooted in the 1960s, it was only in the 1970s that their effects became significant, at least in the United States.

Thomas Kuhn's *The Structure of Scientific Revolutions* (1962, second edition 1970) had its origins in the attitudes of the 1950s. It was published in Rudolf Carnap's *Encyclopedia of Unified Science* and, like logical positivism, was concerned with the question of meaning.[46] The difference was that although logical positivism sought meaning in the structure of scientific theories, Kuhn argued that it was learned through practice. Kuhn's ideas could be taken in a radical direction, rejecting the notion that foundations could be provided for knowledge, yet did not have to be. A philosopher

---

[44] Psychoanalysis fascinated many social scientists on the other side of the Atlantic as well. To give but one significant example, the founders of the Harvard Department of Social Relations were all very much interested in Freud. On the influence of Freud on American psychology, in particular, see Shakow and Rapaport (1964).

[45] It is telling that only 10 years earlier, Fernand Braudel (1958), who found much merit in Lévi-Strauss's *Anthropologie structurale* and its capacity "to go beyond the surface of observation to reach the area of the unconscious or hardly conscious elements" (p. 745 – translation ours) exhorted his social-scientist and historian readers to stop arguing about what is and what is not a structure to concentrate instead on long duration as one of the possibilities of a common language for the confrontation of the social sciences (p. 752).

[46] Andresen (1999) has insisted on the significance of the relationship between Kuhn's "inner crisis," a result of his move from a pacifist to an interventionist stance during the Second World War, and the centrality of the notion of crisis in his view of scientific change in *Structure*. Fuller (2000) has emphasized the roots of Kuhn's work in the Cold War scientific environment.

who spelled out a constructivist view of knowledge far more explicitly than Kuhn was Richard Rorty, whose *Philosophy and the Mirror of Nature* (1979) came to be widely cited in the social sciences and in the humanities more generally. Knowledge, whether scientific, social-scientific, or general, could not be understood apart from the communities in which it was created.

This view of knowledge chimed with critiques of knowledge that came under the movements summarized by Hollinger as antiracisim and feminism. Though Rorty might offer a liberal, democratic view of the communities in which knowledge was created, focus on communities raised questions of how power was exercised within those communities. Those concerned with race and gender linked knowledge with established power structures, linking the social sciences more closely with political movements and with identity debates within those movements.[47] The notion that the analysis of knowledge was inseparable from considerations of power appeared in much more general form in the work of Michel Foucault, which became widely known in Anglo-American social science in the 1970s through works such as (in translation) *The Order of Things* (1970) and *The Archaeology of Knowledge* (1972). Knowledge was, for Foucault, linked to material institutions, not something to be considered in abstract terms. The 1970s also saw the emergence of the radical social constructivism of the Edinburgh School, represented by David Bloor's *Knowledge and Social Imagery* (1976).

Though these developments profoundly altered the social sciences as a whole, anthropology was especially affected, for in the 1970s one of the main vehicles for the development of these ideas within the social sciences was Clifford Geertz's *Interpretation of Cultures* (1973). This helped promote the idea, taken up in other social sciences, that culture should be understood not in the traditional way, as pertaining to literature and the arts, but to societies in general. Sociology was profoundly affected as well – indeed, it was significant that the developments that created the sociology of scientific knowledge (as opposed to the more traditional, Mertonian sociology of science) expanded the domain of sociology into matters that, in the 1950s, were still within philosophy. Reflexivity became a problem that social scientists could hardly avoid. Here the contribution of the French sociologist Pierre Bourdieu deserves to be mentioned especially because his core theoretical concepts influenced empirical research in the

---

[47] There was no simple relationship between political and epistemological commitments. "Enlightenment" values of universalism were cited by some scholars as essential to the political movements that others wanted to link with postmodern ideas.

United States (Sallaz and Jane Zavisca 2007).[48] His theoretical project has been described as bridging "the deep philosophical divide between the structuralism of Lévi-Strauss and the existentialism of Jean-Paul Sartre" (p. 23), but perhaps it is better to describe Bourdieu's effort in his own terms, using the distinction between objectivism and subjectivism, which does not coincide exactly with this divide. Bourdieu was eager to go beyond the distinction between objectivism and subjectivism, which he found damaging for social science in general, by unveiling the objective conditions, which not only make possible and meaningful the subjective experience of the social world but are also implied by the very idea of an objective observer. His views on the subject were expressed in some detail in the first three chapters of *Le Sens Pratique* (1980), in which he proposed to go beyond the antagonism between objectivism and subjectivism as modes of knowledge. It is interesting to note that in criticizing the neglect of what is implicit in the distance introduced between social scientists and their object of study, Bourdieu took the example of Samuelson, who perhaps represented one of the most accomplished attempts to establish the superiority of scientific over lay knowledge, to the point where the latter is often seen as no more than a set of ill-conceived preconceptions.

Though the above developments were pervasive in the social sciences, from the core disciplines of sociology and political science to "applied" fields such as area studies, social history, and business studies, in economics they were confined to a fringe of what, from the 1970s, were increasingly seen as heterodox groupings. The complaint of the radical economists who formed URPE was that economists as a whole ignored (among others) issues of class, gender, and power. The fact is that whereas such challenges had a significant effect on other social sciences, their impact on economics was minimal.[49] Indeed, it was at precisely this time that the rational choice model became firmly entrenched as the basis for economic theorizing in a way that separated economics more clearly from the other social sciences except insofar as they adopted that framework.[50] In the 1970s and 1980s, cross-disciplinary engagements between economists and other social scientists were generally limited to the movements often labeled "economics

---

[48] A very helpful analysis of Bourdieu's sociology can be found in the book edited by Lahire (2001), most notably his chapters on the notions of *champ* and *habitus*.

[49] The case of political science is complicated by the fact that radical developments were contained essentially to the political theory subfield and to the establishment of the Caucus for a New Political Science. We are grateful to Robert Adcock for this point.

[50] On the advances of rational choice theory in political science, see Amadae and Bueno de Mesquita (1999); and in sociology see Hechter and Kanazawa (1997).

imperialism," involving the extension of the self-interest model to a number of topics outside the usual scope of economics. The situation changed in the 1990s when experimental economics began to offer a behavioral alternative to the rational choice paradigm but, even then, rapprochement with psychology was very limited.

Psychology as the Driver of Cross-Disciplinary Social Science

Though the Second World War serves as a convenient watershed in the history of American social science because of the significance of wartime projects involving several disciplines and their multiplication afterward, notably with the creation of nearly 250 cross-disciplinary social science research institutes in the twenty years after 1945 (Crowther-Heyck 2005, p. 421), it should be remembered that similar endeavors took place in the wake of the Great War as well.[51] Yale's Institute of Human Relations (IHR), set up in 1929, is a good case in point. It is of some significance to recall that Robert Hutchins, then dean of the Yale's law school, played a role in its organization before leaving, the following year, for Chicago, where he later prompted other cross-disciplinary projects. Though the Institute intended to transcend disciplinary boundaries, its creation was not meant to challenge existing departments (May 1971, p. 143).[52] The fact that its formation was publicized by *The New York Times* "as dismantling the disciplinary

---

[51] As Craufurd Goodwin has correctly reminded us, the following discussion overlooks important cross-disciplinary ventures in long-established institutions, of which the Brookings Institution and the National Bureau of Economic Research were perhaps the most important examples. In these organizations, economists were always important even if they worked closely with other social scientists. There are also numerous institutions, from those focused on academic research to think tanks and pressure groups, employing social scientists from different disciplines and focusing on problems such as economic development, industrial relations and race. Though we believe that this does not affect our conclusions, it should be noted that the picture we paint here is far from comprehensive.

[52] Also in 1929, but on the other side of the Atlantic, was launched the journal *Annales d'histoire économique et sociale*. Its creators, Marc Bloch and Lucien Febvre "intended to create an open forum for interdisciplinarity research and to promote concrete, collaborative work that would not be tied to the 'positivism' of traditional historical scholarship in France. ... After the war, the journal was associated with the newly founded Sixth Section for economic and social sciences of the Ecole Pratique des Hautes Etudes" (Hunt 1986, p. 209), with Braudel succeeding Febvre as its head from 1956 to 1968. The journal deserves mention because of its place in the overall *Annales* paradigm centered on the belief in a unified interdisciplinarity, a paradigm that began to disintegrate in the 1970s (p. 213). Coutau-Bégarie (1989, p. 8) recalls that the success of the *Annales* was facilitated by the decline of the Vidalian school of human geography from the late 1930s. This is not to say, however, that Vidal de la Blache's geography did not inspire the historians of the *Annales* (see Robic 2003, p. 385).

'Great Wall of China' " (quoted by Morawski 1986, p. 219) should therefore be taken more as an expression of the novelty of the enterprise and its deliberately problem-oriented nature than of the impediments departmentalism supposedly placed on cross-disciplinarity.[53] Despite the vision of Yale's president, James Angell, that the Institute would help "make greater progress in the understanding of human life from the biological, psychological, and sociological points of view" (May 1971, p. 151), it took almost a decade for the Institute to give body to that vision and yet, as noted by Morawski (1986, p. 220), "its inaugural ideals had been replaced by a search for universal and mechanical laws of individual behavior."[54] After 1935, the Institute, thanks to various efforts to explore the intersections between learning theory, psychoanalysis, culture theory, and cultural anthropology, was more successful in promoting its goal of a unified science of behavior, but this was not enough to ensure its survival "as an integral part of Yale University." As May (1971, p. 168) explains, "the University administration frowned at that time upon all those parts of the University which did not fit into the formal structure of departments and schools." By the end of the Second World War, following the development of multidisciplinary efforts, the belief that had accompanied the creation of Yale's IHR – the idea that interdisciplinarity and specialism could go together, and that the former could even strengthen existing departments – seemed more problematic.

Whether the Institute should be regarded as a precursor to postwar ventures is of less interest than the part taken by psychologists in its organization and development, for the striking feature of postwar cross-disciplinary ventures is the omnipresence of psychologists. A few examples are in order. Though it implied the cooperation of a number of social scientists, the London-based Tavistock Institute of Human Relations was mostly the work of psychiatrists. At Michigan, the Survey Research Center (SRC), established in 1946, was run by Rensis Likert, who had received his Ph.D. in psychology from Columbia University. When his group, working for the Department

---

[53] Two years before the Yale Institute was created, Ogburn and Goldenweiser (1927, p. 1) emphasized the increasing difficulty of synthesis in an age of specialization. At the same time, they were able to put together a collection of essays in which the interrelations of the main social sciences seemed incredibly rich and varied. As Abbott (2001, p. 131) usefully recalls, "the Social Science Research Council and the Laura Spelman Rockefeller Foundation were already focused on the problem of eliminating barriers between the social sciences by the mid-1920s."

[54] Morawski (1986, p. 230) notes that there were 21 original IHR members. In addition to psychologists there were "individuals from law, economics, history, medicine, sociology, political science, and psychiatry." And for some time cooperative work was difficult to implement.

of Agriculture's Division of Program Surveys and composed mostly of psychologists, moved to Ann Arbor to increase the impact of survey research methodology, it received the support of eminent faculty there, including social psychologists Donald G. Marquis and Theodore M. Newcomb. The Research Center for Group Dynamics (RCGD), which joined the SRC from Massachusetts Institute of Technology (MIT) in 1948 to form the Institute for Social Research, was under the leadership of social psychologist Dorwin Cartwright, who had worked with Likert in Washington, D.C. Originally, RCGD operated under the leadership of experimental psychologist, specialist in child development, and German émigré Kurt Lewin, who, after advising the Office of Strategic Services (OSS) on personnel selection criteria during the War, moved to Massachusetts in early 1945 to study group processes.[55] Lewin was probably one of the most influential social psychologists of the twentieth century. Still at Michigan but a few years later, the Mental Health Research Institute, another interdisciplinary venture, was headed by James G. Miller, who, after serving as instructor in psychology in the newly created Department of Social Relations at Harvard, had spent some time in Chicago, where he put together another interdisciplinary group. At Harvard, sociologist Parsons chaired the Department of Social Relations, but social psychologist Allport and clinical psychologist Henry A. Murray were heavily involved.[56]

Perhaps the MIT Center of International Studies is the exception that proves the rule. Psychologists there were not especially involved even though some of the activities of the Center, under the intellectual influence of political scientist Lasswell, denoted a form of psychologizing (Gilman 2003, chap. 5). It is often argued that economics, political science, and sociology were the "core social sciences in the U.S." (Ross 1993, p. 99), but, as far as postwar cross-disciplinary ventures were concerned, it is no exaggeration to suggest that psychology was almost always central. Psychologists, notably

---

[55] Marrow (1969, pp. 178–90) provides a detailed account of the origins of the RCGD at MIT. It should be noted that the "Center was located in the Department of Economics and Social Sciences, which had little concern for disciplinary boundaries within the social sciences" (pp. 181–2). At MIT, Lewin also took part in the cross-disciplinary Cybernetics Group (Heims 1993). On Lewin's work in the United States before his appointment at MIT, see Ash (1992).

[56] Though we limit ourselves to examples of cross-disciplinary ventures in social science, it should be remembered that psychologists as well as other social scientists also participated in groups including mathematicians and physicists. The most obvious example would be the Macy meetings (see Galison 1994, pp. 254–6; and, more generally, Heims 1993). Interestingly, Norbert Wiener's *Cybernetics* (1948) had a Chapter on "Cybernetics and Psychopathology."

social psychologists, at Yale and elsewhere, could hardly find themselves foreign to projects that strove to develop an integrated theory of the individual and social behavior.

Reporting on the relations between psychology and the newly created Department of Social Relations (DSR) at Harvard, psychologists Allport and Edwin G. Boring (1946) mentioned IHR and a couple of prewar institutions created to deal with the "administrative perplexities" resulting from the synthesis of various social sciences.[57] Yet, after the war, the context was different:

It seems inevitable that urgent and increasing demands will be laid upon the University for the study of the "human factor" in a technological and atomic age. The pressure will come in part from the federal government, in part from the local community, and in part from the social conscience of the university itself. An efficient Department of Social relations with its adjunct laboratory, will be needed to help to select, implement and execute the most worthy projects among those that will be pressed upon the University. (p. 120)

This new multidisciplinary venture had antecedents at Harvard itself with the so-called "Pareto Circle" from the early 1930s to the early 1940s. As Heyl (1968, p. 317) has reminded us, "One aspect of the university climate during the thirties was the widespread popularity of large-scale historical framework employed to describe socio-political phenomena." Parsons, the would-be chair of DSR, was a member of that group, which, its strong interest in Pareto's work notwithstanding, was notably influenced by Harvard physiologist Lawrence J. Henderson. It is Henderson who took the initiative of organizing a seminar on Pareto's sociology, some participants of which ended up at the DSR later on. As pointed out by Heyl, the group was interested in the concepts of social system and social equilibrium, and it put special emphasis on the connections between the physicochemical system and the social system. Here one sees that natural scientists played at least an indirect role in later efforts at integrating the social sciences, not necessarily that Parsons was thus prolonging Henderson's hope for a science of society, but rather that his participation in the "Pareto Circle" convinced him of the benefits associated with collaborative work of a multidisciplinary nature.

---

[57] In the spring of 1945 Paul H. Buck, the Dean of the Harvard Faculty of Arts and Sciences, asked Parsons "to visit and report back on government and university [interdisciplinary] programs." Interestingly, "Parsons studied the programs at the Yale Institute of Human Relations, the Columbia Bureau of Applied Social Research, the North Carolina Institute of Social Research, the Research Branch in the Information and Education Division of the War Department, and various others" (Johnston 1995, p. 156).

Officially opened in January 1946, less than a couple of years after Parsons replaced Pitirim Sorokin at the head of the Sociology Department, the DSR built on the previous experience of multidisciplinary cooperation within the "Pareto Circle," but its ambitions were broader and reflected the convergence during the Second World War of a number of research activities, "including community analysis, attitude assessment, the process of socialization in childhood and youth, the study of group conflict and prejudice, factors in national and institutional morale, the nature of institutional behavior, aspects of communication and propaganda, ethnic and national differences and similarities, problems of social and mental adjustment of the individual in his social situation" (Allport and Boring 1946, p. 120).[58] More or less, that is what "social relations" meant. These research activities concerned several departments and that is why the new department included all of the former sociology department, the social and clinical psychology part of the former psychology department and the social anthropology part of the former department of anthropology. One thing that is clear when one compares the DSR and IHR is that the former contested disciplinary boundaries when the latter hoped that multidisciplinary projects would rest on, and might even strengthen, existing departments. As Gilman (2003, p. 73) suggested, it is perhaps more appropriate to speak of omnidisciplinarity (multidisciplinarity) rather than interdisciplinarity to characterize DSR. That is an important distinction as not all postwar enterprises going beyond the realm of individual social sciences meant to challenge disciplinary boundaries in the way the DSR did.

Michigan offers a good example. As at Chicago and Harvard, it was believed that putting together different social scientists would bring about substantial benefits. However, there was no suggestion either that this would cause departmental boundaries to disappear or that some disciplines had to be subsumed under a more general social science. Since the close of the war, well-known researchers, such as sociologist Robert C. Angell (editor of the *American Sociological Review* from 1946 to 1948), social psychologists Marquis and Newcomb, and a few others, had initiated various enterprises at the boundaries of the traditional social science disciplines. Established in 1946, the same year as DSR, the SRC represented the culmination of these various efforts. SRC meant anything but disciplinary specialism. Under Rensis Likert, and with the help of Angus Campbell, George Katona, and

---

[58] Crowther-Heyck (2006b, p. 313) notes the "establishment of dozens of Departments of Social/Human Relations in colleges and universities across the nation during the 1950s and 1960s. These interdisciplinary departments typically replicated the structure of the Harvard Department of Social Relations."

a few others who likewise explored the intersections between economics, sociology, and psychology, the SRC applied the sample survey methodology that had been developed during the Second World War to a variety of human behaviors, from economic to organizational and political.

The Research Center for Group Dynamics deserves special mention as well. As we have seen, the Center was founded by Lewin at MIT, a few miles away from the Harvard DSR, in 1945.[59] Interestingly, even before the latter was established, Lewin presented the RCGD as the outcome of two necessities, a scientific and a practical one. "Social science," he wrote, "needs an integration of psychology, sociology, and cultural anthropology into an instrument for studying group life. Modern society demands a deeper understanding and a more efficient and less prejudicial handling of group problems" (1945, p. 126). In comparison with the DSR, one notes the emphasis on cultural anthropology, whose interest for differences between modern cultures had made a rather appealing discipline. Though social anthropology and cultural anthropology were associated with different traditions before the Second World War – the European for the former and the American for the latter – after the war differences were less glaring, allowing for more exchanges. And the fact that "social anthropology" at the DSR was represented by Kluckhohn, who had written his thesis on "Some Aspects of Contemporary Theory in Cultural Anthropology," suggests even greater similarities between the project of the DSR and that of the RCGD. In the highly internationalized context of the mid-1940s, the concept of culture may have had more appeal than that of sociality characteristic of social anthropology. And by the 1950s, it had currency beyond the disciplinary boundaries of anthropology and sociology (Weinstein 2004, p. 23).

On a different level, it should be noted that the RCGD was established in the Department of Economics and Social Science, which combined economics, sociology, and psychology. With that multidisciplinary department, Lewin found at MIT what Parsons and others had to create at Harvard. Lewin was especially aware of the benefits of being in an engineering school. To him, the Second World War had demonstrated "the discrepancy between our ability to handle physical nature and our lack of ability to handle social forces" (1945, p. 128). Awareness of that discrepancy was central to the creation of the RCGD, its endorsement of the "field theory" approach, and its choice of research area as small groups dynamics. These orientations were different from those of SRC, but there were many intersections and, after

---

[59] Marrow (1969, p. 182) notes that "close working relations were established with Henry Murray, Gordon Allport, and others at Harvard."

Lewin died, Michigan, with its strong sociology department and some of its members being interested in psychology, followed Rikert's suggestion that RCGD, under the new directorship of Dorwin Cartwright, join the SRC in July 1948, with the two centers forming the Institute for Social Research one year later.

Finally, mention should be made of the Mental Health Research Institute formed at Michigan in 1955. Though mental health was then regarded as the most important health problem in the country and the discussions prior to its creation, mostly for institutional and political reasons, emphasized a better understanding of the causes and means of prevention of mental illness as one of the goals of the Institute, its activities went largely beyond problems of mental health. For its main protagonist, James G. Miller, but also his two acolytes, neurophysiologist Ralph W. Gerard and mathematical biologist turned social scientist Anatol Rapoport, one of the functions of MHRI was "to fill the gap … between the biological and social sciences."[60] This is clear from the proposal for a "Center for Mental Health Sciences," as it was still described in January 1955. The proposal had a broad coverage: it included a four-part division between the "Cell and Organ," the "Individual," the "Small Group," and the "Social and Community Aspects of Mental Health," with the implicit idea – common among advocates of the general systems theory – that the Center "will emphasize identification of general principles, which extend across various levels of systems" (Miller 1956, p. 3).[61]

The proposal emphasized mental health, but it was articulated in such a way as to open up the possibility for numerous interactions with a wide range of social-science studies of human behavior. Interestingly, Miller, Gerard, and Rapoport were all at Chicago a few years earlier, participating in some of the University's cross-disciplinary ventures. Miller, the founding director or MHRI, was there from early 1948, following his appointment at the Harvard DSR as a faculty instructor in psychology. Under the influence of Enrico Fermi, who felt that a better understanding of human behavior was needed and that it implied the building of general theories, Miller started a new cross-disciplinary group of senior faculty members from the biological- and social-sciences divisions – the Committee on the Behavioral Sciences. The latter considered the possibility of developing empirically general testable theories of behavior, an orientation most evidently associated

---

[60]　Miller to Gerard, February 3, 1955, Box 1, Folder "History," Mental Health Research Institute Records, Bentley Historical Library, University of Michigan.

[61]　[Miller], "Proposal for a Center for Mental Health Sciences at Ann Arbor, Michigan," Dec. 1954–Jan. 1955], Box 1, Folder "History," Mental Health Research Institute Records, Bentley Historical Library, University of Michigan.

with the work of Bertalanffy at the time. The Committee began to operate in the early 1950s and continued its activities well into 1955 when some of its leading members, among whom Gerard, Miller, and Rapoport, moved to Ann Arbor after unsuccessful attempts to establish a behavioral science institute at Chicago and Berkeley.[62]

This description of the institutionalization of cross-disciplinary efforts is biased toward the United States, but other countries, notably Britain, developed similar ventures, some of them having close connections with their U.S. counterparts. That was the case of the Tavistock Institute of Human Relations (TIHR).[63] Founded in 1946, it was but one of the organizations that came out of the Tavistock Institute of Medical Psychology, established in 1920.

From the 1920s to the outbreak of the Second World War, members of the Tavistock Clinic sought to utilize explanations and techniques derived from psychoanalysis and dynamic psychologies in order to explain and remedy problems of disturbed and delinquent children, and troubled adults, and in order to address the difficulties that confronted a wide rage of professionals working with human beings – notably social workers and probation officers – and to train them in appropriate ways of understanding and intervening in difficulties of human conduct. (Miller and Rose 1994, p. 32)

Thanks to a grant from the Rockefeller Foundation, in 1946, which was interested in capitalizing on the experiences of institutions associated with war medicine to develop social psychiatry, the TIHR emerged as a division of the Tavistock clinic (Trist and Murray 1990, p. 5). As it turns out, the innovations introduced during the war gradually convinced a number of psychiatrists and social scientists that some of the synergies revealed by wartime collaborative work could be expected from similar work in a peace context. Following the war, the Clinic's mission was redefined in view of the creation of the National Health Service with, in particular, the decision "to incorporate the Institute of Human Relations for the study of wider social problems not accepted as in the area of mental health" (p. 5), among which

---

[62]   Before coming to Michigan, Miller had the project of creating an Institute of the Behavioral Sciences at Chicago. In that project, the question of mental health was second in comparison with "[t]he problem of the maintenance of peace and the prevention of international misunderstanding." Undated, Box 1, Folder "History," Mental Health Research Institute Records, Bentley Historical Library, University of Michigan.

[63]   According to Jacques (1998, p. 251), The Tavistock Institute had two strong sets of intellectual connections: one with the work of psychoanalyst Melanie Klein and her associates, and the other with group dynamics and personality theory, in particular British psychoanalyst Wilfred Bion's theory of group dynamics and, on the American side, Kurt Lewin at MIT, Henry Murray at Harvard and Jacob Moreno in New York.

industrial relations and organizational functionings were prominent. What makes the story of the TIHR especially interesting for postwar social science is precisely that it embodied the conviction that some of the practical problems inherited from the Second World War could not be understood and solved without first combining the conceptual frameworks of several social science disciplines. The interdisciplinarity of the Institute went together with the variety of issues it dealt with.

Cross-disciplinary efforts were also be institutionalized through journals. Here, the launching of *Human Relations*, interestingly subtitled "Studies Towards the Integration of the Social Sciences," in 1947, comes to mind. The journal was the result of a joint effort between two well-known interdisciplinary institutions – the TIHR in London, and the RCGD in Cambridge, Massachusetts. A few years later, *Behavioral Science* was launched. Published by the Mental Health Research Institute at the University of Michigan, the journal had a multidisciplinary editorial board, most of whom had taken an active role in the production and diffusion of interdisciplinary knowledge. With the exception of human geography, all the social sciences represented in this volume had a representative on the editorial board. The editorial in the first issue, in 1956, noted that the "rise of natural science and the flood of its applications have been paced by the creation of broad theories. It is to the development of such theories of behavior and to their empirical testing that this publication is dedicated" (p. 1). In effect, the actual focus of the journal was not the natural sciences themselves but rather the fact that they could inspire a similar movement in the social sciences. The editorial, probably written by psychologist James G. Miller, betrayed orientations that he took from Enrico Fermi when they both were at Chicago. It read: "Man's most baffling enigma remains, as it has always been, himself. He has been unable to fathom with any precision those laws of human nature which can produce social inequality, industrial strife, marital disharmony, juvenile delinquency, mental illness, war, and other widespread miseries" (p. 1). It is hard to imagine that the social sciences had little to contribute to this. Among the three main figures behind the creation of the journal – James G. Miller, Gerard, and Rapoport – one notes a shared belief in the virtues of the general systems theory (Hammond 2003, p. 169) and its idea that general principles operated across various levels of systems.

Following the Second World War, many social scientific beliefs about human behavior were shaken, leaving researchers with the feeling that human behavior remained a largely unsolved mystery. Drawing on wartime experience, social scientists strove to bring together teams in which psychologists could inform work by other social scientists. The centrality of psychology in these enterprises can be explained by what historians of psychology have called its "protean" identity (Capshew 1999, p. 54; Ash 2003, p. 269). The fragmentation of psychology proved to be an asset, facilitating adjustments to other research cultures and disciplinary traditions. But, as the example of economics amply shows, a far less protean identity could likewise support multidisciplinary ventures.

Economics-Centered Interdisciplinary Ventures

By the late 1940s, the seeds of the most significant cross-disciplinary ventures in social science had been planted. The Second World War and its immediate aftermath were central to their establishment, but the Cold War brought to the front new issues, which opened up new research horizons. With the Truman doctrine of containing Russia in place as of 1947 and the loss of China following in 1949, the issue of getting a better understanding of Russia and to a lesser extent China became central to American foreign policy, as did the connected issue of development. These two issues were interrelated, as economic growth was then seen as preventing the propagation of communism; they raised the question of the U.S. capacity to deal with the rapid changes affecting the world. If all the research centers, institutes, and academic departments mentioned so far were in one way or another the outcome of the war and its immediate aftermath, the MIT Center for International Studies (CENIS), established in 1952, following the critical late 1940s and early 1950s, was above all a Cold War research unit.

Interestingly, economists took little part in the cross-disciplinary ventures in social science in the early postwar years, but they were central in the creation and activities of CENIS (Lodewijks 1991, pp. 286–7).[64] The Center emanated from an anti-communist propaganda project conducted in the fall of 1950 in the midst of the Korean War (Blackmer 2002; Gilman 2003). It was MIT president James Killian who, only one year after his inauguration, was approached by the State Department to tackle the problem of how best to communicate with populations behind the Iron Curtain. Killian accepted the offer. Like several of his

---

[64] It should be noted, however, that the economists involved were not necessarily in the mainstream, though what this comprises has changed significantly during the period we are considering. Lodewijks (1991, p. 307) describes Rostow's approach as "non-neoclassical as well as non-Marxist," an approach that "involves a great many endogenous variables ... all influenced by noneconomic factors and to be handled through a multidisciplinary approach, a development that disturbs economists."

contemporaries, he believed in the possible integration of liberal arts and sciences.[65] Accordingly, with the help of Harvard (hence the association of Kluckhohn, who was running the recently established Harvard Russian Research Center), an interdisciplinary team was formed in the summer of 1950, including notably psychologist Alex Bavelas and economist Max Millikan from MIT, to work on the question raised by the State Department. Later, the activities of the team were referred to as "Project TROY." Its top-secret report, submitted in early 1951, considered a number of ways to improve U.S. propaganda abroad and warned against too intransigent positions toward the Soviet Union. The report from Project TROY encouraged Killian to support three follow-on research initiatives, including a study of Soviet society, under the directorship of MIT economist W.W. Rostow, a defector interview and research program led by Kluckhohn, and the "overload and delay" program (on disrupting communications within the Soviet Union) conducted by Bavelas. It likewise suggested that a permanent research center, the CENIS, should be established under the leadership of Millikan, in early 1952, following his one-year service as assistant to the director of the CIA (Needell 1993, pp. 416–7; Needell 1998, pp. 22–4).[66]

Economists may have been important in the work of CENIS, they were not the only sources of intellectual inspiration behind its activities. Political scientists Lasswell and Lucian Pye, as well as sociologist Daniel Lerner,

---

[65] Allan Needell (1998, p. 3) maintains that "Project Troy also served powerfully to reinforce postwar efforts to associate the social with the natural sciences, not only in terms of the assumed reliability and objectivity of the research methodologies employed, but also in terms of the potential contributions they could make to promoting American interests around the globe."

[66] The connection with Harvard and its Russian Research Center was of great importance if only because the latter, based on the OSS model, had formally opened in February 1948, following the efforts of psychologist John Gardner of the Carnegie Corporation and encouragements from Parsons who believed Harvard was the right place for such a center. As of mid-1947, following the creation of the Harvard Department of Social Relations, Gardner was trying to find ways to increase the interest of psychologists, sociologists and anthropologists in Russian studies (Diamond 1992, p. 65). Placing the president of the American Anthropological Association for 1947 at the direction of the planned center and including in its executive committee Parsons, probably the most influential sociologist of the postwar era, could help in that respect. The two men were very close and Parsons and Vogt (1962) wrote Kluckhohn's obituary for the *American Anthropologist*. In the latter, one reads that Kluckhohn "felt the absolute necessity of the empathetic understanding of the attitudes of people living in cultures other than his own, which he carried out so outstandingly in his work on the Navaho" (p. 144), and likewise in his research on the Japanese morale within the Foreign Morale Analysis Division during the Second World War and on the Soviet Union as the first Director of the Russian Research Center from 1948 to 1954.

were also crucial to the whole project. The committee appointed to advise CENIS on a project running from 1962 also included Lazarsfeld, Edward Shils, and psychologist Jerome Bruner (Planning Committee of CENIS, 1954). Lasswell's view of politics as a specific place for the manifestations of private psychological troubles, in particular, lent itself well to the depiction of foreign leaders as unreasonable and it could likewise justify the occasional difficulties involved in understanding them.

In addition, that view suggested that the seductions of communism may have had less to do with its own characteristics as with the psychological tensions, indeed imbalances, encountered by some people (see Gilman, chap. 5).[67] Some of these tensions could result from the uncertainties associated with periods of transition especially in "underdeveloped" countries. That explains in turn why the role of economists at CENIS, notably Rostow's, has been taken as exemplary of the modernization literature developed there. Gilman has rightly nuanced that view, preferring instead to depict modernization theory as "the initial social scientific rationalization of the post–World War II American drive to achieve global free trade and American geopolitical hegemony" (p. 191). But even if we accept Gilman's characterization, the seductive power of Rostow's *The Stages of Economic Growth: A Non-Communist Manifesto* (1960), is not diminished. Not only did it provide a simple reading of Western industrialization, but it suggested likewise a ready-to-use alternative to communism, which American policymakers could use at will at the attention of developing countries.[68]

As in CENIS, economists were also significant at what was perhaps the archetypal Cold War think-tank, Project RAND, established in early 1946 by the U.S. Air Force as a way of continuing the Second World War practice of bringing together scientists working on problems they believed important, but in an environment more like academia than a military

---

[67] The attractive power of Communism was largely discussed in the early 1950s. At MIT, the "Appeals of Communism Project," directed by Almond, put together a number of scholars who tried to fathom the complexities of the phenomenon. An illustration of their work is provided by Herbert E. Krugman who, drawing on data derived from interviews with former members of the American Communist Party, discussed the question of what makes an individual become a communist and what communism makes of the individual. Interestingly, among the 50 interviewees in the article, "The Appeal of Communism to American Middle Class Intellectuals and Trade Unionists" (1952), 24 were journalists, writers, artists, professionals, and students. Two years later, Almond published his own *The Appeals of Communism* (1954).

[68] The subtitle of *The Stages of Economic Growth* was suggested to Rostow by his editors at CUP. We are grateful to David Engerman for this point.

institution. Originally, Project RAND gathered physicists, mathematicians, and engineers to work on a research program devoted to air warfare, with the objective of making recommendations to the U.S. Air Force, but with no particular pressure in terms of their practical applications. If anything, in the eyes of its progenitors, Project RAND meant to consolidate the cooperation between science and the military, as witnessed during the Second World War, but the return to peace occasioned notable changes to the overall climate that surrounded the scientists' war effort. Social scientists, in particular, had to fight hard to maintain the credit accumulated during the war. Given the nature of Project RAND, it was hard to think of it as a natural habitat for social scientists in general, but the scientist pretensions of some economists and their expertise in quantitative methods made them possible candidates for participation.[69]

Many of the postwar profession's leading quantitative economists ended up working for Project RAND. Along with Princeton University, where the mathematics department was home to John Nash, RAND was the major center for the development of game theory and its applications to problems of atomic warfare. Even before Project RAND became the RAND Corporation in 1948, economists had a foot in the door thanks to "the network of alliances and influences that had grown around economics and economists in the wartime context …: OSS in Washington and London, and SRG [Statistical Research Group] in New York" (Leonard 1991, p. 270). And following economist's Charles Hitch appointment as head of RAND's new Economics Division, it was clear that economists were there to stay.[70]

It was less so, however, that they would be able to give structure to much work being done at RAND. In the late 1940s, economists (and political scientists) represented no more than 5 percent of the research staff, and RAND maintained its original orientation toward hardware analysis. "By the end of the 1950s, however, economists had become the dominant professional group at RAND, outnumbering physicists and mathematicians; 'systems analysis' was now RAND's unique product" (Amadae 2003, p. 40). That success was above all that of the systematic application of economic principles to the treatment of a number of practical issues in an era of increased sensitivity to rational pricing. The adoption of economic criteria in the making of engineering choices was

---

[69] On the creation of RAND, see Mirowski (1991, pp. 241–2), Leonard (1991, pp. 269–71; 1992, pp. 67–9). More detailed analyses of RAND are provided by Jardini (1996), Hounsell (1997), and Amadae (2003, chap. 1).

[70] On SRG, see Wallis (1980).

also facilitated by the social engineering ambitions of the RAND economists, which eventually brought them great influence in the shaping of defense policy.

Finally, another example of an interdisciplinary community in which economists played some role is the Carnegie Tech's Graduate School of Industrial Administration (GSIA).[71] In the early postwar period, it was widely held, in the light of wartime experience, that trained management was important to mobilizing resources, and that, despite the enormous expansion in business education, the average quality of business schools was low and needed to be improved. The major change came in the mid-1950s when the Ford Foundation announced a program to develop four "centers of excellence" in the field. The Harvard Business School obtained the major share of Ford's largesse, but more significant was the attention paid to the newly established GSIA (at what later became Carnegie-Mellon University), which received the first grant. In contrast to the case-study method based on business experience that formed the core of Harvard's MBA teaching, the GSIA sought to follow the example MIT had set in engineering, where underlying disciplines were integrated into a professional curriculum through technical problem solving. This was the model that Ford sought to spread through all elite business schools (Khurana 2007, pp. 252–3).[72]

A feature of the GSIA approach that distinguished it from Harvard was to ground business education in rigorous disciplinary scholarship and quantitative methods, focused on practical problems, out of which cross-disciplinary research could emerge. The approach was thus cross-disciplinary, though driven by economists. The main inspiration behind GSIA was its dean, Lee Bach, an economist, in conjunction with two young recruits, Herbert Simon (trained in political science at Chicago) and William W. Cooper (trained in economics at Chicago) who shared Bach's interest in applying technical methods to the solution of management problems. Though their focus was on applied management problems, it did not mean that they became detached from the main social sciences, as had sometimes happened with applied work. Though fully involved in management science, Simon became a major figure in psychology and political science (Crowther-Heyck 2005), and GSIA's economists (who included Robert Lucas, Thomas Sargent, and Franco Modigliani) became

---

[71] This and the next paragraph draw extensively on Khurana (2007).

[72] Crowther-Heyck (2006b) explores Simon's effort to build GSIA into a center for interdisciplinary social research.

major figures in their own discipline.[73] It is tempting to link the ideas produced by social scientists at GSIA to the concern with information processing and organizational behavior that arose directly out of the attempt to develop quantitative management tools.[74]

Because of its strong identity, economics was able to give structure to cross-disciplinary research. More importantly, however, was its capacity to combine a theoretical framework, conceptual tools, and quantitative techniques to a degree that perhaps no other social sciences could achieve. That meant that, although they could contribute to cross-disciplinary ventures, economists, unlike psychologists, found it more difficult not to be in the driver's seat.[75] Whereas psychologists' satisfaction with equal partnership allowed for their almost ubiquitous presence in most cross-disciplinary social scientific research after the Second World War, the reluctance of economists made their association with other social scientists more difficult.[76]

Conclusions: Cross-Disciplinary Ventures and Disciplinary Identity

Contrary to the assumption that is implicit in much writing on the history of the postwar social sciences, they need to be considered alongside each other. As we have seen, the Second World War exerted a profound influence across the social sciences, not just because of the wartime experiences of social scientists (though these were extremely important) but because the Second World War changed the contexts in which

---

[73] Lucas and Sargent were key figures in the transformation of macroeconomics that took place in the 1970s, deriving the idea of "rational expectations" from their colleague Muth. Modigliani was at the heart of the transformation of finance in the same period. See this volume, chap. 3.

[74] On Sargent, see Sent (1998). On GSIA's links with the economics profession, see Fourcade and Khurana (2008).

[75] We do not explore the issue of whether research at GSIA should be considered interdisciplinary or multidisciplinary (on the distinction between "interdisciplinary" situations, involving the exchange of intellectual tools, and "multidisciplinary" situations, implying researchers working in parallel, see Cohen-Cole 2007). There was clearly an attempt to develop new methods that transcended existing disciplines, the hallmark of interdisciplinarity. However, when disciplinary boundaries are under negotiation, such terminology, though invaluable, has to be used with care.

[76] Leonard (1991, p. 265) notes that the "intolerance and at times belligerence towards the 'blindness' of other disciplines was to become a recurring theme for the next twenty years in the involvement of economists in military affairs ... economists remained loath to cooperate significantly with others, such as historians or political scientists, and only those who adopted the tools of economic analysis commanded their professional respect."

social science was undertaken. The Cold War continued trends established during the 1940s. Both the patronage of the social sciences and the agendas to which they responded had changed substantially since the 1930s. Moreover, not only did the social sciences develop in response to political, social, and intellectual pressures that affected more than one discipline, but also, and this is perhaps more important, there was much cross-disciplinary interaction that helped define the boundaries and identities of the different social sciences. Cross-disciplinary ventures should be seen less as forays across rigidly defined disciplines than as activities that help shape the social sciences' conceptions of their different identities.[77]

There is, of course, a sense in which individual social science disciplines proceeded largely independent of each other: the dividing lines between the social sciences discussed in this volume had by then been laid down and institutionalized. Had this not been the case, the preceding chapters could not have been written in the way they have been. However, it would be wrong to assume that by 1945 the pressures for disciplinary autonomy had become overwhelming. This was emphatically *not* the case. The two decades following the Second World War saw a profusion of ventures that bridged different social sciences. It is because we consider cross-disciplinary ventures a key factor in postwar social science that we have explored some of them in detail: challenging the neglect of such ventures helps contextualize many of the claims of influence from one social science to another that one finds in disciplinary histories. Cross-disciplinary social scientists such as Boulding, Kluckhohn, Lasswell, Myrdal, Parsons, and Simon were, to a certain extent, not isolated mavericks, but part of a wider network of well-funded, cross-disciplinary institutions that formed a more significant part of the social sciences than is commonly understood.

Though these developments involved all the social sciences, the part each took in cross-disciplinary work was uneven. It is commonly believed, no doubt because of Parsons's vision, that sociology must have been at the heart of this process.[78] However, in the immediate postwar period, because of the centrality of the human factor to social science research, it was psychology that was at the center of most cross-disciplinary activities. It is worth noting that Lazarsfeld, a key figure in both sociology and political science, thought of himself, by the time that he became established in the United States,

---

[77] See Backhouse and Fontaine (2010).

[78] Of some importance as well is the "interstitial quality of sociology," as described by sociologist Abbott (2001, p. 6), which plays a significant role in its claims as a general social science.

as a psychologist.[79] As Herman (1998, p. 98) rightfully notes, "[t]o their roles as Cold War military advisers and researchers, psychological experts brought evolving insights into human irrationality. A unified conception of behavior – a conviction that the relevant underlying variables were much the same whether conflicts were geopolitical or personal, whether the actors were the nation-states or individual humans – was central." Economics, likewise, had its part in cross-disciplinary ventures, but it came in different ways – through the spread of economic metaphors through society and through the application of economic language and techniques to disciplines from sociology and political science to law and philosophy. Needless to say, the cross-disciplinarity initiated by economists did not dictate the kind of cooperation psychologists had in mind when they joined in similar undertakings.[80]

It is arguable that the extent of cross-disciplinary activity reflects indistinct demarcations between certain social sciences (at what point, for example, does sociology become social psychology or political science become political sociology?), but that is not the whole story. As we have seen, economics, which, unlike psychology, had made human rationality its province, and which by the 1950s was rapidly developing methods that would set it apart from other social sciences, was involved. The reason is that cross-disciplinarity has to do with cooperation as much as with competition. Whether the initiative came from patrons (government or foundations) or from academics – indeed, given the role played by academics within foundations, this distinction is not always easy to draw – the practical problems to which solutions were sought were occasions for social scientists to claim disciplinary expertise.[81] Following the Second World War, the commonality of problems accounted for most cross-disciplinary research ventures. Yet, the difficulties in transforming multidisciplinary efforts into interdisciplinary achievements reminds us that, beyond the personal penchants of social scientists, cross-disciplinarity should be understood as the struggle by various social sciences to force their own conception of society on each other so as to emerge as the main providers of solutions to its problems.

---

[79] We are indebted to Jennifer Platt for pointing this out.

[80] On the dissemination of economic metaphors through society from the 1960s, see Fourcade (2009).

[81] Patronage and funding are issues that merit more attention than we have been able to pay them. Much research remains to be done on bodies such as Research Councils in different countries, the role of national academies and other bodies sponsoring social science research.

REFERENCES

Abbott, Andrew. 2001. *Chaos of Disciplines*. Chicago, IL and London: The University of Chicago Press.

Abbott, Andrew and James T. Sparrow. 2007. "Hot War, Cold War: The Structures of Sociological Action, 1940–1955." In Craig Calhoun, ed., *Sociology in America: A History*, pp. 281–313. Chicago, IL and London: The University of Chicago Press.

Allport, Gordon W. and Edwin G. Boring. 1946. "Psychology and Social Relations at Harvard University," *American Psychologist* 1.4:119–22.

Allport, Gordon W. and A. Hadley Cantril. 1935. *The Psychology of Radio*. New York and London: Harper and Brothers.

Almond, Gabriel A. 1954. *The Appeals of Communism*. Princeton, NJ: Princeton University Press.

Almond, Gabriel A. and Wolfgang Krauss. 1999. "The Size and Composition of the Anti-Nazi Opposition in Germany," *PS: Political Science and Politics* 32.3:562–69.

Amadae, Sonja M. 2003. *Rationalizing Capitalist Democracy: The Cold War Origins of Rational Choice Liberalism*. Chicago, IL and London: The University of Chicago Press.

Amadae, Sonja M. and Bruce Bueno de Mesquita. 1999. "The Rochester School: The Origins of Positive Political Theory," *Annual Review of Political Science* 2:269–95.

Andresen, Jensine. 1999. "Crisis and Kuhn." In M. Rossiter, ed., *Catching Up with the Vision: Essays on the Occasion of the 75th Anniversary of the Founding of the History of Science Society*, Supplement to volume 90 of *Isis*. Chicago, IL: The University of Chicago Press.

Applebaum, Herbert. 1987. "Overview." In H. Applebaum, ed., *Perspectives in Cultural Anthropology*. New York: SUNY Press.

Ash, Mitchell G. 1992. "Cultural Contexts and Scientific Change in Psychology: Kurt Lewin in Iowa," *American Psychologist* 47.2:198–207.

2003. "Psychology." In T. M. Porter and D. Ross, eds., *The Cambridge History of Science*, vol. 7 (*The Modern Social Sciences*). Cambridge: Cambridge University Press.

Backhouse, Roger E. and Philippe Fontaine (eds). 2010. *The Unsocial Social Science? Economics and Neighboring Disciplines since 1945*. Annual Supplement to volume 41 of *History of Political Economy*. Durham, NC: Duke University Press.

Barnes, Trevor J. 2006. "Geographical Intelligence: American Geographers and Research and Analysis in the Office of Strategic Services, 1941–1945," *Journal of Historical Geography* 32.1:149–68.

2008. "Geography's Underworld: The Military-Industrial Complex, Mathematical Modelling and the Quantitative Revolution," *Geoforum* 39.1:3–16.

Barton, Allen H. 1979. "Paul Lazarsfeld and Applied Social Research: Invention of the University Applied Social Research Institute," *Social Science History* 3.3/4:4–44.

Bates, Robert H. 1997. "Area Studies and the Discipline: A Useful Controversy?" *PS: Political Science and Politics* 30.2:166–9.

Berelson, Bernard. 1963. "Introduction to the Behavioral Sciences." In B. Berelson, ed., *The Behavioral Sciences Today*. New York and London: Basic Books.

Berghann, Volker R. 2001. *America and the Intellectual Cold Wars in Europe*. Princeton, NJ: Princeton University Press.

Blackmer, Donald L. M. 2002. *The MIT Center for International Studies: The Founding Years, 1951–1969.* Cambridge, MA: MIT Center for International Studies.

Bloor, David. 1976. *Knowledge and Social Imagery.* Chicago, IL: University of Chicago Press.

Boas, Franz. 1919. "Scientists as Spies." Letter to *The Nation*, December 20, 1919. Reprinted in C. Simpson, ed., *Universities and Empire: Money and Politics in the Social Sciences during the Cold War.* New York: New Press.

Bonnell, Victoria E. and George W. Breslauer. 2003. "Soviet and Post-Soviet Area Studies." Location: Global, Area, and International Archive. Retrieved from: http://escholarship.org/uc/item/4ct4x896 (Last accessed March 1, 2010).

Braudel, Fernand. 1958. "Histoire et sciences sociales: La longue durée," *Annales. Économies, Sociétés, Civilisations* 13.4:725–53

Brewer, John D. 2004. "Imagining The Sociological Imagination: The Biographical Context of a Sociological Classic," *British Journal of Sociology* 55.3:317–33.

Britt, Steuart Henderson and Jane D. Morgan. 1946. "Military Psychologists in World War II," *American Psychologist* 1.10:423–37.

Camic, Charles. 1989. "Structure after 50 years: The Anatomy of a Charter," *American Journal of Sociology* 95.1:38–107.

Capshew, James H. 1999. *Psychologists on the March: Science, Practice, and Professional Identity in America, 1929–1969.* Cambridge: Cambridge University Press.

Coats, A. W. Bob. 2002. "The AEA and the Radical Challenge to American Social Science." In J. E. Biddle, J. B. Davis and S. G. Medema, eds., *Economics Broadly Considered: Essays in Honor of Warren J. Samuels.* London: Routledge, pp. 144–58.

Cockett, Richard. 1995. *Thinking the Unthinkable: Think-Tanks and the Economic Counter-Revolution, 1931–1983.* London: Fontana Press. First published in 1994.

Cohen-Cole, Jamie. 2007. "Instituting the Science of Mind: Intellectual Economies and Disciplinary Exchange at Harvard's Center for Cognitive Studies," *British Journal for the History of Science* 40.4:567–97.

Cohen-Solal, Annie. 2000. "Claude L. Strauss in the United States," *Partisan Review* 67.2:252–60.

Colander, David C. and Harry Landreth, eds. 1996. *The Coming of Keynesianism to America: Conversations with the Founders of Keynesian Economics.* Cheltenham: Edward Elgar.

1998. "Political Influence on the Keynesian Revolution: God, Man and Lorie Tarshis at Yale." In O. F. Hamouda and B. B. Price, eds., *Keynesianism and the Keynesian Revolution in America.* Cheltenham: Edward Elgar, pp. 59–72.

Converse, Philip E. 2006. "Researching Electoral Politics," *American Political Science Review* 100.4:605–12.

Coutau-Bégarie, Hervé. 1989. *Le Phénomène Nouvelle Histoire: Grandeur et décadence de l'école des* Annales, second edition. Paris: Economica.

Crowther-Heyck, Hunter. 2005. *Herbert Simon: The Bounds of Reason in Modern America.* Baltimore, MD: Johns Hopkins University Press.

2006a. "Patrons of the Revolution: Ideals an Institutions in Postwar Behavioral Science," *Isis* 97.3:420–46.

2006b. "Herbert Simon and the GSIA: Building an Interdisciplinary Community," *Journal of the History of the Behavioral Sciences* 42.4:311–34.

Cumings, Bruce. 1998. "Boundary Displacement: Area Studies and International Studies During and After the Cold War." In C. Simpson, ed., *Universities and Empire: Money and Politics in the Social Sciences During the Cold War*. New York: The New Press.

Dahl, Robert A. 1961. "The Behavioral Approach to Political Science: Epitaph for a Monument to a Successful Protest," *American Political Science Review* 55.4:763–72.

Diamond, Sigmund. 1992. *Compromised Campus: The Collaboration of Universities with the Intelligence Community, 1945–1955*. New York and Oxford: Oxford University Press.

Economic and Social Research Council. Undated. *SSRC/ESRC: The First Forty Years*. Available at http://www.esrcsocietytoday.ac.uk/ESRCInfoCentre/about/esrccontext/index.aspx. Last accessed 1 March 2010.

Engerman, David. 2003. "Rethinking Cold War Universities: Some Recent Histories," *Journal of Cold War Studies* 5.3:80–95.

2007. "American Knowledge and Global Power," *Diplomatic History* 31.4:599–622.

2009. *Know Your Enemy: The Rise and Fall of America's Soviet Experts*. Oxford: Oxford University Press.

Foucault, Michel. 1970. *The Order of Things*. London: Tavistock Publications. Reprinted London: Routledge, 1989.

1972. *The Archaeology of Knowledge*. London: Tavistock Publications. Reprinted London: Routledge, 1989.

Fourcade, Marion. 2009. *Economists and Societies: Discipline and Profession in the United States, Britain, and France, 1890s to 1990s*. Princeton, NJ and Oxford: Princeton University Press.

Fourcade, Marion and Ragesh Khurana. 2008. "*Scientific and Merchant Professionalism in American Economics*," working document.

Friedman, Milton 1953. "The Methodology of Positive Economics." In M. Friedman, ed., *Essays in Positive Economics*. Chicago, IL: University of Chicago Press.

Fukuyama, Francis. 1992. *The End of History and the Last Man*. London: Penguin.

Fuller, Steve. 2000. *Thomas Kuhn: A Philosophical History for Our Times*. Chicago, IL: University of Chicago Press.

Galison, Peter. 1994. "The Ontology of the Enemy: Norbert Wiener and the Cybernetic Vision," *Critical Inquiry* 21.1:228–66.

Geertz, Clifford. 1973. *The Interpretation of Cultures*. New York: Basic Books.

Geiger, Roger L. 1993. *Research and Relevant Knowledge: American Research Universities Since World War II*. Oxford: Oxford University Press.

Gerhardt, Uta. 2002. *Talcott Parsons: An Intellectual Biography*. Cambridge: Cambridge University Press.

2007. *Denken der Demokratie: Die Soziologie im atlantischen Transfer des Besatzungsregimes*. Stuttgart: Franz Steiner Verlag.

Geuter, Ulfried. 1992. *The Professionalization of Psychology in Nazi Germany*. Translated by Richard J. Holmes. Cambridge: Cambridge University Press.

Gilman, Nils. 2003. *Mandarins of the Future: Modernization Theory in Cold War America*. Baltimore, MD and London: The John Hopkins University Press.

Gordon, Scott. 1991. *The History and Philosophy of Social Science*. London and New York: Routledge.

Gouldner, Alvin W. 1970. *The Coming Crisis of Western Sociology*. New York & London: Basic Books.

Guglielmo, Mark. 2008. "The Contribution of Economists to Military Intelligence During World War II," *Journal of Economic History* 68.1:109–50.

Gunnell, John G. 2004. *Imagining the American Polity: Political Science and the Discourse of Democracy*. University Park, PA: Pennsylvania State University Press.

Hagemann, Harald. 2000. "The Post-1945 Development of Economics in Germany." In A. W. Bob Coats, ed., *The Development of Economics in Western Europe since 1945*. London: Routledge.

Hammond, Debora. 2003. *The Science of Synthesis: Exploring The Social Implications of General Systems Theory*. Boulder, CO: The University Press of Colorado.

Harvey, David. 2005. *A Brief History of Neoliberalism*. Oxford: Oxford University Press.

Hayter, William. 1975. "The Hayter Report and After." *Oxford Review of Education* 1.2:169–72.

Hechter, Michael and Satoshi Kanazawa. 1997. "Sociological Rational Choice," *Annual Review of Sociology* 23:191–214.

Heims, Joshua. 1993. *Constructing a Social Science for Postwar America: The Cybernetic Group, 1946–1953*. Cambridge, MA: MIT Press.

Hempel, Carl G. 1942. "The Function of General Laws in History," *Journal of Philosophy* 39.2:35–48.

Herman, Ellen. 1995. *The Romance of American Psychology: Political Culture in the Age of Experts*. Berkeley / Los Angeles / London: University of California Press.

——— 1998. "Project Camelot and the Career of the Cold War Psychology." In C. Simpson, ed., *Universities and Empire: Money and Politics in the Social Sciences During the Cold War*. New York: The New Press.

Heyl, Barbara S. 1968. "The Harvard 'Pareto Circle'," *Journal of the History of the Behavioral Sciences* 4.4:316–34.

Hollinger, David A. 1996. *Science, Jews, and Secular Culture: Studies in Mid-Twentieth-Century American Intellectual History*. Princeton, NJ: Princeton University Press.

——— 1997. "The Disciplines and the Identity Debates, 1970–1995," *Daedalus* 126:333–51.

Homans, George C. 1964. "Bringing Men Back In," *American Sociological Review* 29.5:809–18.

Hounshell, David A. 1997. "The Cold War, Rand, and the Generation of Knowledge, 1946–1962," *Historical Studies in the Physical and Biological Sciences* 27.2:237–68.

Hunt, Lynn. 1986. "French History in the Last Twenty Years: The Rise and Fall of the Annales Paradigm," *Journal of Contemporary History* 21.2:209–24.

Isaac, Joel. 2007. "The Human Sciences in Cold War America," *Historical Journal* 50.3:725–46.

Jacques, Elliott. 1998. "On Leaving The Tavistock Institute," *Human Relations* 51.3:251–7.

Jardini, David R. 1996. "*Out of the Blue Yonder: The RAND Corporation's Diversification into Social Welfare Research, 1946–1968*," Ph.D. dissertation, Carnegie Mellon University.

Johnston, Barry V. 1995. *Pitirim A. Sorokin: An Intellectual Biography*. Lawrence: University Press of Kansas.

1998. "The Contemporary Crisis and the Social Relations Department at Harvard: A Case Study in Hegemony and Disintegration," *American Sociologist* 29.3:26–42.

Johnston, Ron, Malcolm Fairbrother, David Hayes, Tony Hoare and Kelvyn Jones. 2008. "The Cold War and Geography's Quantitative Revolution : Some Messy Reflections on Barnes' Geographical Underworld," *Geoforum* 39.6:1802–6.

Judt, Tony. 2007. *Postwar: A History of Europe since 1945*. London: Pimlico.

Katz, Barry M. 1989. *Foreign Intelligence: Research and Analysis in the Office of Strategic Services, 1942–1945*. Cambridge, MA and London: Harvard University Press.

Kelley, John L. 1997. *Bringing the Market Back In: The Political Revitalization of Market Liberalism*. New York: NewYork University Press.

Khurana, Ragesh. 2007. *From Higher Aims to Hired Hands: The Social Transformation of American Business Schools and the Unfulfilled Promise of Management as a Profession*. Princeton, NJ: Princeton University Press.

Krohn, Claus-Dieter. 1993. *Intellectuals in Exile: Refugee Scholars and the New School for Social Research*. Translated by Rita and Robert Kimber. Amherst, MA: The University of Massachusetts Press.

Krugman, Herbert E. 1952. "The Appeal of Communism to American Middle Class Intellectuals and Trade Unionists," *Public Opinion Quarterly* 16.3:331–55.

Kuhn, Thomas. 1962. *The Structure of Scientific Revolutions*. Chicago, IL: University of Chicago Press. Second edition, 1970.

Kurzweil, Edith. 1980. *The Age of Structuralism: Lévi-Strauss to Foucault*. New York: Columbia University Press.

1986. "The Fate of Structuralism," *Theory, Culture & Society* 3.3:113–24.

Lahire, Bernard, ed. 2001. *Le travail sociologique de Pierre Bourdieu*. Paris: La Découverte et Syros. Originally published in 1999.

Lazarsfeld, Paul F. 1957. "Public Opinion and the Classical Tradition," *Public Opinion Quarterly* 21.1:39–53.

1969. "An Episode in the History of Social Research: A Memoir." In D. Fleming and B. Bailyn, eds., *The Intellectual Migration: Europe and America, 1930–1960*. Cambridge, MA: The Belknap Press of Harvard University Press.

Lazarsfeld, Paul F., Bernard Berelson and Hazel Gaudet. 1944. *The People's Choice*. New York: Columbia University Press.

Lazarsfeld, Paul F. and Wagner Thielens, Jr. 1958. *The Academic Mind: Social Scientists in a Time of Crisis*. Glencoe, IL.: The Free Press.

Leonard, Robert J. 1991. "War as a 'Simple Economic Problem': The Rise of an Economics of Defense." In Craufurd D. Goodwin, ed., *Economics and National Security: A History of Their Interaction*, Annual supplement to volume 23 of *History of Political Economy*. Durham, NC and London: Duke University Press.

1992. "Creating a Context for Game Theory." In E. Roy Weintraub, ed., *Toward a History of Game Theory*, Annual supplement to volume 24 of *History of Political Economy*. Durham, NC and London: Duke University Press.

Lewin, Kurt. 1945. "The Research Center for Group Dynamics at Massachusetts Institute of Technology," *Sociometry* 8.2:126–36.

Lipset, Seymour M. and Neil Smelser. 1961. "Change and Controversy in Recent American Sociology," *British Journal of Sociology* 12.1:41–51.

Lipsey, Richard G. 1963. *An Introduction to Positive Economics*. London: Weidenfeld.

Lodewijks, John. 1991. "Rostow, Developing Economies, and National Security Policy." In Craufurd D. Goodwin, ed., *Economics and National Security: A History of Their Interaction*, Annual supplement to volume 23 of *History of Political Economy*. Durham, NC and London: Duke University Press.

Loewenberg, Gerhard. 2006. "The Influence of European Émigré Scholars on Comparative Politics, 1925–1965," *American Political Science Review* 100.4:597–604.

Longchambon, Henri. 1958. "Les Sciences sociales en France. Un bilan, un programme," *Annales. Économies, Sociétés, Civilisations* 13.1:94–109.

Lowen, Rebecca S. 1997. *Creating the Cold War University: The Transformation of Stanford*. Berkeley / Los Angeles / London: University of California Press.

Lundberg, George A. 1945. "The Social Sciences in the Post-War Era," *Sociometry* 8.2:137–49.

Manicas, Peter T. 1991. "The Social Science Disciplines: The American Model." In P. Wagner, B. Wittrock and R. Whitley, eds., *Discourses on Society: The Shaping of the Social Science Disciplines*. Dordrecht / Boston / London: Kluwer.

Marrow, Alfred J. 1969. *The Practical Theorist: The Life and Work of Kurt Lewin*. New York and London: Basic Books.

Mata, Tiago. 2009. "Migrations and Boundary Work: Harvard, Radical Economists and the Committee on Political Discrimination," *Science in Context* 22.1:115–43.

May, Mark A. 1971. "A Retrospective View of the Institute of Human Relations at Yale," *Cross-Cultural Research* 6.3:141–72.

Mazon, Brigitte. 1988. *Aux origines de l'École des Hautes Études en Sciences Sociales: Le rôle du mécenat américain (1920–1960)*. Paris: Éditions du cerf.

Merelman, Richard M. 2003. *Pluralism at Yale: The Culture of Political Science in America*. Madison, WI and London: The University of Wisconsin Press.

Merriam, Charles A. 1926. "Progress on Political Research," *American Political Science Review* 20.1:1–13.

Merton, Robert K. 1942. "A Note on Science and Democracy," *Journal of Legal and Political Sociology* 1: 115–26.

1945. "Sociological Theory," *American Journal of Sociology* 50.6:462–73.

Miller, James G. 1996. "My Role in the Assessment Program of the Office of Strategic Services," *Behavioral Science* 41.4:245–61.

(and other members of the editorial board). 1956. "Editorial: Behavioral Science, A New Journal," *Behavioral Science* 1.1:1–5.

Miller, Peter and Nikolas, Rose. 1994. "On Therapeutic Authority: Psychoanalytical Expertise Under Advanced Liberalism." *History of the Human Sciences* 7.3:29–64.

Miller, J. and R. J. A. Schlesinger. 1949. "Editorial," *Soviet Studies* 1.1:1–2.

Mills, C. Wright. 1951. *White Collar: The American Middle Classes*. New York: Oxford University Press.

1956. *The Power Elite*. Oxford: Oxford University Press.

1959. *Sociological Imagination*. New York: Oxford University Press.

Milne, David. 2008. *America's Rasputin: Walt Rostow and the Vietnam War*. New York: Hill and Wang.

Mirowski, Philip. 1991. "When Games Grow Deadly Serious: The Military Influence on the Evolution of Game Theory." In Craufurd D. Goodwin, ed., *Economics and National Security: A History of Their Interaction*, Annual supplement to volume

23 of *History of Political Economy*. Durham, NC and London: Duke University Press.

2005. "How Positivism Made a Pact with the Postwar Social Sciences in the United States." In G. Steinmetz, ed., *The Politics of Method in the Human Sciences: Positivism and Its Epistemological Others*. Durham, NC: Duke University Press, pp. 142–72.

2009. "Postface: Defining Neoliberalism." In P. Mirowski and D. Plehwe, eds., *The Road from Mont Pèlerin: The Making of the Neoliberal Thought Collective*, pp. 417–456. Cambridge, MA: Harvard University Press.

Monkkoonen, Erich H., ed. 1994. *Engaging the Past: The Uses of History across the Social Sciences*. Durham, NC and London: Duke University Press.

Morawski, Jill G. 1986. "Organizing Knowledge and Behavior at Yale's Institute of Human relations," *Isis* 77.2:219–42.

Morgan, Mary S. 2003. "Economics." In T.M Porter and D. Ross, eds., *The Cambridge History of Science*, vol. 7 (*The Modern Social Sciences*). Cambridge: Cambridge University Press.

Moss, Laurence S. and Andrew Savchenko, eds. 2006. *Introduction to Talcott Parsons: Economic Sociologist of the 20th Century*. Malden: Blackwell.

Needell, Allan A. 1993. " 'Truth Is Our Weapon': Project TROY, Political Warfare, and Government-Academic Relations in the National Security State," *Diplomatic History* 17.3:399–420.

1998. "Project Troy and the Cold War Annexation of the Social Sciences." In C. Simpson, ed., *Universities and Empire: Money and Politics in the Social Sciences During the Cold War*, pp. 3–38. New York: The New Press.

Nichols, Lawrence T. 1998. "Social Relations Undone: Disciplinary Divergence and Departmental Politics at Harvard, 1946–1970," *American Sociologist* 29.2:83–107.

Ogburn, William F. and Alexander Goldenweiser, eds. 1927. *The Social Sciences and Their Interrelations*. Boston / New York / Chicago / Dallas / San Francisco: The Riverside Press.

Parker, Richard. 2005. *John Kenneth Galbraith: His Life, His Politics, His Economics*. New York: Farrar, Strauss and Giroux.

Parsons, Talcott and Edward A. Shils, eds. 1951. *Toward a General Theory of Action: Theoretical Foundations for the Social Sciences*. Cambridge, MA: Harvard University Press.

Parsons, Talcott and Evon Z. Vogt. 1962. "Clyde Kay Maben Kluckhohn, 1905–1960," *American Anthropologist* 64.1:140–61.

Planning Committee of the Center for International Studies at the Massachusetts Institute of Technology. 1954. "A Plan of Research in International Communication: A Report," *World Politics* 6.3:358–77.

Platt, Jennifer. 1996. *A History of Sociological Research Methods in America, 1920–1960*. Cambridge: Cambridge University Press.

Platt, Jennifer and Paul Hoch. 1995. "The Vienna Circle in the USA and Empirical Research Methods in Sociology." In M. G. Ash and A. Söllner, eds., *Forced Migration and Scientific Change*. New York: Cambridge University Press, pp. 224–45.

Porter, Theodore M. and Dorothy Ross. 2003. "Introduction: Writing the History of Social Science." In T. M. Porter and D. Ross, eds., *The Cambridge History of Science, vol. 7 (The Modern Social Sciences)*. Cambridge: Cambridge University Press.

Prewitt, Kenneth. 2005. "The Two Projects of the American Social Sciences," *Social Research* 72.1:219–36.

Price, David H. 2008. *Anthropological Intelligence: The Deployment and Neglect of American Anthropology in the Second World War*. Durham, NC and London: Duke University Press.

Robic, Marie-Claire. 2003. "Geography." In T. M. Porter and D. Ross, eds., *The Cambridge History of Science*, vol. 7 (*The Modern Social Sciences*). Cambridge: Cambridge University Press.

Robin, Ron. 2001. *The Making of the Cold War Enemy: Culture and Politics in the Military-Intellectual Complex*. Princeton, NJ and Oxford. Princeton University Press.

Rorty, Richard. 1979. *Philosophy and the Mirror of Nature*. Oxford: Basil Blackwell.

Ross, Dorothy. 1993. "An Historian's View of American Social Science," *Journal of the History of the Behavioral Sciences* 29.2:99–112.

Rostow, W. W. 1960. *The Stages of Economic Growth: A Non-Communist Manifesto*. Cambridge: Cambridge University Press.

Runciman, W. G. 1969. "What Is Structuralism?" *British Journal of Sociology* 20.3:253–65

Sallaz, Jeffrey J. and Jane Zavisca. 2007. "Bourdieu in American Sociology, 1980–2004," *Annual Review of Sociology* 33:21–41.

Saunders, Frances S. 1999. *Who Paid the Piper? CIA and the Cultural Cold War*. London: Granta Books.

Schrecker, Ellen W. 1986. *No Ivory Tower: McCarthyism and the Universities*. New York and Oxford: Oxford University Press.

ed. 2004. *Cold War Triumphalism: The Misuse of History After the Fall of Communism*. New York and London: The New Press.

Schulten, Susan. 2001. *The Geographical Imagination in America, 1880–1950*. Chicago, IL and London: University of Chicago Press.

Selcer, Perrin. 2009. "*The View from Everywhere: Disciplining Diversity in Post-World War II International Social Science*," *Journal of the History of the Behavioral Sciences* 45.4:309–29.

Sent, Esther-Mirjam. 1998. *The Evolving Rationality of Rational Expectations: An Assessment of Thomas Sargent's Achievements*. Cambridge: Cambridge University Press.

Sewell, William H. 2005. "The Political Unconscious of Social and Cultural History, or, Confessions of a Former Quantitative Historian." In G. Steinmetz, ed., *The Politics of Method in the Human Sciences: Positivism and its Epistemological Others*. Durham, NC: Duke University Press.

Shakow, David and David Rapaport. 1964. *The Influence of Freud on American Psychology*. New York: International Universities Press.

Skinner, Quentin, 1985. "Introduction: The Return of Grand Theory." In Q. Skinner, ed., *The Return of Grand Theory in the Human Sciences*. Cambridge: Cambridge University Press.

Smith, Neil. 2003. *American Empire: Roosevelt's Geographer and the Prelude to Globalization*. Berkeley/Los Angeles/London: University of California Press.

Snow, Charles P. 1959. *The Two Cultures and the Scientific Revolution*. New York: Cambridge University Press.

Solovey, Mark. 2001. "Project Camelot and the 1960s Epistemological Revolution: Rethinking the Politics-Patronage-Social Science Nexus," *Social Studies of Science* 31.2:171–206.

——— 2004. "Riding Natural Scientists' Coattails onto the Endless Frontier: The SSRC and the Quest for Scientific Legitimacy," *Journal of the History of the Behavioral Sciences* 40.4:393–422.

——— 2009. "Senator Fred Harris's National Social Science Foundation Initiative: Reconsidering the Road Not Taken," working document.

Steinmetz, George, ed. 2005. *The Politics of Method in the Human Sciences: Positivism and its Epistemological Others*. Durham, NC: Duke University Press.

Steuer, Max. 2003. *The Scientific Study of Society*. Boston/Dordrecht/ London: Kluwer.

Stouffer, Samuel A. 1955. *Communism, Conformity, and Civil Liberties*. Garden City, NY: Doubleday.

Sturrock, John, ed. 1979. *Structuralism and Since: From Levi-Strauss to Derrida*. Oxford: Oxford University Press.

Suppe, Frederick, ed. 1977. *The Structure of Scientific Theories*. Urbana, IL: University of Illinois Press.

Tribe, Keith . 2009. "Liberalism and Neoliberalism: Britain, 1930–1980." In P. Mirowski and D. Plehwe, eds., *The Road from Mont Pelerin: The Making of the Neoliberal Thought Collective*. Cambridge, MA: Harvard University Press.

Trist, Eric & Hugh Murray. 1990. "Historical Overview: The Foundation and Development of the Tavistock Institute." In E. Trist and H. Murray, eds., *The Social Engagement of Social Science*, vol. 1 (*The Socio-Psychological Perspective*). London: Free Association Books, pp. 1–34.

Vout, Malcolm. 1991. "Oxford and the Emergence of Political Science in England, 1945–1960." In P. Wagner, B. Wittrock and R. Whitley, eds., *Discourses on Society: The Shaping of the Social Science Disciplines*. Dordrecht / Boston / London: Kluwer, pp.163–91.

Wagnleitner, Reinhold. 1994. *Coca-Colonization and the Cold War: The Cultural Mission of the United States in Austria after the Second World War*. Chapel Hill, NC and London: The University of North Carolina Press.

Wallis, W. Allen. 1980. "The Statistical Research Group, 1942–1945," *Journal of the American Statistical Association* 75.370:320–30.

Weinstein, Deborah F. 2004. "Culture at Work: Family Therapy and the Culture Concept in Post-World War II America," *Journal of the History of the Behavioral Sciences* 40.1:23–46.

Weintraub, E. Roy. 1999. "How Should We Write the History of Twentieth-Century Economics?" *Oxford Review of Economic Policy* 15.4:139–52.

Weyer, Johannes. 1984. *Westdeutche Soziologie 1945–1960*. Berlin: Duncker und Humblot.

Wheeler, Stanton. 1994. "The Commitment to Social Science: A Case Study of Organizational Innovation." In D. C. Hammack and S. Wheeler, *Social Science in* the *Making: Essays on the Russel Sage Foundation, 1907–1972*. New York: Russel Sage Foundation, pp. 81–139.

Wiener, Norbert. 1948. *Cybernetics or Control and Communication in the Animal and the Machine*. New York: Wiley.

Winch, Peter. 1958. *The Idea of a Social Science and Its Relation to Philosophy*. London: Routledge & Kegan Paul.

Winks, Robin W. 1964. *The Cold War: From Yalta to Cuba*. New York and London: Macmillan.

Worcester, Kenton W. 2001. *Social Science Research Council, 1923–1998*. Available at http://www.ssrc.org/publications/view/1F20C6E1–565F-DE11-BD80–001CC477EC70.

Index

Abbott, Andrew, 109, 113, 187
Abend, Gabriel, 127
Aberystwyth University, 161, 162
academic freedom, 194
action research, 27
Adcock, Robert, 6, 7, 11, 71, 72, 88, 90, 93
Addams, Jane, 120
Adorno, Theodor W., 27
Afghanistan, 172
Africa, 3, 4, 20, 44, 87, 93, 107, 137, 142, 146, 193, 194
  see also nationalism, African; South Africa
African Political Systems (Fortes and Evans-Pritchard, 1940), 144, 145
After Tylor (Stocking, 1995), 141
Agnew, J., 162
Agricultural Involution (Geertz, 1963), 151
Alatas, S.F., 120, 126
Allison, Paul, 125
Allport, Gordon, 26, 209, 210, 211
Almond, Gabriel, 71, 79, 80, 81, 87, 88, 185, 200
Althusser, Louis, 202
Amadae, Sonja, 47, 200, 219
American Commonwealth, The (Bryce, 1888), 75
American Economic Association (AEA), 1, 38, 49, 50, 57, 58, 59, 196

Committee on the Status of Women in the Economics Profession, 57
American Economic Review (AER), 1, 38, 57
American Geographical Society, 157
American Geological Society, 160
American Historical Association (AHA), 73
American influence, 40, 129, 152, 185
  see also Americanization, narrative of
American Institute of Public Opinion, 95
American Journal of Sociology, 112, 187
American People and Foreign Policy, The (Almond, 1950), 81
American Political Science Association (APSA), 1, 11, 72, 73, 76, 77, 200
  Committee on Political Parties, 77
  presidents, 76, 80, 82
American Political Science Review (journal), 1, 72, 81, 82, 92
American Psychological Association (APA), 9, 18, 22
American Sociological Association (ASA), 1, 105, 109, 115, 117, 120
  membership, 112
  presidents and politics, 117
  section on Sex and Gender, 109
American Sociological Review (journal), 112, 211